new retail

new retail

rasshied din

WITH CONTRIBUTED TEXT BY JACKIE WILLS

conran
OCTOPUS

00001503

DEDICATION

To John and Jackie for their help and support; and to Tim for everything.

Page 1 **Interior of Johan, London, designed by Claudio Sylvestin.**

Page 2 **Market in India.**

Page 5 **Pleats Please, Issey Miyake store in SoHo, New York, designed by Toshiko Mori.**

First published in 2000 by
Conran Octopus Limited
2–4 Heron Quays
London E14 4JP
Reprinted in 2003
www.conran-octopus.co.uk

ISBN 1 84091 042 9

British Library Cataloguing-in-Publication Data
A catalogue record for this book is available from the British Library

Colour origination by Sang Choy International, Singapore
Printed in Hong Kong

Commissioning Editor Denny Hemming
Managing Editor Kate Bell
Senior Editor Emma Clegg
Executive Art Editor Tony Seddon
Senior Art Editor Carl Hodson
Picture Researchers Rachel Davies and Helen Fickling
Picture Research Assistant Marissa Keating
Production Controller Sarah Tucker

Main text written by Jackie Wills in collaboration with the author.

contents

Introduction

The way we dress, furnish our homes, the foods we eat, the books we read, the music we listen to and the cars we drive...all point to the people we are. Moreover each of us has at some time looked at the contents of another supermarket trolley or looked at someone's home in a magazine and been curious, or judgemental, about the lifestyle that the images suggest. We draw conclusions from such visual evidence drawn from our own knowledge and assumptions that are in turn based on our instincts and experiences.

Shopping has always been a social and highly personal activity. So much more than just a practical necessity, it is a communal activity, about people coming together in markets, malls or streets. It encompasses the buying of essential commodities and being tempted by a luxury item that has no use other than to raise our spirits and give our lives an extra sparkle. In addition to this, shopping is an opportunity to meet friends, to gather information or to just watch the world go by at our leisure.

The inevitability of change is a feature that underlines the world of retail and makes design such a challenging profession. *New Retail* has been an interesting book to write and in its evolution I have met a number of retailers with different businesses and personal perspectives and learned about how other designers work. I have also visited and analysed many of the projects included in the book, and have been intrigued by the creative solutions that designers arrive at, while at the same time working within very similar processes. I have been struck by how cyclical the retail world is and this awareness has helped formalize many of my viewpoints about the origins of, inspiration for and influences on various design projects.

As I point out throughout the book, there are underlying basic principles which recur even in the most sophisticated design projects. These principles are used throughout to respond to the complex requirements and characteristic responses of the human psyche. The way that people interact and how they express their personalities and character dictates the quality of environments, product or service they are given. What shoppers remember about their experiences can be intangible.

Why do people keep going back to one place or reject it in favour of another? The answer is not as simple as price, location or products. What is important is a sense of relationship, which, as with any human relationship, is a complex issue made more so by the assumption today that shoppers do not have relationships with retailers in the way they used to. The scale of retailing and the vast choice available now affords many more options than any single person needs. The final choice of retailer or the definitive trigger to buy could be quite subjective and arbitrary.

Looking to the future, which we are told is firmly based in information technology, 'E' commerce (electronic commerce) will play an increasing role. However, I doubt it will ever replace the social experience of shopping which has, worldwide, created trade routes across continents, and

Opposite **A shopping car park in 1940s Canada. A typical Sunday activity, evangelist families gathering to worship at the centre of their community.**

Below **'Art Market' window promotion at Harvey Nichols, London. A wall of soup tins provides the repetitive image, into which tableaux are formed.**

been the reason for the growth of market towns and gathering places in the most remote, rural communities. I believe technology's most useful role, if it is used properly, will be to help the humanization of retail. This will result in people being instantly recognized, and catered for, as individuals in a personal, caring and efficient way.

Furthermore, I believe it is important to realize that the future is happening now. There are many innovations in place which have not been widely taken up and which retailers and consumers, generally, could benefit from before contemplating the longer-term future. One of the most critical elements of the future is the separation which is emerging between shopping for basic commodities and shopping for pleasure which appeals to consumers as individuals. It is obvious that we will create our own time frames to allow more quality time for ourselves.

Researching the book I have drawn widely on my experience and relationships with clients, particularly with instinctive retailers such as George Davis, Vittorio Radice

and Stephen Marks, each of whom are highly successful individuals with characteristic approaches to their business. All three of them have made important contributions to the development of retail within the UK, and arguably, further afield: George Davis as founder of Next and George, Vittorio Radice in Habitat and Selfridges and Stephen Marks with French Connection and Nicole Farhi. All three also share a true commitment to high quality design and understand, instinctively, its importance in driving their brands forward. Their approaches, too, are singularly democratic in that they have shown that it is not necessary for good design to be solely confined to the top end of the market. Indeed some of the case studies, such as Boots the Chemist, Tesco, Vinegar Factory, Hema and Opaque, illustrate that the public is more design aware than ever and that good design is not a luxury, but a necessity.

In choosing the case studies for *New Retail* I have endeavoured to select the best examples of their kind, regardless of when they were first opened. The projects I

Below **A tantalising display of fish-shaped chocolates found in the window of Rococo Chocolates on the Kings Road, London.**

Below right **The futurist Li Edelcourt creates and informs retailers on the future needs and desires of consumers. Picture from** Interior View *published* **under United Publishers.**

examine in detail have, to date, not been bettered. Almost unique, they bear the stamp of particular individuals. All are worth a visit for anyone interested in retail merchandising, product selection, interior design, graphics and how these elements combine. These are the types of projects which influence and inspire people within the industry.

Perhaps one of the most critical lessons from the projects, research and interviews undertaken for *New Retail* is that good design works best when it is backed up by entrepreneurs with vision and style. In this context, design is considered at a strategic level and applies to every aspect of the retail operation, from point of sale and advertising, to visual merchandising and the store interior. By incorporating design so fundamentally into a strategy, a retailer can make powerful statements to the consumer which will reinforce the values of the brand.

When retail design was in its infancy in the sixties and seventies, it was generally art based and less concerned with function. Today, it has developed into more of a creative science aimed at facilitating economies of scale and enabling a retailer to reproduce multiples of the same experience globally.

In addition, new technologies are having a greater impact in the industry with retail design benefiting from enormous advances in lighting and materials technology. Multiple channels of retailing are also making demands on businesses to ensure they communicate a consistent brand message across different media. New channels require different design solutions and offer retailers an opportunity to innovate further, particularly in the way that they convey service and choice to the consumer. Good interior and packaging design has proved its cost effectiveness by increasing profit margins and improving communications.

Authenticity, sensory appeal and an understanding of people are what retailers must have to succeed. Many of these attributes can be found in traditional retail environments. The challenge today is to combine new technology with these values.

*Below left **A shopping bag becomes a must-have accessory. A mundane functional item is imbued in this way with style and quality. Designed by Michael Nash for Space NK.***

*Below **A Samsung laptop computer is depicted here as a fashion accessory with sex appeal. This synthesises I.T. style and humour within a creative ad with impact. Designed for Samsung by the Arnell Group.***

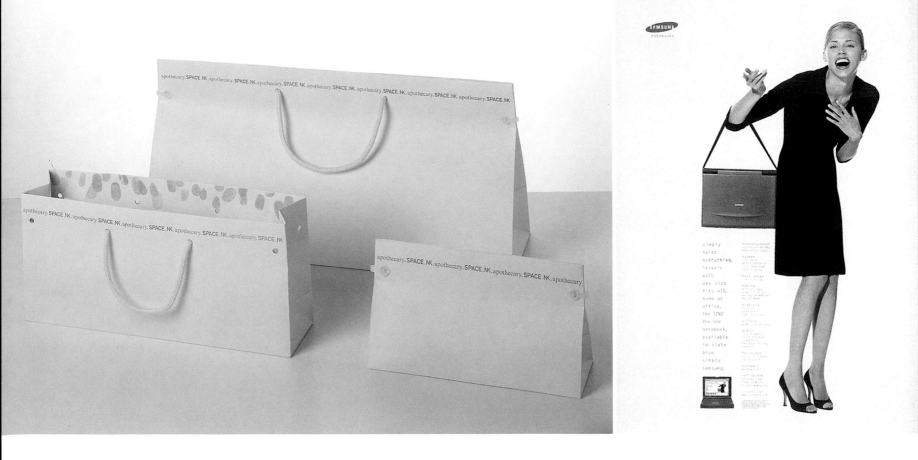

principles of
retail design

The role of contemporary retail design is to link instinct, art and commerce. Designers must understand the innate techniques gleaned from years of first-hand contact with customers, while satisfying the objectives of those corporations whose chains of outlets have turned retailing into a science. The skills of a retail designer are used to stimulate a consumer's natural instincts to persuade him or her to consider a product or service, and then to facilitate its purchase or use so that the consumer feels comfortable with the choice made. The challenge is to invent new kinds of retail environments which are both efficient (in terms of space, flexibility and cost) and effective (to communicate the retailer's brand values and encourage consumer activity), in order to meet ever-tougher consumer demands.

The retail designer's task is to combine elements of psychology, technology and ergonomics with the retailer's knowledge of the market to develop an interior which is most likely to fit the consumer profile. While it is true that the basic principles of retail design may be divided between intuition, aesthetics and practicality, in all three areas responsiveness is the key factor. In many ways the retail designer's skill as an artist is to draw on a diversity of sources and experiences to achieve a successful result. Retail is a complex study which incorporates the management of people and space with the ability to respond to retail's most essential characteristic: change. Of most industries, retail is perhaps the most susceptible to the ever-changing demands of consumers, the economy, public policies and even the weather.

Constant reinvention

Previous page **A Bathing Ape Busy Work Shop, Osaka, Japan 1998, designed by Masamichi Katayama.**

Below **Louis Vuitton's flagship store, Bond Street, London. Designed by American architects, Peter Marino, the 'new look' for this luxury brand adopts a contemporary classic style. Opened in 1999, the design is a blueprint for the new millennium, with stores opening in major cities throughout the world.**

Retailers who do not encourage new consumers through innovative products and services will suffer, as their existing clientele may not be sufficiently large or loyal to support future plans. In fashion retail, consumer requirements continually change so that even the most loyal customer may lose interest or feel neglected if their requirements are not met. One of the hardest jobs in retail design is to attract new customers while maintaining existing ones. This is especially true in the fickle world of fashion, where a designer has to understand the marketing of brands, and in particular the need for those brands constantly to develop and reinvent themselves. Gucci, Louis Vuitton and Prada have all rationalized their products and remarketed themselves as modern, luxury brands in order to remain one step ahead of their competitors (see also page 114).

In the past five years these three companies, and many others, have developed new products and created new markets because society's perceptions of luxury have changed. The old symbols of exclusivity – furs, diamonds and big cars – were fast becoming irrelevant and ostentatious symbols in the late twentieth century. 'Luxury' has become another glib sales pitch and, along with the word 'designer', an overused marketing term. This is not to say that luxury goods are less desirable, but that retailers have had to change their products to suit what modern consumers want in their lives today.

Change, therefore, is essential, but the development of a new design concept must be carefully planned. The relationship between retailer and designer is critical: the two must work together to understand who the customers are and to identify new markets. Products are designed and manufactured months in advance, and stores may be planned seasonally to coincide with product deliveries, so any delays can cause huge losses in trade.

In retail, 'product is king'; the design must never overshadow what is on sale, and the interior should complement and communicate without dominating. Just as product is central to design, so is the management within any retail organization. If other aspects of the organization do not work, a new design – however innovative or remarkable – will not succeed. Old products and complacent relationships generally produce tired formats and, for the designer, this is a potentially difficult area. A retailer whose only motive for redesigning is short-term gain by imitating the success of another retailer, for instance, may have a fundamental problem with management and consequently with product. The designer should be prepared for the eventuality that such a client may not be ready for change, and therefore to back out if necessary. A designer is in many ways a facilitator: a means of helping a retailer to develop and produce a strategy to reposition his product, enter new markets or sustain market share. A design company needs to become part of the retail team which analyses the problems and reviews the target market, so as to turn the retailer's objectives into a three-dimensional reality.

Retail strategy

The importance of retail design, as opposed to shopfitting, emerged during the 1970s. It continued to extend its influence during the following decade, when it became essential to retailers' development strategies. In essence, the retail designer became involved in 'communication' rather than simply being the means for finding solutions to physical problems. Designers became involved in brand marketing and advertising through the manipulation of architectural volumes of space, and the effects that these environments had on consumer psychology. Today, however, there is ongoing debate as to whether a designer should specialize in retail, and even on whether the importance of interior design is overestimated. I would argue that retail design is a complex area, requiring increasing knowledge and experience – not readily available to most practitioners of interior design – to produce commercially viable working solutions for some very difficult retail operations. The retail sector is growing in sophistication. It is highly specialized in some sectors, and requires understanding, speed and

practical skills which take years to develop. Designers with such abilities are of increasing value to retailers, and support the retailers' decisions to invest substantial sums of money in the industry every year.

Many retailers invest in extensive market research and analysis. On the basis of these findings the designer and retailer will work out a strategy, which may vary depending on the analysis and on the retailer concerned. The designer can adopt many approaches, from creating a new brand to initiating a strategy which evolves an existing brand over a period of years. Some design companies have extended their businesses into strategy development (this will be explored in greater depth in Chapter 5). Strategy may also include the use of style-prediction agencies and futurists such as Faith Popcorn and Lynne Franks (see page 209). The advantage gained by the design consultancy as strategist is communication with the retail company at a much higher level. The designer can then ensure that the way that the brand develops is understood at board level.

Above **Harvey Nichols, Knightsbridge, London. This exterior shot shows a sculptural window treatment by Thomas Hetherington, the winning design for the 1998 Design and Art Directors' Gold Award. Constructed of veneered polystyrene it brought London traffic to a standstill when it was launched during London Fashion Week.**

The new consumer

Below left **New consumers are time starved and cash rich; they seek value for money, the best reward schemes, and are unlikely to be loyal.**

Below right **Barnes and Noble bookstore, New York, USA. The new consumer is re-defined by his or her individual interests and chosen specialist pursuits.**

Retail design is increasingly seen as a powerful resource. The illusion of multiple retailing is that the consumer is king. However, retailers' indepth customer knowledge now gives them the power to dictate who comes to their doors.

Retailing today is about people – their lifestyles, attitudes and beliefs – and design is part of the experience of shopping. The important aspect of all retail design lies in understanding both the product and the aspirations of the customer, so that the vehicle and the message are clearly focused. Some may dispute that customers wish to have a relationship with retailers, yet this is undoubtedly the new language of corporate retail. This sector has become based on emotional response rather than on need, because of the general rise in living standards throughout the northern hemisphere. What consumers want from retailers can only intensify: as each expectation is realized, another will replace it, to the extent that some retailers are now fulfilling quasi-spiritual, educational, social and even medical needs. A stroll along the high street may comprise

a weekend outing; a trip to the new supermarket can encompass the dry-cleaner, chemist, bank, newsagent, cobbler and photographic supplier. For the elderly and lonely it may be the only opportunity of the day to speak to another person.

Modern consumers tend to confound the old socio-demographic groupings of ABCD/123, and some of them are less influenced by cheap commodities than they used to be. Instead, they are guided by style aspirations, and so will be more likely to fit into a type such as modernist, purist, techno and so on. Entire service industries, including advertising and market research, are now devoted to defining the consumer, and the indications are that consumers increasingly defy mass-marketing categorization. Societies no longer operate on simple divisions, although there is increasing economic polarity. The decline in mass markets will result in more segmented and niche markets, while youth culture has outgrown the image built up from the late 1950s onwards as a sector defined by

rebellion. Although a sense of exclusivity is still important for young consumers, 'youthfulness' has also become a style which may be adopted by older adults. Society no longer accepts 'growing old gracefully'; people are healthier, fitter, and want to look and feel younger for longer.

Young consumers today are generally more visually aware, and will respond cynically to overt advertising. They will be increasingly unwilling to accept the second-rate, whether in product quality or service. They will shop around with sophistication – seeking value for money, credit and the best loyalty schemes. The child at school today will be able, quite effortlessly, to read behind a marketing message. Furthermore, as that child grows up he or she will be a confident brand-user, having been brand-conscious from an early age. This young adult will be adept at seeking information about products and may well turn away from the narrow, status-driven brand-building which characterizes so much contemporary marketing in favour of brands which carry more sophisticated messages.

Doubt is even being shed on the concept of the consumer, and on whether he or she should instead be defined as a 'user' or a 'citizen'. What is clear is that, whichever term is used, the modern consumer is promiscuous rather than loyal, and is considerably more likely to evade definition than in the past. Retailers also need to bear in mind that the new consumer will not necessarily be based within a radius of a few hundred miles from headquarters. Retailers producing new products, and those with international aspirations, need to consider these new markets. They may need to be prepared to alter production, sizes and colours to suit differing cultures and climates.

The difficulty of defining today's consumer provides a good illustration of how retailing works: using both the scientific and intuitive approaches. Whereas data is essential to understand the consumer, the designer must also make use of knowledge that is drawn from an awareness of current affairs, of trends in popular culture and of human behaviour and habits.

Below left **San Francisco, USA. Young consumers defy categorization and define themselves by style and image.**

Below right **Debenhams department store, Leeds. Retail for the older consumer can mean a day out or an opportunity to socialize.**

The fundamentals of retail

Above **Habitat bean bags in the 1970s. Conceived, designed and produced by Terence Conran, Habitat was respected for its contemporary-style home furnishings and went on to become a household name.**

Far right **The French Connection advertising campaign of 1997. The new trade name FCUK and subsequent ads created problems in America, but have subsequently been a great success for the brand improving its recognition and authority in the market place.**

For a product to be successful, a retailer must know what the public wants, understand the market and establish who the customer is. Furthermore, a product has to communicate the values of the retailer. Through market research the retailer will target his consumer group, identifying his customers and whether they match the profiles that have been set. Market research will also be used to communicate with established customers about what they want, so that the retailer can ascertain how to fulfil their needs with products or services – either new or extended. The retailer will also be aware of forecasters' information, and of what independent designers at the top end of the market are doing – using them as a barometer of trends – as well as making extensive use of product and materials research.

Even if a company has been in business for years, it still has to reassess and move on. For example Habitat was a well-established and successful retailer for many years but, through a lack of investment and without continuous product development, its products became tired and old during the 1980s. Many other retailers were starting to sell the same and similar products at cheaper prices, and so it began to lose its unique selling point, which was providing contemporary design at affordable prices. The products and stores began to lose their way and, following the involvement of a succession of management teams, was eventually sold to the IKEA Foundation in 1995. Habitat has since redeveloped its products and stores, and has regained its position as a retailer with vision, confidence and integrity.

Finding an image

The product concerned will itself suggest an image, on which the marketing department and the retailer will work; it then becomes the task of the retail designer to communicate that image effectively. Sometimes the image will be working 'with' the identity of the product, and sometimes against it. Establishing an appropriate image in fashion, for example, will involve the right selection of models and stylists, while in home furnishings it will centre on choices such as whether a catalogue or brochure is used and on how windows are created to display the products.

Image is also conveyed through advertising, and this communication method can equally be used to introduce a brand new image. Ralph Lauren's diverse product ranges show how this can be done effectively: for instance, different images apply to the company's Blue, Polo, childrenswear and Sport ranges. French Connection's advertising campaign launched in 1997 using the F&C theme was based on selected images using themes of colour, sexiness, warmth and comfort. The image shots used in their advertising were intentionally consistent with those in brochures and on point-of-sale reference cards.

An example of how a product has successfully engineered an image change – and thus found itself a new market – is Absolut vodka. Now ingrained in youth culture as a 'cool' drink, this image has been achieved by endless promotions at events attended by young people. Brands can

also successfully ally themselves with a particular market through sponsorship and, increasingly, retailers are employing the same tactics.

Levi's is a company which has been forced continually to reinvent its product image during the long history of its garments, from working clothes to the 'must-have' red tabs and button-flies of the 50s and 60s. The company's marketing campaigns have become so sophisticated that

Above **The DKNY logo was a fantastic success both for the designer, Peter Arnell, and for the company itself (Donna Karan New York). Indeed, now it has become synonymous with New York City, and reflects the American preoccupation with patriotism and with all things big.**

they are guaranteed media coverage in their own right. Yet this is a market which has changed dramatically. Levi's no longer has a monopoly over 'the jeans to be seen in' as designer labels, more retro styles and high-street retailers all threaten the supremacy of the famous Levi studs and pockets. Furthermore, younger consumers no longer automatically consider jeans for casual wear: they have considerably greater choice. James Dean may once have been an icon of rebellion, but even his charisma would have had to work hard to reach across five decades.

Levi's is, however, a good example of how brands which speak directly and frankly to their target customers will be rewarded with more than loyalty: they can become a part of popular culture.

Staying ahead

It is clear that retailers can never take their customer loyalty for granted. Instead, as the market reaches saturation point (particularly in grocery and food in general), they are increasingly forced to seek out what will make them the retailer of choice. That quest may be centred on sourcing new products and brands or on launching services which broaden the customer base. It may also take into account existing customers' needs – should they be rewarded for their loyalty and if so, how?

Consumers are more able and willing to shop around than ever and as a result, retailers need to find ways to ensure that those consumers make an active choice to spend money with them. A retailer can create a point of difference in a number of ways by listening to customers and ensuring that any suggested ideas or voiced complaints are acted upon. Retailers also need to listen to suggestions from within their organisations and therefore create a culture of empowerment which rewards creative thinking from employees. Some retailers have done this by giving employees share options, others by paying bonuses for money-making (or saving) ideas. There is no easy equation which ensures a retailer will stay ahead, other than that of being in touch both with consumers and staff and being proactive with trends.

Below **Absolut Vodka advertising** *stretches the boundaries between art and advertising. The ads are witty and always feature the bottle with two- or three-word captions. The Absolut Cities of Europe campaign appeared in* Newsweek *featuring one city in every other issue.*

Ultimately, staying ahead means taking risks, although the more in touch a retailer is, then the more informed those risks will be. Take, for example, the anti-mall concept behind the Lab opened in California, USA in 1994, aimed at teenagers and other consumers who had had enough of suburban shopping malls. It simulated urban dereliction, concentrating on local retailers with Tower Records and Urban Outfitters representing the national chains, and provided space for concerts, films, poetry readings and fashion shows. Another risk-taking venture was the launch of Lush, based on the sale of beauty products which looked more like chunks of cheese and vats of yogurt than soaps and conditioners. There are many UK retail observers who have questioned the wisdom of the department store, Selfridges, for not launching own-brand fashion. The store promotes itself as a destination for brands, but this decision goes against the trend, certainly in the UK.

When Tim Waterstone founded the UK's leading bookseller, Waterstones (which was then subsequently bought by the HMV group), he ran up against some major obstacles in raising the funds to support the project. However, his wide experience in bookselling combined with self-belief and a willingness to take risks resulted in what proved to be an enviable success.

Above **Paul Smith campaign of autumn/winter 1996. These graphic enhanced images by designer Alan Aboud used to promote this fashion brand are direct and provocative. Their eccentric use of colours and alternative style gives a clear brand value.**

Finding a focus

The fashion industry has a crucial role in dictating contemporary style and taste. These trends will in turn inform the rest of the retail industry – whether for home furnishings, food or DIY. Essentially design assimilates the hierarchy of information and social history. In the UK the historical traditions of trading, travel and the extended Commonwealth have introduced a rich variety of cultural influences – including foods, fabrics, jewellery and homewares – to the public. Many European families have links across the world's continents, with old colonial associations now

Above **World markets have strongly influenced many designers and stylists who travel the world looking for cultural inspiration, manufacturing expertise and artefacts to export.**

replaced by more fundamental family ties, bringing Indian, Caribbean and Far Eastern culture into the mainstream; in the USA, the search for cultural roots has become a national preoccupation. Retailers are not excluded from this social phenomenon and need to respond actively to it. In addition, cheaper, more accessible global travel has resulted in consumers who wish to replicate at home what they have experienced overseas.

The development of retail design

Trends in retail design eventually come full circle, but also reflect the concerns of the time. Just as the 1980s was a period of excess, mirroring the economic boom, in the 90s retail design was expected to communicate changing values such as the family, ecology and the environment. This was evident in the evolution of eco-friendly products and the use of natural materials. The challenge facing retailers and designers is continually to invent new formats and scenarios which are exciting and stimulating. Shop environments are used as vehicles of communication; to inform, educate and entertain as well as to promote and sell products.

The flagship store

Flagship stores are a relatively new phenomenon, emerging in the last 10 years from the retailers' desire to make a larger-than-life statement about their companies and their brands. This is the most dramatic statement a retailer can make: space will be used to impress, and furniture and fittings will be of the highest quality. Such stores will generally be located in prime retail sites. Financed jointly from a company's development and marketing budget, they are more recently expected to be loss leaders – their value is as a billboard for the brand. Flagship stores such as Nike Town in New York achieve impact through media coverage and as tourist attractions.

The flagship store is the brand extended to its limit in retailing terms, and its importance lies in the wider influence that it can exercise on consumers. The reason for the enormous scale of flagship stores is simply that space impresses, and the trend is for sites to be even bigger. Developers and landlords have taken advantage of this trend, and are combining smaller units to provide accommodation for larger retailers. Size is not the only important factor, however: location is of prime significance, and premiums are being paid for the right site in a specific location. Many retailers cannot, of course, compete in this respect with the global players, whose enormous funds can define shopping streets in major cities all over the world.

The value of good design

Good design challenges people's perceptions, supports retail strategies and accelerates consumer activity. In the UK, the Design Business Association runs annual awards to assess design effectiveness. In 1996, the retail-interiors winner was the clothes store Oasis, whose Covent Garden outlet saw sales per square metre increase by 40.2 per cent after the introduction of its new look, by RSCG Conran Design.

The chief executive of the DBA had previously pointed out that key benefits of good design should include increased sales per square metre, increased spend per customer, reduced operating costs and reductions in theft.

The same principle – the vital importance of good design – is also true of packaging. Lewis Moberly developed the brand name and packaging of Italia hosiery for Pretty Polly. For every £1 spent on design, the subsequent

Below **The Nike Town flagship store in Manhattan, New York. This fantastic piece of retail theatre is highly influential in communicating the core values of the brand. The store is more promotional than commercial, as the actual retail sales square footage is unusually disproportionate.**

Above **Helmut Lang, SoHo, New York.**
This intelligent and creative use of
space is defined by its uncompromising
layout. Expanses of sculptural space are
left for art installations.

Right **Joseph, Sloane Street, London.**
This store, designed by Eva Jiricna,
made an impressive visual statement,
strong in imagery and evoking power,
strength and individuality. The glass
and steel stairway encouraged
circulation and light penetration
through to the lower floor.

turnover increased by £36.20 and additional profits by £8.60. The design managed to pay for itself in the first six weeks of the launch.

It is clear, therefore, that good design can support the commercial aspirations of retailers. The choice of designer is another central factor, and a high-profile designer can add value. There are many instances of a designer's style being adopted and translated into a brand value: in the world of fashion, Peter Marino's work for Donna Karan in London, New York and Hong Kong, Antonio Citterio's designs for Esprit in Amsterdam, John Pawson's work for Jigsaw in London and Calvin Klein in New York, and Eva Jiricna's Joseph store in London are just some examples. This approach can be problematic, however: the imposed style could overshadow the content – particularly if the designer has a strong 'signature'. Equally, if a designer who has well-known 'trademarks' works for several retailers, the results could appear similar, and promote the designer more than the retailer. Retailers may also be influenced by successful concepts elsewhere, and will adopt elements for their own stores. This runs through all retail activities, from materials and production to distribution and sales.

Consumers respond to good design, and expect environments which complement their moods and choices as well as supporting their lifestyle. Sir Terence Conran has commented that the successful retailer should 'define', rather than 'anticipate', what consumers will desire. Good retail design is an evolutionary process, produced through teamwork. At the centre of the process is the product; if the product is wrong, out of date or inappropriate, no amount of stunning visual imagery will increase its appeal. The processes which support contemporary retailing are more complex than they have ever been, but the need to have the right product on offer at the right price remains unaltered.

*Below **Pretty Polly hosiery packs designed by Lewis Moberly. The value of good design can sometimes be measured by its effectiveness in changing perceptions. This was reflected in direct sales of this new product which outsold all its competitors when it was re-launched.***

A global market

The 'price-promise' contract between customer and shopkeeper, underpinning mass-market retailing throughout the twentieth century, has resulted in some of the most fundamental social changes in Western societies. The cost of food and other goods has been incessantly driven down by competition between multiple retailers and by the economies of scale established by negotiating with suppliers. Intensive farming has changed agricultural landscapes worldwide, with vast tracts of land being sacrificed to ever-more-demanding consumers. Strawberries are available all year round; roses are grown in Kenya for European venues; mange-touts are produced in Zimbabwe; fields of cotton dominate the landscape in Turkey and India; and Barbie and Action Man dolls indirectly employ thousands in China. American and European manufacturers and retailers therefore play crucial roles in the economies of developing countries. The London-based Henley Centre, a consumer-trends consultancy, points out in its report, 'Planning for Social Change 98', that 51 of the world's largest economies are corporations, not nations.

For the average UK family, the result of these dramatic shifts is that the week's food shopping now accounts for significantly less of the household spending than it did immediately after World War II. The Henley Centre points out that, in 1940, 30 per cent of the average British household income was spent on food, whereas in 1990 this had fallen to 12 per cent. Real-term prices of clothing and household goods also fell significantly between 1974 and 1991. According to the US Department of Labor, the average US family spent 13.8 per cent of the household income on food in 1995. The University of Missouri's 'Consumer Update' newsletter in September 1998 also showed that 5.5 per cent of household income in 1995 went on clothing. The public has rewarded retailers for these achievements by embracing shopping as a leisure activity. The more often retailers induce consumers' feeling of well-being, the more often these consumers will visit and spend money – yet there is still no room for complacency. It has already been made clear that, when retailers become stagnant, the public is quick to shift allegiances.

Social change and demographics

The world's population growth is now almost exclusively taking place in Asia, Africa and Latin America, and the economic power wielded for so long by the northern hemisphere – or by so-called Western societies – has now given way to the southern. In developed countries the birth rate has fallen, whereas an increased lifespan is most noticeable in the over-45 age groups. Some societies have polarized, creating greater distinctions between rich and poor as demonstrated by, in the USA and Europe, the increased sales of luxury goods but by less dramatic changes in sales of other products. Social polarization has also been mirrored in the significant increase of sales experienced by discount retailers. In the US, Wal-Mart and Target experienced double-digit growth during 1998, while in Europe discount food retailers have expanded dramatically, particularly in Belgium, Germany, Spain, Italy and eastern European countries.

The discounters' influence has been on middle-market retailers. Research by the leading German retail group, Tengelmann in 1998 revealed that in Germany discounters had a 30 per cent market share of food sales, while in Norway the figure stood at 37 per cent. Discount grocery outlets prompted further growth of own-label ranges by mainstream supermarket groups, while, in fashion, discounters forced mid-market chains to re-evaluate their pricing policies. One of the reasons given for the decline in the mid-market fashion sector in 1998 and 1999 was that consumers responded to the lack of excitement in the offer by opting for cheapness.

The UK discount department store T.J. Hughes has declared its intention to double its store numbers from 20 in 1998 to 40, opening new stores at the rate of four or five a year. Its pre-tax profit for 1998 nearly doubled to £3.01 million (compared with £1.82 million in 1997). The company sells a range of brands, around one-third of which are sourced from clearing houses and the 'grey market' (this market uses parallel traders who deal in luxury branded goods but without the licence to do so). In 1998 the Danish discounter Netto moved into twenty-ninth place in a top-50 European food-retailer ranking set out by the UK consultancy Strategic Vision.

A report in the UK trade magazine, *In-Store Marketing* in March 1999 also pointed out that discount stores have begun investing considerably more in shopfitting and visual merchandising, as well as in product development. They are building their own brand names and are targeting specific groups of customers using the same techniques as more upmarket stores.

Youth culture has exerted one of the most dramatic influences on all aspects of society since the 1950s. Its impact has intensified in the latter part of the century, and is now embedded in the spheres of media, retail and entertainment. Other factors, however, have changed the way in which society is structured. The traditional family has been overtaken, and a range of different households has emerged: double-income couples without children, single parents, a huge increase in single-person households and a wealthy group of retired people with plenty of leisure time. All have different needs and requirements. As journalist

Christopher Field points out in his *Financial Times* report 'The Future of the Store' (1997), a consumer who once fitted into a single niche now fits into a number of categories and may even switch from one to another, according to circumstance.

Ageing 'baby boomers' have become a considerable force within societies in the northern hemisphere, which experienced the 1960s' baby bulge. In March 1998, the US National Retail Federation's magazine, *Stores*, reported on a growing consensus within the marketing community of the need to redefine strategies for this group. It suggested that marketing strategies which worked for their parents would risk alienating this substantial and affluent group, and pointed out that service-orientated or health-product retailers would be well positioned to appeal to these consumers, but that clothing and music retailers would have to be aware of the danger of losing them. It also said that baby boomers were not ready to grow old or to be perceived as old: they might have grown-up families but, equally, could have young children or be preparing for second careers. What is certain is that they defy definition.

Below **Some of the biggest global brands have untapped potential. Manchester United, having won an unprecedented range of competitions, has a loyal global audience. By association and sponsorship such brands can achieve massive exposure, and penetrate markets worldwide.**

Above **This Levi Strauss campaign presents an interesting play on pre-conceived notions of image. From the rear a youthful, desirable blonde, but from the front an old lady, raising the issues of ageism, sexual taboo and product placement. Whatever your opinion, the image has great power.**

New consumer habits

In a 1998 study entitled 'The Consumer Paradox', Wendy Liebmann found that consumers aged 55 and over represent 33 per cent of adults in the USA and 50 per cent of the nation's disposable income. She pointed out that this group was shopping less and therefore contributing to the decline of department stores and malls as well as to specific product categories. She suggests that another influencial group for US retail consists of 'ethnic' consumers – Hispanics, African-Americans and Asians – who today represent almost 30 per cent of the US population. This group is shopping more, offsetting the decline in department stores and malls, and positively influencing key product categories, particularly clothing retail.

An important factor in the changing face of retail is the pressure on time experienced by consumers. Time is a precious commodity, and many people no longer have the opportunity or the will to scour the high street and mall for the shops and products they need. They increasingly prefer to shop with retailers who have invested time in making choices for them, and are therefore looking for stores they can trust to give them what they want.

There is also a greater emphasis on the home and, as many have pointed out, on the search for a sense of community to replace the family. In its report, 'Planning for Social Change 1998', the Henley Centre notes that consumers' security has been threatened by violent events, and that many people take a pessimistic view of society as a whole. Furthermore, although there may have been a waning of community activities, it seems that affection for the idea of community is strong. Paradoxically, this trend is being reinforced by globalization, which tends to intensify local and regional awareness and identities. Companies have begun to respond to this by including elements of local distinctiveness in brand, service and product identity.

Economic change

Throughout the 1980s and 90s there have been substantial changes to working practices. In theory this means more leisure time, but flexible ways of working. More people working from home or freelancing mean that it is less easy to predict when that time is available – and shopping is just one activity competing for it. With the emergence of shopping during the late twentieth century as one of the prime leisure activities, and the rise of intense competition for a share of disposable income, retailers now have to work even harder to attract consumers. It is no longer merely the ability to buy, but the 'desire' to buy that counts.

Consumer behaviour over the last 30 years has also been strongly dictated by economic performance. Financial stability has been uncertain at different periods, and the economy has swung between boom and bust periods: inflation has become an important word in our vocabulary and simple patterns of human behaviour have become blurred. Furthermore, changing ownership within large retail companies has turned the industry into a highly professional sector. Many retailers are now publicly listed on the stockmarket, and retailing dynasties have been replaced in the boardroom by professional accountants with little or no knowledge of merchandise. Many family-owned groups have lost control and, as a result, personality, character, idiosyncrasy and values have altered in turn.

New directions in public policy

In the 1980s there was a boom in out-of-town retailing in Europe. In the UK, incentives were offered to developers to build on brown-field sites on the edges of towns, and to tap into the expanding car culture. Pressures on high street infrastructures exacerbated the situation, and massive malls were planned to which people could drive and then park easily. Unfortunately, however, this had a negative effect on the long-term development of town centres, and the boom had to be curbed by changes in government policy to stop the flow of consumers out of the city centres. Retail traditions have therefore moved full circle, with current planning laws reconfirming the value of the high street and blocking significant out-of-town retail development.

In the USA, where there is no shopping-street culture, there have been recent attempts to create street activity through artificial means, particularly with factory-outlet centres. Disney's regeneration project in Manhattan (still in its planning stage) also illustrates a move towards the culture of the traditional street.

One of the lasting effects – and benefits to retailers – brought about by out-of-town retailing in the UK was a more leisure-focused approach to shopping, which translated to a number of different retail formats such as Children's World, Toys 'Я' Us, and the Disney and Warner Brothers stores. While the shopping mall in the USA has traditionally been more of a leisure centre, in the UK this was more the exception than the rule. Yet regional shopping centres such as the Metro Centre in Newcastle and a number of factory-outlet centres have made a point of becoming leisure destinations in their own right and, as a result, have captured consumers for longer periods. Jane Lamacraft, in her 1998 report 'Retail Design: New Store Experiences' for the *Financial Times* Retail and Consumer Publishing division, points out: 'The leisure aspect of shopping is one that is being emphasized not only by the individual retail chains, but also in shopping centres and retail parks. Proponents of the entertainment/retailing mix believe that it enhances earnings for both types of operator and helps to bring life to the shopping centres after the shops close in the evening.'

Above **Discovery Channel flagship store, Washington DC, USA. This store, designed by Ron Pompei, is an association of museum, television and retail. It draws on the imagery and resources of the TV channel dedicated to the natural world, and on this basis becomes a brand building exercise.**

Retail traditions

The architecture of retailing inevitably reflects social, cultural and economic changes. One of the most fundamental examples is the architecture of shopping streets, arcades and department stores; another is the development of chain stores and their impact on traditional family-owned shops. The much-maligned open shopping precincts of the 1960s were, in the UK, the first steps towards a purpose-built out-of-town mall. In the USA malls were the obvious answer to shopping – as soon as car ownership became more widespread – and centralized commercial developments built up on the intersections of roads and highways.

The shopping centre has had a great impact on retailing, and new, covered centres offer shopping and leisure experiences which encourage interaction and participation. The effect on retail design has been to create new environments in which leisure time and retail activity are combined. The objective is a balanced mix of the two, and there are many concepts used to achieve this, including ice-skating rinks, water features, multiplex cinemas, restaurants, bars and night clubs.

A sense of place

Prior to the Industrial Revolution, shops and stores did not exist in an organized or centralized way. Dressmakers, cobblers and tailors worked from home, so that their businesses were simply an extension of their domestic arrangements. Subsequently, craftsmen had workshops which opened up into side streets which customers could visit to place their orders. Products were often commissioned and made to order for a specific purpose.

The Industrial Revolution and the migration from the countryside into the cities changed craft-based skills and culture into a mass-produced and automized manufacturing process. Outlets had to be found in which products could be amassed for viewing by the public. Open markets had existed for many centuries and were accepted as part of everyday life, but the bazaar or arcade reflected, for the first time, a more permanent concentration of retail activity.

Arcades became covered public spaces, protected from the elements and often linking two or three busy streets. They later developed into more prestigious buildings. The 'gallerias' and arcades in Paris and Milan were the forerunners of the atrium spaces we know today.

Department stores

Of the traditional retail formats, the most forward-thinking department stores have enjoyed the greatest renaissance in recent years. The first department store, Au Bon Marché, was built in Paris in 1860. It openly encouraged access and became a place to meet, rather than merely being a means of supplying goods, and was so successful that a rival store, Le Printemps, opened five years later.

Japan's oldest department-store chain, Mitsukoshi, dates back to a seventeenth-century Tokyo kimono shop. In more recent years, department stores carry considerable

*Below **Place des Vosges, Paris, France.** This historic square has been a social and retail gathering point since the eighteenth century. Small shops surround the square, which is protected by covered walkways allowing access to other streets nearby, and intimate boutiques spill out into the passage.*

prestige in Japan with exclusive services such as the ritualistic treatment of money, and the 'customer-as-guest' approach, arising from cultural idioms of Japanese life.

From the 1950s, the department store developed in the UK through Marshall & Snelgrove and Selfridges, and in the USA with Macy's, Bloomingdales, and Lord and Taylor. Intended to attract the middle classes, these stores were beautifully designed and fitted out, and customers came to expect ever-growing spectacles of invention in window-dressing, displays and co-ordinated livery. The stores became the 'quality' shopping environment, offering huge choice, comfortable surroundings, good service and home delivery.

Department stores today fulfil a broader function. In the Far East they are often open 24 hours a day. Selfridges in London plans to glaze cover the back of the store connecting it to a hotel at the rear to allow 24-hour access to a planned leisure centre and restaurant facilities.

In the 1960s, with the emergence of independent teenagers rebelling against parental role models, department stores lost their appeal to younger people; they were replaced by new lifestyles, the sexual revolution and shops offering goods that young people wanted, such as Mr Freedom, Biba, Vidal Sassoon and Mary Quant. Although department stores still offered everything for sale in one place, they were too big and slow to take advantage of youth trends. What has made them attractive to the youth market once again is the control that they now exercise over the brands they sell, in addition to the independent development of own-brand labels. A store such as Selfridges, for instance, with its new look – including bigger open spaces and improved vertical access – can cover every stage of menswear from youth to maturity, incorporating every fashion brand. The selection in department stores is phenomenal because of the stores' buying power; another attraction is that they offer a friendly environment and social opportunities (in almost every case there will be at least one coffee bar or restaurant in which to relax, and customer-services personnel who arrange social evenings or special promotions). This is a strength on which they continue to build.

Above **De Bijenkorf department store in Amsterdam was designed by Virgile and Stone. Department stores today fulfil the same retail and social requirements as they did in the eighteenth century, providing variety and spectacle and enabling product comparisons under the same roof.**

The distinctive image of a department store also comes from the total control exercised over display and general merchandising. It can offer space to new, young clothes designers with small collections; in furnishings, it can offer designer one-offs and, because the space is available, can use such pieces to create impact. This ability to be distinctive sets the department store apart from other retailers, and is therefore a valuable asset.

There are a number of examples of how department stores have further defined their differences. In London, for instance, Lillywhites is a total-concept sports department store; Harvey Nichols is a fashion-lifestyle store, which has also became renowned for its fifth floor restaurant; while Harrods is set apart for its exclusivity as well as its history.

In the USA, however, the success of some department stores has recently been in question. Department-store designer Edward Hambrecht – responsible for Dickens and Jones, and Derry and Toms, among others – believes that the country's department stores are outdated because they attempt to offer all things to all people. He believes that even shopping malls in the USA have realized the importance of having a niche market, and that department stores should be following the same principle.

Management Horizons Europe, a research organization based in Richmond, Surrey, argues in its report 'Retailing Perspectives from America 1998' that the past two decades have seen a shake-out in ownership of department stores. The report points out that half of the corporate chains in the USA have disappeared as a result of this trend, with five companies – Dillards, Sears, J.C. Penney, May & Co and Federated (which includes Macy's and Bloomingdales) – controlling 73 per cent of sales in the sector. Only a few including Neiman Marcus, Nordstrom, Saks and

Right **Harrods' menswear department, Knightsbridge, London, 1930. A typical retail scene from this period with rows of glass-fronted cabinets and counters lining the perimeter walls, behind which stand servile salesmen in formal dress. Chairs were provided for customers while they waited to be served.**

Bloomingdales, continue to expand. Department stores in Asia have also been under pressure as a result of fierce competition from other retail formats as well as from rising property costs during the mid-1990s.

Some European department stores have also been under pressure, particularly Karstadt and Kaufhof in Germany, Printemps and Galeries Lafayette in France and House of Fraser in the UK. This is reflected in falling sales figures, and in the inability of such stores to change their retailing methods to fulfil contemporary requirements. During the 1980s, many large store groups suffered, failing to keep up with the consumer in terms of the product service and ambience. In addition goods and services were provided that were out of date and not targeted at specific consumers. Many lost sight of their core values, and attempted to compete with their rivals on all fronts. Many were also late in adopting technology, or could not justify the cost of upgrading their equipment. Stock-control systems were outdated, inaccurate and slow, so that stores had no way of knowing what was on sale, what had been sold, or how long products had been on the shelves. Indeed, many stores relied on their suppliers to provide goods continuously, without a buying guide or an overall plan.

Debate centres today on how department stores can continue to build their influence. In the USA, there is a belief that major stores are more likely to expand overseas through mail order and by opening 'shops in shops'. (For example, Harrods, Selfridges and Liberty are opening satellite stores in airport tax-free zones, and are considering shop-in-shop expansions); while Saks Fifth Avenue announced in 1998 that it was aiming to become a global brand name. The announcement came after a merger with the department-store group Proffitts. In the UK, own brands are the route being pursued by the majority of department stores – with the exception of Selfridges, which is basing its strategy on the concept of being a top-brand outlet.

*Below **Harrods' menswear department, Knightsbridge, London, 1999. This space in the lower ground floor is cool, modern and streamlined, with concealed lighting and artificial daylight. Large photographic images are shown here, lining the walls to the entrance of the department.***

Chain stores

The alternative which emerged to upmarket department stores was mass-market retailing. Chain stores established a different retail format from the department store selling mass-market products, and this remains typical of the shops we know today. Frank Winfield Woolworth opened his first five-and-dime store in Utica, New York in 1879, and by 1919 he had opened 1,081 stores across the USA and in Europe. Between 1910 and 1931 in the USA there was a dramatic rise in the number of chain stores.

The chain-store principle – originally based on a single commodity and price point – appealed to the working classes. The approach was simple, the product was inexpensive and attainable, and the formula was widely reproduced. The result was outlets which were instantly recognizable and far more accessible to most people than exclusive department stores. The object was to establish familiar formats which standardized quality, service and delivery. Chain stores were inexpensively fitted out, and rarely offered the implied luxury of the department stores. The defining feature was usually the fascia, and most

people would regard the names of, among others, Woolworths, Boots, the Co-op, J.C. Penney and Albert Heijn (see page 34) as being part of their neighbourhood. However, in 1998, the historic name of Woolworth disappeared from US storefronts when the company changed its name to Venator, shut its 'dime stores' and prepared to move out of New York following acquisition of the Florida-based retail group, Sports Authority.

Passages and arcades

Arcade architecture throughout Europe during the nineteenth century developed from the potential offered by open iron framework and glass. The two forms of retailing developed alongside one another, using similar architectural techniques. The difference lay in their functions: open-ended covered passages were used to fill in stretches of land between buildings and, like arcades, were built by landowners and let out as individual units to small retailers and designers/makers. In the old glass-roofed arcades, it is easy to make the jump forward to the covered shopping malls of the mid- to late twentieth century.

Below left **Woolworths, Lancashire, England 1945. The chain store originally appealed to a price-conscious public. The formula was inexpensive, accessible and instantly recognizable throughout the world.**

Below right **Exterior of Marks & Spencer, Shoreham, England, designed by Aukett and Associates. This British chain store has a long history, but in recent years it has suffered huge losses of its market share to its smaller and more fashionable competitors. It is now updating its image by developing new format stores and interiors.**

Shopping centres (malls)

The shopping centre originated in the USA in the 1950s. Huge covered shopping streets, they incorporated large department stores and chain-store tenants as anchors, in order to attract more diverse and smaller independent retailers. These stores, which were surrounded by huge car parks, were attractive to car-owning families. As car ownership increases today, the centres become even more popular, especially because they offer a safe environment free from the danger and debris often associated with the streets of inner-city America.

Malls boomed in the UK and in suburban America during the 1970s and 80s, but suffered as they outgrew demand and became uniform, partly as a result of the 'developers' retail formula' which was cost-effective but became predictable and boring. There was also a recognition that the malls were failing to address the social needs of their communities, and they turned into 'hang-outs' for bored and disillusioned young people. They suffered further from the growth of factory-outlet stores and discount retailers, offering designer brands at lower prices.

In general, shopping centres come in three types: the town-centre precinct, the edge-of-town retail park and the out-of-town shopping centre or retail park. The precinct was formulated to encourage safe, pedestrianized shopping areas dedicated to family shopping. They are often centrally located in towns and cities, linking a number of streets or other shopping areas.

The edge-of-town retail park is a format used in the UK in the late 1970s and in the following two decades, as derelict or cheap land was used to build speculatively. These simple steel-frame buildings could be used for a number of activities provided that they complied with local-authority policies. They have little or no external architectural features and were built as quickly and cheaply as possible in order to maximize rental potential.

Although, in the UK, the growth of out-of-town shopping malls – such as the Metro Centre in Newcastle, Lakeside at Thurrock and, more recently, centres in Bristol, Manchester and Essex – was halted by a change of public planning policy, their impact continues to be felt and they have radically altered shopping and leisure patterns.

Below left **Shopping malls are developing as branded centres in their own right. They show interesting similarities in the use of design elements such as glass, daylight, multi levels and the use of curved forms. This mall in Feldspauch, Zurich was designed in 1994 by New York architect Peter Marino and Associates.**

Below right **Some of the best preserved passages and arcades are found in the industrial towns and cities in the north of England. This one is in the Victoria Quarter in Leeds, Yorkshire.**

Factory outlets

Factory outlets evolved in the USA during the 1980s as a means of selling excess and returned stock from major manufacturers, many of whom made branded goods for designers. Originally, these places lacked any character and were no more than big warehouses. As they became more popular, however, retailers took responsibility for controlling the quality of their brand image – even though goods were being sold at discounted rates. Many sites originally only opened at the weekend but subsequently became very popular all-week attractions. Today, many of these outlets, like malls, seek to combine leisure with shopping. The first such centre in the UK was in Street, Somerset, with numerous outlets of various sizes following throughout the 1990s. Many of them use a leisure attraction as a selling point, such as the historic interest of the site: for example, the Great Western Designer Village in Swindon is based in former railway yards.

Factory-outlet malls offering a range of designer labels also operate in France (A L'Usine Roubaix and Boutique des Fabricants in Troyes, near Paris) and Italy (Pelletiere d'Italia in Tuscany and Salvagente in Milan). Further expansion is anticipated in France, where a centre is scheduled to open near Disneyland Paris in the summer of 2000; centres are also planned for Barcelona, Madrid and Munich and plans are afoot for sites in Austria and Belgium.

Supermarkets

The Dutch supermarket Albert Heijn was established in 1887 when Albert Heijn took over his father's grocery store in Zaandam in The Netherlands, where the company is still based. He sold a great variety of products, including groceries, wooden shoes, liquor, dredging nets and tar. In

Left **J Sainsburys, Plymouth. Designed by Jeremy Dixon and Edward Jones, this amazing structure is striking against the coastal skyline of Plymouth. Sainsbury has had a corporate redesign by the London Consultancy 20/20 which aims to re-establish them as the biggest food retailer in the UK.**

1897 further stores were opened under his name in Alkmaar, the Hague and Amsterdam; within 10 years there were 23. The first Albert Heijn self-service supermarket opened in 1955 in Rotterdam, and there was significant expansion from that date onwards. In the USA, the first supermarket – King Cullen – was opened in New York in 1930 by Michael Cullen. During the 1930s' Depression, supermarkets became popular for their low prices.

Supermarket groups, in business terms, are setting the pace in relation to their use of technology and diversification into new areas. The numbers of products on offer have been substantially increased, as well as the product areas: independent butchers, bakers, pharmacists, off-licences, greengrocers and delicatessens have all suffered as a result. Newer areas of diversification will be examined in Chapter 2 (see page 71), but this is now the principal motivating force for supermarkets faced with market saturation. Top food retailers are also actively seeking new markets overseas in order to grow. These include Delhaize le Lion in Belgium, Dairy Farm International in Hong Kong, Ahold in The Netherlands, Carrefour and Promodes in France, and Metro and Tenglemann in Germany.

The majority of supermarkets have, however, started to address – in design terms – the dramatic shift in their role in domestic markets. Ahold, for example, through its revolutionary design has changed the concept of supermarket shopping. Part of the Royal Ahold Group in The Netherlands, Albert Heijn has generated considerable interest in its 'World of Worlds' concept store in Haarlem, which breaks away from the traditional supermarket-aisle layout and has substituted a layout based on how consumers shop, or based on themes. For example, there are sections for breakfast which include cereals, fruit juice, butter, coffee and jam. Other features include self-scanning, electronic shelf-edge labelling, a children's play area, a wine-information service, Internet points and trolleys fitted with 'fridges' for chilled foods.

Other significant changes in food retail in recent years have included meeting the growth in demand for ready meals, and the rise of convenience shopping; an increase

in the amount and variety of organic food available, in response to an increasingly health-conscious public; the recognition by supermarkets of consumers' needs for town- and city-centre sites during the working day; and the development of forecourt shopping. The emergence of discount food retailers has also threatened the supermarkets and led to development of economy own-brand labels. One of the pinnacles of this battle was the baked-bean 'price wars' in the UK that took place during 1996.

Food retailers have also become increasingly involved in community-based activities through recycling schemes, a trend towards supporting local suppliers, and educational initiatives. With the addition in some cases of shoppers' crêches, cafés and cookery demonstrations, and support for charities, as well as special events for loyalty-card holders, they are beginning to meet social needs as well.

Above **Dean and Deluca, Broadway, New York. This specialist store has established strong credentials with the population of New York. Located in the downtown district of 'SoHo', it provides a stylish environment for the freshest and most attractive food displays.**

'Category killers'

This term describes everything that the consumer would want in a particular category within a single venue, with a huge choice available. A result of US trends for bigger and better stores, among the best known is Toys 'Я' Us, which, when established promised unrivalled choice.

Minimalism and high fashion

The paring away of pastiche, unwanted detail and decoration in favour of a mix of contemporary design with handcraft skills adds respect and value to a product. The search for purity has a link with a new and purist form of architecture known as minimalism, referring back to traditional Japanese architecture. Such an environment can be intimidating because it rejects and challenges accepted views. For certain leading retailers, however, it is essential to develop a point of difference, and many continue to look further afield for their ideas and take more risks.

Above **Urban Outfitter, Kensington, England. This was the first London-based outlet store for this American group, established in 1970. The open-plan format presents a deconstructed aesthetic where the structure is stripped out and exposed, aimed at a young lifestyle market.**

Far right **Nowhere, Shibuya, Tokyo. This store, which is designed by Masamichi Katayama of H Design Associates Inc., reveals a notably minimalist interior. A beautifully defined space featuring concealed lighting, the atmosphere is cool and the environment is defiantly unfriendly; the excitement of the interior comes through the detailing and the sensitive use of materials.**

Lifestyle retailing

One of the buzzwords of the 1980s, 'lifestyle retailing' was a term coined by the media for the prevalence of chain stores indulging in product diversification. This aspirational technique, aimed at stimulating customers' desire to spend by selling a co-ordinated lifestyle, helped these shops to become specialist mini-department stores.

The UK group, Next, was an important exponent of this form of retailing. The Next brand became a market leader in the 1980s, as well as a chain store credited with the introduction of many new product innovations, including fully co-ordinated seasonal products, fresh flowers, café bars, homewares and children's wear, within a focused format. The US store, Urban Outfitters, has sought to do the same with its stores. Founded in 1970 as The Free People's store (its name was changed in 1976), the first London outlet, which was opened in High Street Kensington in 1998, aimed to be a one-stop shop for 18 to 25 year olds, featuring labels from a wide range of new designers in the UK and music by the Ministry of Sound.

Traditional stores

Traditional outlets have survived precisely because they offer an alternative to mass consumerism. In London, stores such as J.J. Fox Cigars in St James Street, Smith's Umbrella Shop in New Oxford Street, and Swayne and Adie selling guns and saddlery in Mayfair, or in Tokyo the Toraya Hat Shop in Ginza Central Street survive because they offer traditional values and belief systems alongside traditional products. They refer back to a time when service was highly valued and when class was clearly defined. With loyal customers, they tend to remain at the upmarket end.

Youth retailing

Youth culture first began to be commercially exploited by retailers such as Mr Freedom during the 1960s. Clothes, music, publishing and the arts began to expand as a result of the new presence occupied by young people reacting to the austerity that their parents had known. The full potential of this market was realized in the 1970s, when 2001 Space Odyssey, Chelsea Girl, Top Shop and Biba were launched to create a mass market for teenagers.

Youth culture has always been led by independent thinking. Punk style was the obvious reaction to the commercialization of a movement which had shifted out of the hands of the young. Vivienne Westwood's Seditionaries and Sex in London's World's End became the focus for another shift, but by the end of the 70s there was further commercial activity, with Benetton and Fiorucci following a new, more European style. During the 1980s, Paul Smith catered for young people with more money, while the Burton Group (now Arcadia) and Next catered for a larger market.

Throughout the 1980s, 'lifestyle' was the buzz word exemplified by Ralph Lauren and Next in the UK. By the end of the 1980s, however, recession hit the USA and Europe and many lifestyles changed. Gap bridged the shift into the 1990s with its ranges of quality, fashion, utility clothing. By the early 1990s, there was a sense that youth culture was burning out, yet the sportswear market took over and boomed with the transfer of icon status from pop to sport stars, a trend epitomized by Nike Town flagship stores.

What the development of youth culture illustrates in retail terms is that young consumers' needs are fulfilled through independent outlets which subsequently encourage commercial exploitation. These independents cannot compete in bulk, but exert a substantial cultural influence.

The entrepreneur

Movers and shakers are individuals who have stamped their views on the organizations: French Connection's Stephen Marks, the Bennet brothers (at Warehouse and Oasis), Roger Saul at Mulberry, Margareta Ley at Escada, Issey Miyake and Yoji Yamamoto. Others include cosmetics and fashion houses: Estée Lauder, Coco Chanel, Yves St Laurent, Calvin Klein, Ralph Lauren and Donna Karan.

Above **Traditional épicerie store, France. Such stores exist as independent and often family-owned businesses worldwide. They are perhaps most visible in countries where mass-market retailing predominates – namely in Europe. They are generally pitched at the upper end of the retail spectrum.**

NOWHERE

Retail boom

The expansion of choice

From fashion to electronics, DIY, home furnishings, perfume, cosmetics, books and records: there is a chain store or an independent retailer to cater for every taste. Indeed, choice is the key to successful contemporary retail and has been an important element in the increasing floor-space demanded by major retailers in the USA and Europe.

Globalization of retail has also increased choice. It has resulted in brands such as Esprit, Morgan and Kookai from France, Gap from the USA, Episode from Hong Kong and Mango and Zara from Spain, all establishing themselves in the UK, and in large numbers of UK retailers moving overseas. Moves abroad can be motivated by the potential benefits of selling into the new markets of Poland, South America and Russia, as well as into the more established retail markets in Europe and the Far East. Other retailers have spotted opportunities in the UK: these include the discount food retailers, Aldi and Lidl, which recognized the economic polarization of the population; as well as enter-tainment-led retailers such as Disney and Warner Brothers from the USA; and the Swedish furnishing retailer, Ikea.

The 1980s was the decade for expansion by fashion retailers, including Benetton, Levis, Laura Ashley and Sears, as well as brands such as H & M, Bata, Armani, Donna Karan, Louis Vuitton and Hermes. In the 1990s, this movement slowed down, with the exception of a number of medium-sized chains seeking outlets abroad, among them Jigsaw, Oasis and Next from the UK; Cortfeil and Zara from Spain; and Kookai and Morgan from France. The American brand, Calvin Klein, has opened outlets in London, Madrid, Barcelona, Lisbon, Milan and Moscow (it was the first American designer to open in the Russian capital). Of non-fashion retailers, The Body Shop has expanded throughout the USA, South America, Asia and Europe; other leading international players from within the UK have been HMV and Vision Express.

Food retailing is the second-largest sector to have developed internationally. The grocery groups are Europe's largest retailers, and possess the most power to expand since they are sought-after by developers to anchor shopping centres. These are now the dominant economic forces in European retail.

Below **Virgin is a successful example of brand stretch diversification. Founder and entrepreneur Richard Branson has successfully developed a group of companies trading on the established and trusted Virgin brand – these include Virgin Rail (below left), Virgin Cola (below centre), Virgin Atlantic, Virgin Cinema, Virgin Music and Virgin Brides (below right).**

Methods of expansion

Four of the methods used by retailers moving overseas are organic expansion, acquisition, joint venture and franchising. There is still huge potential for international growth, particularly with the expansion of the European Union, and opportunities for global brands, worldwide advertising and advances in technology.

Extension of brands

The proliferation and variety of today's media mean easier access to high fashion and to brands previously regarded as being beyond the reach of most consumers. The Recession and popularization of brands such as Chanel, Armani and Donna Karan worldwide led to consumers wanting top designs at affordable prices. In order to feed this growing interest a number of diffusion lines were created, which were lower in price and therefore more accessible. Designers were also lured by multiples into translating their ideas into accessories so that, while the brands retain a certain exclusivity, the lower priced items by designers had a much larger audience.

Brands and international choice are central to global competition. The phrase 'Think Global, Act Local' is the message for new retail which has been expounded by international companies such as MTV, BA, Virgin and DKNY. Multi-media access through cable, Internet and digital TV is common across continents. MTV can deliver a message globally to the youth of all nations, and fads and trends can become global movements within hours. The influence on youth culture is enormous, but brands are also heavily influenced by different cultures, which leads to a constant cross-fertilization of ideas. Retailers and designers must learn to harness these images: communication is a vital tool. New retail is multi-layered: it is about cross-cultural collaborations and fusions, and about experimentation, continually testing consumers' basic assumptions.

The use of branding by retailers is a complex issue. While, historically, retailers have provided vehicles for manufacturers to sell brands, they have also needed to brand themselves in order to offer diverse products to a particular audience. Manufacturers have also increasingly become retailers in their own right; examples of such companies include Levis and Nike. Such manufacturers have used the flagship stores (see pages 20, 56 and 132) to communicate their values and image on a large scale; as well as small 'shops in shops' – a tactic used to build up consumer recognition of, and confidence in, a brand before a stand-alone store is launched in a high street or mall. Among the manufacturers which have taken these two routes are Nike, which progressed from being a supplier to a retailer by building a range of flagship stores to promote the company's brand values and philosophy; and Escada, which opened 'shops in shops' to launch Escada Sport.

During the 1990s, department stores and food retailers launched a wide range of own-brand labels. In the case of department stores, many of these labels have their own image and operate as if they were independent of the store. In food retail, own-branded goods may be designed as part of a price-led or economy range where the packaging is basic and clearly identifies the items as cheap options, or may be an attempt to copy a well-established brand.

Above **Muji, Covent Garden, London, designed by Harper Mackay. This 'no name' brand provides simple, stylish basics – with products covering furniture, storage, food and fashion. The brand has now established itself internationally with particular popularity in the Far East.**

In fashion, most department stores carry ranges of own-brand labels. A retail designer's job in this instance will be to develop graphics, labelling and a 'shop-in-shop' environment to fit these lines. A number of exclusive retailers such as Nicole Farhi and Tommy Hilfiger are also extending their brands up by diversifying into even more exclusive versions of their ranges.

In contrast, the reaction by some retailers to the heavily branded environments that are now so common in high streets and malls was to create an impression of no branding at all (Muji is the prime exponent of this: the name actually means 'no brand'). The idea suggests that the retailer is supplying basic products designed for simple, functional jobs. None of the items sold by Muji are branded, but they became fashionable because of their association with quality, integrity and authenticity. In other words, they are products in which design is the most important component. The fashion retailer, Egg, operates in the same way, with the added advantage of having been founded by well-known individuals – Asha Sarebai and Maureen Docherty. Their marketing strategy was to build up Egg's reputation by word of mouth, therefore maintaining a warm, personal association with customers. This rejection of overt branding and fashion suggests exclusivity, but it is not a rejection of branding: it simply takes a different form.

Another manifestation of the reaction against heavily branded interiors is the trash aesthetic: essentially a deconstruction of retail interiors prevalent in the late 1980s and early 1990s, and based on the ideas of architect Rem Coolhouse. This deconstructivism was a reaction against the post-modernist approach, and sought truth in buildings and architecture through disposing of superficial architectural detail, exposing how buildings worked (by removing the cladding from ducting, showing wires and so on) and being honest about how a building interior was designed.

Any new brand or retail concept is a reaction to what is already on the market. What retailers need to be aware of is the public's increasing feeling of vulnerability (see page 26). The image of trust on which retailers have always relied is based today on a different concept: that of ethical business which is responsible to the people who are contributing towards a company's profits (i.e. its employees and customers). New retail entrepreneurs have understood this need for integrity, and are building the ethos into their organizations, both in the way they sell their products and in the way they deal with their customers.

Advertising/marketing

Retailers' advertising options have never been greater than they are today but the difficulty with this promotional approach is one of ensuring that the message reaches the right audience. As well as having the option of mailing customers directly, retailers can choose from a diverse range of mediums, including television and radio stations, the Internet, newspapers, magazines and billboards. Increasingly, too, advertisements are carried in-store, on trolleys, at the point of purchase and even on floors. In addition there are indirect marketing opportunities for retailers, such as the sponsorship of sporting, arts and educational events.

Advertising on the Internet is opening up new approaches for retailers. Levis, for example, uses icons which reveal an entertaining message about the brand; Pampers nappies are promoted by Proctor and Gamble in the USA through an on-line parenting magazine and advice service. Customer magazines are another more indirect method of advertising and of extending a retailer's brand by association with a popular form of media; they are aimed in particular at female customers. Customer magazines can be directly targeted to groups of customers by producing different versions of the core product. There is a blurring of distinction, too, between magazines and catalogues, with some functioning as paid-for titles which effectively challenge established consumer publishing, while others are available free of charge; these are more sophisticated than catalogues, but contain no external advertising.

The fundamental principles of marketing are also changing as brands reassess their relationship with consumers. Much effort is being directed towards keeping customers by convincing them that a solution for their needs is being offered, as opposed merely to a product. For international retailers, cross-cultural marketing (in other words marketing which is not culture-specific) will increasingly become an issue. Cause-related marketing – such as that espoused by The Body Shop (including campaigns on body image and domestic violence) – has become a general trend, most notably among multi-national companies such as Shell and British Nuclear Fuels, as well as among other retailers such as Adams through its link with Save the Children. The UK trade magazine *In-Store Marketing* reported in November 1998 that the advertising agency Saatchi and Saatchi has a department devoted to cause-related marketing. In the USA, Home Depot has stated that community development is as much a part of its business strategy as its products.

Below **The Benetton advertising campaigns in the 1990s created reactions of outrage and disgust. Topics such as race, religion and sex were woven into provocative and sometimes overpowering images, which questioned perceptions of taste and appropriateness within the fashion world. New Born Baby by creative director Oliviero Toscari, 1992.**

UNITED COLORS
OF BENETTON.

new kinds of retail

The guiding principle of new approaches to retail is consumer focus – retailers need to understand and respond to how consumers shop. Technology has clearly played a significant role, but perhaps equally significant is the shift in expectation which has taken place within advanced consumer societies: people now expect better levels of service, more choice and guaranteed quality, as well as an interesting environment.

The consequence of this is that retailers have been pushed into becoming more flexible in how they present their products. There is now the option of shopping 24 hours a day using the Internet, and even in stores to a more limited extent. More retailers are introducing catalogues, brochures or magazines to present a wider range of products, therefore encouraging mail order and telephone sales.

There is a growing awareness of how consumers shop differently at various points in the week, or day. There is also a greater recognition among retailers of consumers' shopping habits – in particular, of their need to be entertained and looked after. This is not simply altruistic, as retailers know that there is intense competition for consumer spending from the leisure industry. More people are eating out than ever before and, if retailers can tap into this with in-store cafés or restaurants, they will encourage shoppers to stay with them longer.

New retail is also about retailers adapting formats to suit different moods or circumstances, and the adage that 'one size fits all' clearly no longer applies.

Cross-cultural influences

Previous page **Joe's Café, London.**

Below **Cross-cultural influences and movements are quickly communicated around the world. Chinese adolescents adopt 1950s' rock and roll and take to the streets during the October Festival.**

As the world becomes smaller due to intercontinental travel, trends, styles and colours can be communicated between countries within minutes. There is access to a breadth of information which was unthought of in previous decades, with the consequence that it is much harder to identify where trends begin or who is responsible for them since more people are dipping into a shared pool.

This is a marked difference from decades such as the 1960s and 1970s when, for example, the Japanese influence could be identified in European designers' clothes and in minimalist shopping environments such as the first Joseph store in the UK. Pop culture within the UK and USA during the 1960s also influenced the world, and deconstructivist and post-modernist international architects were responsible for copycat trends in Europe. US retailer Ralph Lauren was influenced by British traditional retailers, whose characteristics he recycled as a brand. Brands have become global in a relatively short period of time. Where previously it would have taken many years for some brands to achieve an international presence, it is now possible for them to buy their way into new continents by creating a global marketing strategy with saturation advertising and product placement.

Finding the right design

Minimalism will be recognized as an influence in new retail, just as more traditional images will remain as the counterpoint. Which to pursue will ultimately rest on how cohesively each one sits with a retailer's product and style.

Tommy Hilfiger, for example, makes clothes which appeal to gangland Los Angeles and, at the other end of the spectrum, to preppy Middle America. However, the shop environment reflects the latter image. Some retailers have recognized that classic style alone has little future, so they have evolved more youthful ranges. Ralph Lauren's future was assured with the development of the Polo Sport range.

By contrast, Paul Smith sells contemporary collections of clothes but chooses to sell them in a traditional manner. His first shop in Covent Garden was a minimalist concrete interior which proved less successful than a range of clothes sold in a shop retro fitted with old-style furniture.

Men's formal clothing, as a general rule, was sold in traditional environments, because these are what men associate with tailoring. Sporty products need more youthful environments, while women are expected to be more fashion-conscious, to take more risks and to be more able to tolerate minimalism.

Below **The 1999 Diesel advertising campaign uses superimposed images and familiar metaphors of romance, desire, music and flowers.**

Accommodating new technology

The impact of technology can be viewed from two angles: the way in which it relates directly to how a retailer operates, and the way in which it affects consumers. The innovative use of technology is a major force in changing retail strategy: essentially, it is a tool for competing against other retailers and for gaining a market edge. Retailers use technological advances in order to understand their consumers and to improve their environments and margins, whether through better distribution techniques, general managerial efficiency or by generating more marketing information. The technology now available and being used by some of the world's leading retailers, such as Wal-Mart in the USA (see pages 24, 71), enables retailers to cut down dramatically on the staff needed for mechanical tasks.

Information-gathering

Through electronic point of sale (EPOS), loyalty systems and ever-more sophisticated market research, the supermarket retailer can identify the contents of its customers' shopping trolleys on any specific day, week or month, and thus create personal profiles from which to gain data about shopping patterns on individual, local, regional and national scales. This allows the retailer to anticipate shopping behaviour to offer the kinds of products that suit specific stores, as well as to inform individual households of goods that will suit their particular requirements. This is done through the loyalty scheme, which targets known household needs and makes discounted product offers which in turn generate more sales.

In theory the data which can be held on today's households is awesome. Sophisticated data-matching techniques allow retailers to buy information from a number of different sources and, when this information is combined with loyalty-card details, to build up an in-depth profile of their customers. In practice, however, retailers very often fail to exploit the potential that technology has given them – even for updating databases of customer addresses – and have only just begun to experiment with how they can best exploit the techniques available to them.

Information about customers and their buying patterns can ultimately be used either in personalized marketing or to inform visual merchandising strategies in store. Data mining – the use of this information – is being developed to provide personal shopping lists, or to vary merchandise store by store. Self-scanning technology – currently used in some supermarkets – is an example of a development which has benefited retailer and customer alike: used in conjunction with loyalty cards, it can build a picture of a particular customer and enable the retailer to prepare one-to-one promotions which are activated as soon as a customer picks up a scanner. For the customers, it means less time at a till and the ability to keep a check on how much they are spending as they go around the shop. Ultimately, self-scanning linked with swipe-card payments could allow a customer to shop without having any contact at all with store staff. There are many theories about how loyalty schemes will develop in the future. Certain retailers have linked up with credit-card companies and have introduced affinity cards and 'smart' cards. Others maintain that loyalty cards could become a lowest common denominator and a 'must have' for any retailer.

The distribution of loyalty cards as an incentive to customers to shop within a particular store or group of stores developed considerably during the 1990s. From the single store card offering 'points' for purchases made, schemes also evolved which provided benefits for consumers across different sectors, some of them linking in with other services such as free air miles. Retailers are, however, aware of the continuous need to update their loyalty-scheme benefits in order to ensure that the novelty does not wear off. Stores such as Safeway in the UK and

Below **Tesco was the first to launch a supermarket loyalty card in the UK. This approach was a great success in maintaining customer loyalty and the idea was therefore quickly emulated by competing supermarkets.**

Albert Heijn in the Netherlands offer loyalty-card customers real benefits in-store, such as self-scanning to speed up the shopping process.

Some of the most valuable technological advances, from the point of view of retailers, have come from 'intelligent tills' and from the ability of the retailers to collect instant information about what they are selling, at what times of the day and to whom. A direct effect of this is much greater accuracy and speed in what is re-ordered – no small consideration when speed may give a highly competitive retailer the crucial point of difference. Many major retailers use this opportunity to send data about sales directly to a centralized distribution depot or manufacturer so that certain items can be automatically restocked. The information can also be used to move stock around stores to accommodate different sales trends, making a good distribution and transport system essential. This automatic restocking and just-in-time delivery have cut down dramatically on the amount of stockroom space needed. Since all retailers have been striving to reduce gross area (and therefore costs), this means that prime retail space can be used without wastage. Harvey Nichols department store in

London, for example, has sited its management offices away from the store itself, allowing highly expensive space to be put to maximum use. Retailers worldwide have been striving to reduce space needed to hold stock – as is apparent in the move towards 'just-in-time' deliveries.

Above **In-store screens present special offers, information and coupons to shoppers, who can highlight products which offer extra points and larger cash savings. The loyalty cards also inform the retailer of customer shopping habits and buying preferences.**

Left **Sainsbury's interactive kiosks are located conveniently at the entrance of the stores. The kiosks are used to ascertain the current balance of store loyalty cards and to exchange points for cash on purchases.**

Kiosks

Shopping can also be facilitated by interactive kiosks. Those retailers which have installed interactive kiosks have put them to a wide range of uses. One example is the UK DIY chain, Do It All, who developed a system that was aimed at helping customers to put together colours and designs for their homes within the store. A customer can concentrate on one room and make selections of wallpaper, paint and borders in various combinations in order to decorate it. The kiosk will then calculate the quantity of materials needed according to the customer's specified measurements. Kiosks have also been used by Allied Carpets, by the stationery and book retailer WH Smith to provide product information, as well as for self-service at Argos.

In France, the supermarket chain Auchan uses kiosks to help customers locate products within the store; in the USA they have been used for selling shoes, groceries, toys and cosmetics, to preview videos and to order custom-made Levis jeans. The US electronics retailer, Best Buy, uses kiosks to feature all its products and prices, and the information available to customers is the same as that available to employees. For Best Buy, the next stage could be to use

Below **The self-service information kiosks in Carland, designed by Rawls and Co., give relevant and detailed information to the prospective customer. This information is provided on screen and audio delivery is through the clear plastic domes that hover over the customer's head.**

the same system to enable customers to buy directly from their television sets. For the future, there are suggestions that interactive systems could be used on trolleys, in in-store coffee shops and to provide extra nutritional information on foods.

Technology in merchandising

The ways in which technological developments affect the consumer range from improving physical environments by introducing better lighting and air conditioning, to making cash tills more efficient and ensuring that there is more product on the floor, leading to improved choice. Video technology enables customers to be more aware of product promotions, giving them better information and greater visual stimulation with which to make a choice. As the US toy retailer FAO Schwartz shows, technology can help a store to compete on a level playing field with the leisure industry, by turning it into an entertainment destination.

As Jane Lamacraft describes in her report, 'Retail Design, New Store Experiences *Financial Times* Retail and Consumer (1998), FAO Schwartz 'designs its stores as "wonderlands", full of whimsy and entertainment. For example, customers at the flagship stores are greeted by a toy soldier and met by a cast of other characters, while in the background animated clocktowers chime. So unusual are the FAO Schwartz environments that outside retailing hours they are hired out for business parties and corporate events. There are areas where children can test out the toys and where special events and celebrity appearances are held. Lamacraft also describes the Viacom Entertainment Store in Chicago, which has a room in which customers can link to MTV via computer; and the Warner Brothers Studio store, which has an interactive games floor.

Flagship stores such as Nike Town operate on the same principle (see case study on pages 132–35). More prosaically, technology can also speed up service. For example, shoe retailers and some clothes stores are equipping their shopfloor controllers with audio headsets, therefore enabling them to communicate instantly with the sales staff, stockrooms and security to ensure quick,

efficient on-floor information and responses. This assures customers that their requirements are being dealt with on a personal basis.

Increasingly, interactive technology is being used to communicate with customers. For many this is a preferred option, as the technology can quickly provide them with information about products without the need for a sales assistant. The advantage of interactive screens is to give the uninformed, sometimes reticent customer simple, direct advice in an impartial way; this may be particularly appreciated by a man shopping in an overtly feminine domain. The machines' print-out facility is also useful, as product names and categories can be difficult to remember when the customer is faced with a multitude of choices. For retailers, therefore, more advanced technology can continue to improve their relationship with consumers by taking the drudgery out of shopping.

Gains in efficiency, space and more accurate stocking will be reflected in improved choice and availability of products. However, technological advances do contain

Above **Let's Eat, Australia, designed by Landini Associates. This fully computerized work station displays up to 1,600 dishes on screen. Recipes and lists of ingredients can be printed out to ease the buying process. Copies of videos can also be borrowed that show how the dishes are made.**

will allow a virtual-reality experience with quicker and more efficient access to new products, revolutionizing the way we shop; the other that shoppers will not wish to forgo the social, enjoyable experience of shopping, and will purchase only basic products from the computer.

Technological advances can also enable a retailer to adopt a new approach to how their products are sold – in other words, to use technology innovatively for the benefit of its customers. Some stores in the US cover thousands of square metres of retail space, but have fewer highly trained sales assistants. Visual presentation is of an extremely high standard and, while the format is that of a department store, the system is basically self-service. The strategy behind such a technique is to ensure that the visual merchandising is highly advanced, to give customers as much information as they need and to support them in making their choices, with fewer staff, so that all they need to do is to make their selection and then pay for it.

Retail support and security

Advances in security systems have enabled companies to employ a reduced staffing level. With the use of source tagging (in which security tagging is fitted before goods arrive at the store) and CCTV cameras trained on tills, fitting rooms and other vulnerable areas, retailers have less need to involve staff in the prevention of theft. In many busy high-street shopping zones it is now possible to track thieves beyond the store boundaries, with known culprits being identified to other retailers so that their staff are alerted to the imminent danger.

As already mentioned, automated stock replenishment and re-ordering systems are now run by the most advanced retailers with little human intervention at all. In fact, many believe that it is behind the scenes that the developments in technology have proved to be of most use. Computer-based training is another development which has been invaluable in product-knowledge training for staff. Good product knowledge is essential to all categories of retailers. Websites can be used to provide information on products for consumers, while Intranets can support staff in-house.

Above **Adidas kiosk, Wade Smith Outdoor Athletic, Liverpool. This in-store interactive kiosk works as both promotional and interactive screen for young customers to gain the latest information and up-to-date sports news.**

implicit difficulties for retailers, particularly in the extension of home shopping. Supermarkets, for example, make increased sales when the customer is browsing through the store, by offering associated products and enticements through sensory stimulation (see also page 81). The dilemma that they face is how to reproduce that exciting, sensory browsing experience through a home computer. Two opinions are currently being expressed about technological developments of the future. The first is that the advances

Home shopping

Demand for home shopping has come about as a result of broad social changes. These include time-starved customers, more people working from home, single-parent families and elderly people, the lack of transport, advances in home technology, and the need for retailers to compete.

Catalogues

Mail-order catalogues and retailer magazines have changed the image of home shopping. Catalogue agents have traditionally been the means by which people have shopped from home. Mail-order catalogues today provide a direct selling service between the company and the customer. This has been made possible by the development of telesales agencies, which use technology to access information about any individual's credit-worthiness, history and reliability to pay, and to confirm his or her identity and home address.

In the USA, the Sears Roebuck catalogue is almost a national institution and, during the 1980s, mail-order business grew at three times the rate of traditional retail. The decision by major UK retailers such as Marks and Spencer and Debenhams to operate catalogues has also encouraged catalogue companies such as Freemans, Grattan and GUS to refine their offer. All now include a wide selection of high-profile brands and designer ranges. At a certain level, consumer magazines and high-class catalogues have come closer together, with many magazines incorporating 'advertorials' (advertisements with an editorial content and appearance). The style and presentation of catalogues have also changed, with many using magazine formats – guiding their readers towards lifestyle solutions.

Home delivery

In grocery, home shopping can range from simple home delivery by a supermarket to a scheme whereby orders are placed by a company-based workforce, with delivery made to the office. The UK company, Next, was the first to link catalogue shopping to the high street, when it opened small catalogue shops where customers could try on clothes and then order them for home delivery. This was only possible with a promise of delivery within 24 hours of the order and using specially designed hanger clothes bags which allowed the products to be delivered almost crease-free.

Below Home shopping catalogues have created new markets by incorporating good quality design, printing and lifestyle imagery. Banana Republic and Williams-Sonoma from the USA and Alan Chan catalogues from Hong Kong present lively youthful pictures and diagrams of their products.

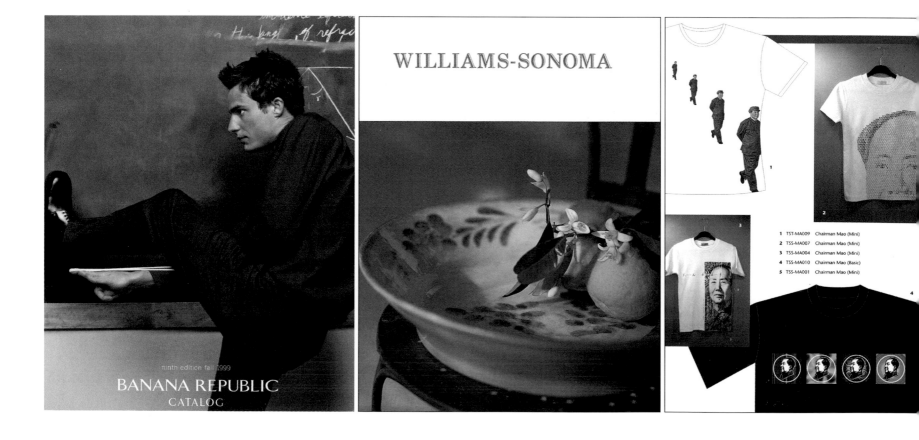

The Internet

Retailers in the UK have been slow to make use of the Internet for selling – largely due to scepticism about its economic potential and because of fears from consumers about the security of payment methods. Nevertheless, there are phenomenal forecasts for an increase in Internet use which retailers cannot ignore, and this is an area that is developing constantly.

According to IBM's Internet division in the USA, growth in Internet use worldwide at the end of 1998 was estimated at 37 per cent a year. In the 10 years from 2000, 500 million people worldwide are expected to be using the Internet. The 1999 Ernst & Young Internet Shopping Study showed that in 1997 in the USA, 12 per cent of retailers were selling on-line, while in 1998 the figure had risen to 39 per cent, with the number planning to sell on-line in 1998 at a further 37 per cent. 'As a result, in just one year, the percentage of retailers either selling or planning to sell on-line has more than doubled from 34 per cent to 76', the study concludes, adding that retailers believe that sales from the Internet will also be more significant.

One of the issues with which retailers have grappled, often unsuccessfully, is website design – the lack of success being because many companies do not understand or use the full potential of the Internet. The sites are often visually unstimulating, with too much text; they are little more than flat, static catalogue pages which fail to exploit the potential to provide fast, eye-catching moving images which could extend the visual impact of the product. Some initiatives have, however, demonstrated the possible value of the Internet. For example, the designer Helmut Lang has used the Internet to broadcast his fashion shows live.

A *Financial Times* report, 'The Future of the Store' (1998), argues that three main areas will generate income from the Internet: information services, financial services and consumer retail. The report identifies one of the key factors in driving the expansion of remote buying as the use of the Internet by women. The report points out that, in future, women will use the Web as a service, going straight to sites which can benefit them.

Digital TV

Digital TV is widely predicted to be the medium by which the general public has access to the Internet in future, since it is the electronic medium with which people are comfortable, and which they associate with leisure. One of its advantages will be better visual quality and the ability to integrate the personal computer, providing a quicker, easier way to access information and to communicate with the Internet. Interactivity is a benefit that will ultimately affect retailers, in the form of direct response. It will be possible for the broadcaster not only to react to consumer interest, but also to give additional, unsolicited information directly related to the enquiry for comparison products or services. Advertising can also be designed and directed specifically at individuals who respond to particular topics.

Below Computer manufacturers are constantly updating packages to make Internet access easier. Apple have created a successful new range of computers aimed at a more casual audience; while they look fun they are faster and more sophisticated and this satisfies the enthusiast.

Home-shopping channels will be offered by all digital TV companies. In the UK, Granada was the first to launch a digital TV shop, called Granada Shop. This brings a magazine format to the screen, integrating live discussions with designers and manufacturers, and offering background information, style tips and demonstrations on screen.

Research by pollsters Mori undertaken in 1998 revealed that 77 per cent of US consumers found it useful to shop outside normal hours, alongside 75 per cent of UK consumers and 64 per cent in France. According to Chris Townsend of PRI Media Group, and former marketing director of BSkyB television, digital TV will create thousands of new channels, with shopping, games and betting being the three key services identified by consumers, who want major high-street brands represented.

Looking ahead

The areas of new technology such as the Internet and digital TV are currently characterized by uncertainty. Home shopping does offer rewards for retailers but, for traditional companies, it also opens up a new set of potential difficulties such as setting up efficient distribution and call centres, and dealing with returned goods. Furthermore, while the Internet has created a new retail platform for various retail products, some companies have taken the opportunity to become successful electronic entities without any presence in a traditional high street or mall (such as, in the USA, Amazon.com, which has thousands of books on offer through its website). For traditional retailers it has meant new approaches to selling their products.

Management consultancy KPMG advises retailers to develop several channels for home shopping: keeping the more traditional, but also exploring the longer-term alternatives. A report by KPMG, produced in association with the Oxford Institute of Retail Management, entitled 'Home Shopping across Europe: Experiences and Opportunities' (1997), gives examples of how organizations can run multi-channel home shopping. For example, Germany's largest mail-order retailer Quelle owns half a satellite and cable shopping channel, has an Internet site, offers a CD-rom

catalogue and in 1996 began an interactive-TV trial, HOT, broadcasting to six million households by cable and satellite, which was applauded for its product quality and upmarket presentation. In another report, 'Virtual Retaility' (1997), property consultants Knight Frank advise that retailers should not underestimate the power of telephone sales. In the UK in 1998, for example, sales of car insurance over the telephone rose to 52 per cent, as opposed to just 16 per cent in 1993. Telephone banking has also increased. The significance of both changes is the ease and familiarity of the technology; however, digital television is not expected to reach critical mass in the UK for at least 10 years and, in the meantime, familiar technology should not be ignored.

As will be shown later (see pages 76, 82, 89), advances in technology have also considerably broadened retailers' visual merchandising options: from talking shelves which give information on shoes when you pick them up, used by UK sports retailer Cobra; to shelf-edge digital pricing which allows promotions to be flashed up instantly.

*Above **Digital TV was launched in the UK in 1998. This service offers better quality pictures, more channels and the opportunity to interact with the TV, therefore offering quicker access to the Internet. Granada Shop is a home shopping channel which launched the service, designed by Din Associates.***

The growing range of retail spaces

Above A typical European shopping precinct built in the late 1960s. It is open to the elements, creating central squares and meeting places. The environment is barren and represents an era of pre-cast modular building systems and faceless architecture.

Urban renewal has played a critical role in opening up the choice of varied and more architecturally interesting retail sites. In the 1980s the focus was on waterfronts and waterways, with their nostalgic trade associations and vast warehouse spaces. In the 1990s other neglected parts of the inner city have been rediscovered, and developers have sought to create mixed-use sites on industrial wasteland. Many of these areas have a local character, and have subsequently been occupied by retailers who find that they offer a richer and more rewarding environment.

In the 1980s many larger retailers had estates departments which got together to create joint development and construction companies to expand their empires. In this way, many developments were created with specific retailers involved at a very early stage. At the other end of the scale, many low-budget, independent retailers often have to find 'off-pitch' sites for cost reasons. As a result, a number of them located together on a particular street can create a specific retail experience which cannot be designed or manufactured. These small colonies – if successful – tend

to attract bigger retailers who have a greater commercial impact on their environment. Unfortunately, this often has a reverse impact: an increase in desirability drives up rents and eventually drives out the independents.

Today there is a wide range of sites available, from high-street locations, shopping malls and department stores to arcades and factory outlets. The huge success in telephone banking has released many former bank buildings, further expanding retailers' options in their search for stimulating sites. There are also converted sites or buildings which have changed their use, such as the Covent Garden area of London, the Farmers' Market area of Boston and the Queen Victoria Building, Sydney. Originally a produce market, the Queen Victoria Building opened in 1898, with shops and rooms available for rent by artists and traders; it is comparable in scale to the main arcade of Galleria Vittorio Emanuele in Milan. After the produce market had closed in 1910, the building had various uses, until in 1979 the city council sought tenders for its rehabilitation into retail. It opened at the end of 1986.

expand and desire more space – whether they are super-markets or fashion multiples. However, there are alternatives which are being trialled, including 'shops in shops' for fashion brands which increases their retail space in a city without the full cost of an independent stand-alone site, as well as a more recent diversion of food supermarkets into local corner shops and forecourts. At present, fashion flagship stores cover areas of 300–3,000 sq m (3,000–30,000 sq ft), and stand-alone large or medium shops may cover 200–500 sq m (2,000–5,000 sq ft), while the small shop-within-shop format could be 50–100 sq m (500–1000 sq ft).

It is an essential part of a designer's brief to show how new concepts translate to different sizes and formats of stores. Retail designs should show how the concept can translate the same brand values into these different formats. Each will have its own specific considerations in terms of features, space and materials, and should be recognizable in each configuration.

Left **The Great Western Designer Outlet Village, designed by Rawls & Co., is an American trend which has been replicated in Europe. This centre was created to offload brands at discounted prices. Often the products are end-of-season items or clearance stock but they must still convey the brand image and values to give authenticity.**

Below **Dean and Deluca set up their first enterprise in SoHo in New York. This area in downtown Manhattan was an industrial zone characterized by huge warehouses, and inhabited by artists and galleries.**

In general, developers are becoming more aware of the need to create an interesting retail mix both in terms of scale and diversity. This allows the smaller specialist to live alongside the bigger retailer, enabling each to feed off the other and adding a distinctive point of difference.

In the UK in the 1990s, the developers of out-of-town malls and sheds built speculatively to take advantage of local-government tax incentives (see also page 27), and had no specific users in mind during design and construction. As a result the buildings had no specific character, and relied on coloured graphics and distinctive signage. Many shopping centres were also planned and some built in the late 1980s, but the ensuing recession caused many to open with little success. The overabundance of retail space caused many local authorities to rethink their policies on out-of-town developments and to reverse planning decisions in order to bring shoppers back to the city centres.

The increasing importance of diversity in retail formats also translates into a demand for a wider range of site sizes. The trend during buoyant economic times is for retailers to

How different spaces work

A major new retail concept will often start from a flagship store which, as described previously (see page 39), is increasingly used as a three-dimensional marketing tool for advertising the retailer's brand, identity, values and philosophy. A flagship-store location has to be second to none; its design should reflect the latest developments in terms of product and brand. The design will often be cutting-edge, and is expected to be special in terms of features, fixturing and materials. These stores are often costly to build, but are important status symbols in the international arena. Smaller and different types of spaces – such as department stores, malls and stand-alone sites – require a different approach towards shopfittings and density, which will be dictated by financial and space limitations. The smaller-spaces route enables the retailer to devise a brand strategy which allows him to build his brand's awareness through department store corners and 'shops in shops', without exposing himself financially on stand-alone stores. This route is taken by many companies which are new to a country or area, and for new product launches.

A large store will have a substantial budget and a designer can therefore produce a strong image, exploiting the shopfront, interior layout, circulation, merchandising, specialist fittings and equipment to develop the brand strategy. In a 30 sq m (300 sq ft) corner of a department store, however, a designer needs to consider carefully how every bit of space is used. In these small areas a different selection of fixturing and furniture may be required to carry more product; there will also be limited space for display, and no shop window. In addition, the designer will need to bear in mind that a department store's attitude towards the retailer will vary: some stores will help an established, branded retailer to maintain his identity and will offer specific locations and contributions to shopfit costs; others may move small, unproven or non-profitable retailers around the store as they choose, and will restrict the retailers' identity by imposing their own fixturing and signage.

In these situations, housekeeping by the department store is important. If this is poor, the product and the retailer will suffer, with the result that there will be little or no distinction between the different concessions. This is a problem experienced by many smaller brands, and by companies which sell their products wholesale – namely that they cannot exercise control over the merchandising or presentation of their product. In order to improve their identity, many companies develop distinctive point-of-sale branding material and gradually devise their own shops and corner concepts. For example, Polo Ralph Lauren, Sony, Wedgwood and most of the cosmetics houses rely on strong identity for their brands.

In Japan and the Far East, where space is very costly, some retail sites are even smaller in scale. In these situations, a designer may use 'soft shops': sites with no permanent perimeter structure, which may be moved around as required. These sometimes have a special identity and are permitted to use their own units, but often they have to adopt the in-store fixtures and fittings. Soft shops are particularly useful for new brands and for start-up businesses. If the range is successful, they can be moved to a more prominent position in a store; if unsuc-

Below **I.S., Tokyo, designed by H Design Associates Inc. This 'shop in shop' is typical of the format. A walkway frontage with a three-sided perimeter creates an enclosed box. This space has an open shopfront with window space. The height has been extended by exposing the ceiling void.**

cessful, they can be moved out without disrupting the space. In Galeries Lafayette in Paris, for instance, positioning within a store is allocated on the basis of sales figures, with the space allocation often changed on a weekly basis until a proven track record can be established.

Shopping mall or off-pitch?

Whichever site a retailer opts for, it will clearly need to be appropriate for its purpose. In a shopping mall, the anchor store will determine which other retailers follow. In areas which are undergoing organic regeneration (that is, which are not backed by any funding), independent retailers will be attracted by like-minded people and businesses. They will choose a location for its buzz, and for affordable and accessible property. Some retailers will deliberately seek these 'off-pitch' sites, but need to be very confident of quality and sales in order to make this kind of decision pay off. UK designer Paul Smith has operated in this way for many years, although more recently he has started to open in more central locations.

Habitat used to occupy off-pitch sites in the same way. This location strategy works very well if the retailer has chosen his site carefully, but retailers must be aware of potential changes in town planning which may affect their location strategy. When a retailer is confident that he has a unique product, consumers will inevitably find their own way to the outlet, but in hard financial times this policy can have an adverse effect.

When retailers search for new sites, two of the most important factors are the turnover and characteristics of any shops nearby. It is no coincidence, for example, that brand flagships cluster together in areas such as London's New Bond Street. In this way, they can feed off one another and guarantee footfall. This concept of clustering is similar to the way in which a department store operates with its internal planning. Other retailers choose to create activity and attract customers by, for example, siting sandwich bars and cafés at the front of their shops. This exploits people's natural curiosity and instinct, which is why retail space is valued on a zonal basis from front to back.

Above A new flagship store for DKNY in Madison Avenue, New York. This is a fantastic location and the site is celebrated and highlighted by a huge builders' hoarding. The space is used to advertise the brand, show new products and inform the public of the opening date of the store.

Finding the sites

Above **Location is vital; it must reflect the brand and project the retailer's image. A corner site is often the best location as it offers a larger exposure to the passing customer. This prime retail shopping location is occupied by Calvin Klein and is on Madison Avenue.**

Right **The OXO Tower on the South Bank of the Thames in London is a prime example of regeneration. Designed by Lifschutz Davidson, it has a rooftop restaurant managed by Harvey Nichols and owned by the Coin Street Community Association.**

The clarion call of all retailers is location, location, location. Those looking for new sites often enlist the expertise of retail-property specialists who have detailed knowledge of shopping habits, property trends and emerging retail centres. In addition to the size and location of the store, other crucial factors are visibility, footfall, the size and number of windows, the type of building and whether the outlet is positioned well in relation to its competitors. However, broader factors will also have an effect on trading patterns: namely the parking situation and town-planning policies. If, for example, changes are made to pedestrian or transport routes or parking availability near a department store, the retailer will need to conduct regular door counts to establish footfall within the store. These changes may necessitate altering the planning of the store.

Geographic Information Systems are becoming more important for retailers looking for new sites, as a means to calculate population and demographic changes, and to map the locations of potential competitors. The regeneration of inner-city or former industrial sites can happen strategically through intervention by local or national government, or organically through the movement of like-minded people into an area who communally alter it to service their needs. Retail features in both cases, but in radically different ways. Whereas in strategic-regeneration projects it is more likely to be multiple retailers who move in because of the high costs involved, the altering of an established community and subsequent involvement of retailers is a more gradual process. Often this latter process is initiated by artists and independent retailers looking for cheaper spaces.

Strategic regeneration

Bluewater Park, the UK's most recently opened regional shopping centre outside London, is a good example of strategic regeneration (see case study on page 190). A former mining site, it was characterized by a vast, empty quarry, which architect Eric Kuhne decided to flood. Every aspect of the design of Bluewater has made water a central theme, from reflections on the ceiling to other representations of earth and sky. The site, which was formerly Europe's largest industrial eyesore, has also been landscaped with one million trees.

Disney's purchase of 42nd Street is another strategic – and financially significant – example of regeneration, with its potential knock-on effect on Times Square and the once seedy theatre district. In a report, 'Urban Leisure Development: Recent American Trends' 1998, Healey and Baker examines Urban Entertainment Centres – large-scale developments seeking to re-create European town centres with a blend of cinema, retail outlets and restaurants. The study found that most UECs benefited from some public money, but some required millions of dollars of investment. For example, San Francisco's Yerba Buena Gardens was mostly the responsibility of the San Francisco Development Agency and incorporates a public garden, Museum of Modern Art, Visual Arts Centre, theatre, 15-screen cinema and stores for book retailer, Barnes and Noble, Transworld Music and Reebok. According to the report, UECs are primarily associated with regeneration or revival. Significantly, design is at the heart of these centres' success. It points out that at Universal City Walk, an UEC built by Universal Studios which expanded to incorporate retail, 'tenants were encouraged to break all the rules and to adopt a style they thought would be challenging'.

London's Oxo Tower is another successful regeneration project. Part of the Coin Street Community Project, the Tower contains a planned mix of low-cost housing units, designer workshops, studios and showrooms. With its prime location by the Thames, the site also includes rooftop restaurants and bars run by the Harvey Nichols restaurant team with uninterrupted views over the City of London.

Organic regeneration

While planned renewal is essential, there are more organic examples of inner-city regeneration which can have an equally dramatic effect. Inner-city regeneration tends to happen where buildings and areas of a community have fallen into disuse. This happens typically around old markets, or where industries have moved on, leaving empty warehouses or factories and workers' houses. The low-cost housing in such areas tends to be inhabited by immigrant families; as one community leaves, another takes over. With each community a different set of values and needs is created: food, health, entertainment and leisure are all reflected in their diverse cultural needs. There are often several different groups which compete to become the dominant culture.

SoHo (south of Houston), an area in downtown Manhattan, used to be an industrial zone supplying goods to the metropolis of New York state. The area is character-ized by massive warehouses, many of which span entire blocks. Infiltrated and occupied by artists, often becoming both living and working spaces, the area quickly absorbed

Opposite to left **Soho, in downtown New York. This once industrial zone was inhabited by artists who needed the inexpensive working spaces. Today it is fast becoming the alternative shopping venue with many independent shops selling one-off and alternative merchandise.**

Below **Cape Town Harbour is still a working harbour. Waterside developments are now big business and there are already many examples worldwide. There is, however, a real danger of overdeveloping these natural locations and turning them into commercial dead ends.**

this creative and lively community. The market for this type of 'open-plan' space grew, and loft-space conversions can now be found worldwide. With the growing community of artists came galleries and showrooms. Often functioning as extensions to the uptown establishments, these alternative venues became popular as interest in contemporary art increased. The buildings also appealed to many artists and sculptors because they provided large, uninterrupted spaces for installation or site-based work. As these artists in turn attracted more visitors, the area became increasingly desirable. While property prices have now forced many artists out, on the whole the area has retained its vigour because of its independent spirit and bohemian lifestyle. SoHo is now established as an entity in itself, and has its own style of shops, restaurants and hotels. Likened to London's Kings Road in the 1960s, it is an area of youthful vitality. The cultural diversity and inspired creative mix attracted numerous unusual and creative retailers in the 1980s, when many stores took advantage of the unique warehouse-type spaces to present their products like works of art. In the 1990s many designer names – such as Miu Miu, Prada, Yves St Laurent and Helmut Lang – have been attracted to the area, although there are fears that, with the influx of multiples such as Banana Republic and Pottery Barn, the character of the area is under threat. Interestingly, the smaller independents are now moving into the area known as Little Italy. At present there are a number of small, unusual retailers in this region, but the area will become increasingly popular – and so will bring in the bigger players – in the future. In Boston, San Francisco and Cape Town, regeneration – largely inspired by existing markets – has been concentrated around docklands areas.

In London, the Notting Hill area has long been home to a Caribbean community as well as to one of Europe's largest street carnivals each summer. The area has a long-established antiques and second-hand market, along Portobello Road, but is also now attracting a number of new and interesting retailers including Ghost, Nick Ashley, the jeweller Dinny Hall, Kath Kidson and Tom Dixon. This has attracted more mainstream retailers such as designer Paul

dying industries and, as a result, the areas attract newcomers looking for cheap space in which to work. However, the neglect they have suffered has also been the means by which their architectural heritage has survived. These areas, passed over for large-scale redevelopment, have retained many interesting buildings which, when converted, create desirable retail space. Wade Smith, a leading fashion retailer based in Liverpool, converted a warehouse into one of the UK's most innovative independent retail sites, complete with a professional standard climbing wall.

Below **Bond Street, London in the 1990s has regained its past position as the most exclusive shopping location in the city. The street has many beautiful and individual examples of historic retail architecture. The new vibrancy shown in recent years is fuelled by a resurging interest of all things British.**

Smith, and now Jigsaw. As in other areas which have successfully reinvented themselves, the Notting Hill area has an eclectic mixture of restaurants and galleries, which have contributed to the regeneration. Another example is the prosperous, bustling Covent Garden area in central London which was once a fruit and vegetable market, while in Camden Town a market based around the canal has also gradually attracted a number of shop-based retailers.

Le Marais in Paris – the old Jewish quarter – is now one of the city's most desirable areas, and the city's fruit and vegetable market, Les Halles, was transformed in the early 1980s into an area that was characterized by the Beaubourg Centre art gallery.

Every city has its industrial quarter, which has grown up around specific skills or social activity – be it lace, jewellery, clothing or printing. These are often neglected,

Going international

Below left **Helmut Lang, downtown New York. Since opening in 1998, the brand has fast become one of the most sought-after labels and the store's location builds on these credentials.**

Below right **Yves Saint Laurent, the well-known luxury brand has established a new concept with this store designed by British designers Virgile and Stone.**

On a global scale, and particularly with the opening up of former Eastern bloc countries, international retailers are now able to benefit from the regeneration of economies such as Russia and Poland, which offer a vast array of new sites and opportunities. Rents in Moscow were once the highest in the world, but today they have come down, enabling speculative retail projects to be set up, and a number of major retail developments have recently opened. Poland has the largest population in central Europe, with a growing middle class. Among the retailers already established there are Jaeger, Benetton, Bata, Levis, Hugo Boss and Tesco. Central and South America have been targets for a number of retailers, including US giant Wal-Mart. In South Africa, there is the Zonk'Izizwe (All Nations) development, due to open in 2000, and this will be the African continent's largest shopping and recreational complex. It is to be sited in Midrand, the administrative capital of Pretoria, an area targeted for other major projects.

The Middle East is another area of the world in which shopping-centre development has grown substantially. According to Simon Thomson, Managing Director of property company Brooke Hillier Parker (Middle East), floorspace increased by 500 per cent between 1987 and 1997.

The giant Dutch food company, Ahold, has expanded into Spain, Portugal and eastern Europe, with the possibility of expansion in Asia and South America. UK consulting group KPMG points out that retailing in Asia is also opening up to international brands and to overseas competition, as a result of a growing middle class and of Western influence on young people. Half the population of Asia is aged under 25, a phenomenon which, KPMG suggests, is stimulating brand awareness in particular. Given the ability of fashion to demonstrate rising affluence, it is also significant that half the profits of European manufacturers such as Louis Vuitton now come from Asia. Mega malls have also made their mark here.

Left **Marks & Spencer, Myslbek shopping mall, Czechoslovakia.** This British institution began expanding into Europe in the 1980s and has established itself in several countries with varying degrees of success.

Below left This Calvin Klein store, located off the Champs Elysées, is in one of the most prestigious shopping locations in Paris and is designed by minimalist architect Claudio Sylvestrin.

Below right Jil Sander opened this store in Paris in 1993 during a period of recession. It was one of the first international brands to open on this scale in Paris for many years.

The role of the shop

Above **This small shop is located within a Grade II listed stable block at Althorp in Northamptonshire. It is a museum shop selling products by Mossman and Sale, specifically created for this location and unique only to this outlet. Designed by Din Associates.**

Shops and shopping satisfy different needs at different times. Whether it is a rushed lunch-hour trip for essentials, a Friday-night family shop to stock cupboards for the following week, or a leisurely weekend stroll for less important purchases, the shop has to fulfil a wide spectrum of requirements, and it is essential for the retailer to understand how customers' requirements alter at different times of the day or week.

For many, especially the young and old, shopping is still essentially a social activity: it could mean a bus ride into town with friends to buy clothes and spend time in a café, or the opportunity to escape home surroundings to be among other people. However, for a large group of society, who are juggling work with endless other responsibilities, traditional methods of shopping are being questioned. Since electronic shopping and home delivery are threatening at least some categories of retailers, the reassertion of

shopping as a social activity is a point of difference which they need to address. The supermarket Waitrose, for example, has linked with BA in an office-based delivery scheme whereby office workers can order the weekly shopping supplies from their desks, which are then delivered to their offices.

Shopping and the community

The UK retailer Boots is experimenting with retail outlets in hospitals, and is even planning to open in-store surgeries for doctors, opticians and dental treatments – in many ways forming a logical extension of the company's diversification into medical-related services and supplies. In-store crèches also provide children with fun and safe care while their parents shop unhindered. The success of leisure-related retail, such as museum shops in the USA and UK, the National Trust chain of outlets in the UK, and Disney and Warner Brothers stores illustrate the demand for retail to be more fully integrated with leisure. Even churches and cathedrals have gift shops, some of which make sizeable profits. Many supermarkets have also taken over the function previously held by local parades of shops and have become more community orientated, providing convenience shops such as a dry-cleaner, chemist, newsagent and tobacconist, together with recycling points and bulletin boards for local information.

During the 1920s' Recession in the UK, the Burton Group opened snooker halls above its stores, both to keep unemployed men occupied and to make use of empty retail space. In other words, hardship forced the company to think of a new approach which was both altruistic and an example of good commercial planning.

Cafés and catering

In recent years, retailers have introduced extra services such as cafés to bring customers into the store. Café areas are becoming much more leisure based and focused – in particular in large bookstores in the USA and, more recently, in the UK. Department stores have also rediscovered the

advantages of providing leisure areas in-store. For a long time such resting areas were neglected when the rest of the store was refitted, but these ancilliary areas are becoming crucial to today's fashion-conscious customer. The type of facility on offer needs to reflect the brand values of the retailer: a large store, for instance, would not want old-age pensioners drinking cups of tea in its new, prestigious fashion department. In other words, the product, customer and services should relate to one another. The proliferation of leisure areas is yet another affirmation of the retailer's authority in understanding and supplying the consumer with what he or she requires. A good example of this is Harvey Nichols, the London department store, which has a fifth floor restaurant, a bar café and a delicatessen with separate access. The fifth floor restaurant has a high-profile chef and attracts customers through its identity alone. It also remains open after the main store has closed. The company has also opened a catering division and become a restaurateur in its

Above **Leisure equals pleasure and this is a retail preoccupation with particular relevance to the 1990s. Cafés and restaurants stimulate and revive customers and also encourage them to stay longer within the store. This bar, designed by Wickham & Associates, is located in the fifth floor of Harvey Nichols in Knightsbridge, London.**

Above **This Soho News Café in New York, designed by Torett Architects, is a newsagent, tobacconist and café. Such a combined purpose encourages browsing and relaxing, for example sipping coffee at the same time as reading the paper or a magazine.**

own right, with restaurants in the Oxo Tower in London (see also page 59) and in Leeds. Selfridges provides cafés throughout their store. The tactic of opening leisure areas when a store is closed, however, can be fraught with problems in the UK. This is because local planning authorities will generally be opposed to mixed-use development. The main reason for this opposition is safety: this is because it is more dangerous to have buildings occupied at different times of day or night unless clear divisions of space are set out; costs can also be prohibitive due to the extra provisions needed for escape routes and codes of

practice. (The Chinese owners of Harvey Nichols have a very different experience of multi-use retail space: in Asia, stores will often incorporate office, leisure, retail and other activities, with facilities sometimes provided 24 hours a day.)

Special events and services

Retailers are constantly seeking new ideas in order to inspire and motivate their customers, to bring them together and develop a common interest or theme. These ideas include discount incentives, previews and special events such as fashion shows, personal appearances, book signings and demonstrations. Habitat, for example, actively promotes work by young artists and designers via a giveaway broadsheet, and has a targeted network for displays and exhibitions of the artists' work in its stores throughout the country. Sponsorship of the arts and universities fulfils a similar function, and as a result of such targeted sponsorship companies such as Habitat, Arcadia and Oasis are generating a profile and cachet with a creatively aware audience. A shop in Milan, Onyx, allows customers to leave messages for one another, and even to communicate through the Internet. Other special events such as singles' nights and promotional days for pensioners create the impression that the retailer cares about each customer's well-being, and wishes him or her to have fun even beyond the retail environment itself.

In many cases, the shop has become significantly more than simply a place in which to buy products, and has developed services that give it the association of a centre for well-being. In-store services such as hairdressing, beauty treatments and alternative therapies that make the mind/body link are techniques which further satisfy customers' need to feel good about themselves.

Such developments as this, which also encompass retailers' links with schools through charitable fundraising or local sponsorship, tie in with a more general social shift towards a rediscovery of community, the importance of local identity and the increased emphasis on friendship networks to replace family networks. These are not trivial options for retailers: the changing role of the shop must continue to mirror the changing role of the shopkeeper. As stated earlier (see page 26) London's Henley Centre has described how the trend towards globalization has created an even more intense need for community, and has engendered a shift of trust towards those companies which are willing to respond to the needs of individuals and their communities. In addition to the flourishing concepts of service and community, however, retailers searching for new strategies will also have to be able to manage information to a sophisticated level: this skill will be at the forefront of retail competition in the future.

Above **Joseph, Sloane Street, London, has used his stores to promote unknown furniture designers. His choice of designer was personal but always seemed to complement his products. Now established designers such as Tom Dixon, André Dubreil and Christian Liaigre were featured during the 1980s.**

New retail concepts

The central principles of retail remain the same today as they have through the centuries. New retail incorporates all the same methods and philosophies, but the difference is that it has developed and changed its imagery for a new contemporary society. Within these new concepts, however, retailers also need to understand how familiarity operates in communicating traditional values. Familiar, classic imagery can engender a feeling of comfort, forming an easy emotional bond which the consumer will recognize. This can be conveyed in many ways, through fittings, lighting materials, service levels, the presentation of products or the comfort level within the shop, and these approaches can apply whether or not a product is modern. As previously explained (see page 45) UK fashion retailer Paul Smith often uses traditional imagery to sell a contemporary product. Minimalism is certainly more challenging, but suits contemporary fashion better because it is generally more

extreme as a product. Many of the factors driving retailers' search for new concepts have already been discussed: the changing perception of shopping as entertainment, the new forms of technology available, and the importance of brand consciousness, diversification and specialization (see pages 112–14). Each one of these issues comes into play when retailers are looking for points of differentiation from their competitors. The most interesting examples of how retailers are rising to this challenge fall into several categories: from fashion to sports shops, car retailing to bookshops, super-markets, niche retailing, travel and convergence technology.

To appreciate the way in which new concepts work, however, it is vital also to remember those retailers – such as high-class jewellers – who maintain a traditional image and methods of operating. These form a small and generally exclusive group, are often independent and are therefore able to rely on a core of customers. Tradition can also be used in the form of pastiche – such as that adopted by Ralph Lauren in the USA, and which was subsequently brought over to the UK.

When developing a new concept, it is clear that the retailer and designer must search for an aesthetic that will suit both the product and the target audience. The public today has a good appreciation of visual imagery, and this has developed from a sophisticated advertising industry, television and the vast amount of printed material now available. The retailer must be highly sensitive to this sophistication, because it is the fine details which make a difference to how a concept is received. Furthermore, given the amount of painstaking work which must go into such a project, the designer and retailer must at all times remain mindful of possible future trends when developing new products. The design concept has to allow for growth and development; whether this will be in the form of a brand with many labels, or new products and sources, flexibility must always be apparent in the approach and handling of the imagery used. Both retailer and designer have to be aware of how far the brand may go, given the success of those brands which have managed to extend themselves into new markets.

Below Paul Smith mixes modern, traditional and individual designs to personify his style. Images are juxtaposed creating an idiosyncratic approach. The children's shop in this Westbourne Grove store is colourful, mixing robotic images with substantial industrial-looking wooden furniture. Designed by Sophie Hicks, with plastic toy installation by Tom Dixon.

It is now widely accepted that a trusted brand can extend into product or service areas which may be far from its original source. The Henley Centre has shown how trust traditionally placed in public institutions and government has been transferred to retail brands because the public has lost faith in many of those institutions which have fallen out of touch with the public mood. This is largely due to the loyalty which retailers have encouraged, and to the frequency with which they are visited by the public. Retail brands have also become established as providing the best choice and quality. It is not surprising, therefore, that retailers such as Sainsbury, Tesco, Virgin, Marks and Spencer, and Delhaize Le Lion in Belgium are also now providing financial services for their customers. Virgin is one of the the most adventurous players in the field in the UK, for extending its brand well beyond music retail into travel, hotels and financial services.

Fashion

Many of the contemporary fashion designers illustrate the way in which a brand develops and then introduce crossover product categories such as accessories, fragrances, home furnishings and decoration. Examples include Tommy Hilfiger, Joseph, Paul Smith, Calvin Klein, Ralph Lauren, Yves St Laurent and Gucci. These new categories have often come into being as a result of fashion-design personalities creating advertising campaigns or 'propping' their shops by buying furniture and artefacts to add interest to their interiors and window environments; the perceived message for the consumer is that this is my world and you can buy into it. Whether an item is a piece of clothing, a perfume or a household object, the fact that it is identifiable as a designer brand makes it all the more desirable. This lifestyle retailing, in the same way as flagship stores (see page 20), has become another successful extension of the retailer's marketing image.

One of the most successful by-products of this extension – fragrance – has become the largest generator of sales and profit for many of the brands which launched them. The tables have now turned, so that the couture

houses which inspired the launch of fragrances as an add-on have actually become the vehicle for promoting the perfume. There are many examples of how this success story has manifested itself, including Chanel, Dior, Polo Ralph Lauren (one of the best-selling men's fragrances in the USA) and Calvin Klein (Klein has produced an individual lifestyle 'attitude' for each of his fragrances, and the choice of name and packaging plays a vital part in extending brand awareness of all his products and philosophy). Joop is an interesting marketing development in which a fragrance manufacturer devised the strategy in reverse and started a company with the fragrances, which then led into a fashion product, with the latter created by Wolfgang Joop, a brilliant fashion illustrator. In many cases the perfume or fragrance has become stronger (financially) than the original product, yet the two are totally

Above **Oswald Boateng is a young British tailor who has attracted a great deal of attention for his classic tailoring. His clothes always have a magical twist and often play on his use of bright colours. The location for this store is Savile Row, London, the bastion of male tailoring. The store was designed by Paul Daley.**

Right **This conversion of a large building into a Borders bookshop in Glasgow, Scotland follows an American trend for leisure bookshops. This was followed by Waterstones of Piccadilly, a bookstore on four floors which has four cafes and a restaurant within the store.**

interdependent. In fact, perfume and diffusion clothes lines can account for up to 80 per cent of sales for companies such as Calvin Klein, Chanel and Yves St Laurent.

Conversely, however, while such retailers diversify into areas that were previously out of their range, there are examples of other businesses diversifying into fashion. *Cosmopolitan* magazine, for instance, has turned the tables and extended its brand by product licensing into 'The Cosmopolitan Collection', which covers towelling, swimwear, eyewear, footwear, home furnishings, jewellery, hosiery, bags, stationery and lingerie. *Cosmopolitan* bed linen has been featured in both the Freeman and the Grattan mail-order catalogues.

Books

The meeting of leisure and technology are two major factors in new bookstore concepts. Mega bookstores in the USA, such as Borders, and Barnes and Noble, have built their identities on blurring the distinction between leisure and retailing, and take on the functions of library, café and performance venue. It is perfectly acceptable for shoppers to stay in a store all day reading, or for whole families to visit the store in the evening for a snack and a performance, and later on to browse for books. Borders superstores trade in and out of town, have floorspace of over 2,300 sq m 23,000 sq ft) and carry up to 150,000 titles. They have substantial free car parking on their free-standing sites, and frequently hold promotion events, including singles' nights. The company also has a tracking system which allows stores to restock shelves continually. This is expected to become the norm in the UK, and Waterstones – in converting Simpsons of Piccadilly in London, and with its superstore in Glasgow – is leading the way. While many smaller booksellers have provided cafés for years, this has become an aspect of their service which is now taken for granted.

Supermarkets

In grocery retailing, a number of different tactics are emerging, including providing home shopping, offering entertainment (such as in-store demonstrations) and developing shops as community centres. For supermarkets in the USA and Europe, new concepts and diversification are a way of life, largely because they have reached saturation point in terms of customer spending. The supermarkets' common aim to become one-stop shops for all manner of purchases is already well underway with their diversification into music, electrical goods, clothing – even designer labels – books, pharmacy, fragrances and restaurants.

The next phase of development may, however, be less economically driven and potentially more difficult. Tesco, the UK leader, is constantly searching for new ideas. Asda, now owned by Wal-Mart, has set itself up as consumer champion in challenging price-fixing on books and over-the-counter medicines, Tesco and other European retailers have challenged the restrictive channels of supply of luxury brands by sourcing goods from the 'grey market' (see page 24). Yet in addition to such moves, supermarkets will need to focus even more on different communities and to understand what people really want. They – and indeed all retailers – will have to invent the format which suits the locality, instead of insisting on national conformity. Wal-Mart did this by launching a smaller 'neighbourhood-market' format in 1998, regarded as particularly suitable for use in Europe and inner-city areas of the USA. Dutch retailer, Ahold, has consistently maintained a policy of retaining local brand names, where it has made acquisitions. Another way in which food retailers in the future

could create a valuable point of difference, according to London's Henley Centre, is by promoting themselves as 'green champions' (with environmental policies) or as 'local heroes' (by supporting local suppliers, operating community bus services, developing the store for community use and giving a percentage of profits to local communities). The recent move by Sainsbury's into village shops is an apt illustration of this image promotion. Similarly in France, Carrefour and Auchan are recognizing the need for smaller stores which cater for different needs, as is Delhaize Le Lion in Belgium. Auchan president, Christophe Dubrulle, in an interview with French business daily *Les Echos* (30 September 1998), pointed out the importance of smaller formats, saying that they would be critical to the expansion of his group in Europe.

In larger stores, the diversification into new product areas and services requires supermarket operators to reconsider the traditional aisle-based layout. While supermarkets are using category management extensively to alter the way stores are merchandised, there is increasingly a body of opinion favouring solution or story-based layouts which are more in tune with how customers shop: certain products, therefore, might be in a number of different areas.

Below **Traditionally supermarkets sold on price advantage, while some retailers started incorporating more activities in-store to create lifestyle choices. Asda, recently bought by American group Wal-Mart, are expanding their discount offers to more products making it an aggressive retailer in the British market.**

Travel retail

Above **Seattle Coffee Company at Heathrow Terminal 4, designed by Arthur Collins Architects. Airport retailing in the UK is very successful. Air terminal sites have a captive audience, and are located for convenience and to gain maximum sales. This café also exemplifies the huge growth in coffee shops in the USA and Europe at the end of the 1990s.**

The scrapping of duty free on luxury goods has forced a reassessment of travel retail within Europe. The future of airports will lie in differentiating their retail offer, in repositioning retail from low-price, tax-free goods to satisfying consumer desires for quality. This can be exploited by designing a memorable store experience, promoting the consumer's desire for quality brands, and innovating in the use of space with sensory appeal and interactive settings. Essentially, travel retail needs to fulfil travellers' expectations of experience. In repositioning, airport retailers also need to be aware of the need for new product-design formats if they are to charge premium prices. Tim Greenhalsch of the international design company Fitch points out that 70 per cent of consumers do not shop at airports. The opportunity for airport retail, therefore, is to

celebrate the opportunity of travel by tapping into the sense of unpredictability experienced by consumers. Greenhalsch says that there are three types of consumer: the fast-track 'lounge lizard' or seasoned traveller who will be interested in a smaller offer, such as books; the comparison shopper; and the browser. He concludes that airport retail should offer good circulation, fast transactions, at-a-glance information and multi-level spaces to improve access for different types of shoppers. The ideal airport retail is a combination of brand experience and mall.

Airports

In terms of airport shopping, the UK is way ahead of other countries. The remarkable success of the British Airports Authority in turning London airports into shopping destinations has shown retailers the potential of other travel-related shopping, and railway and service stations have been examined for their potential as new retail sites. In its turn, particularly as a reaction to the proposed abolition of duty-free shopping, BAA has been forced to look at how it can target retail formats even more closely at particular groups of passengers (whether on scheduled business or family-orientated charter flights). BAA has the advantage of knowing who its customers are and when they will be passing through its doors; it is also in the almost unique position of knowing its customers' sex, age and nationality from air-ticket sales, passport information and flight destinations. For example, in Heathrow's Terminal 4, which is used for international, scheduled and long-haul flights, BAA knows that the passengers – a large percentage of whom come from countries which are wealthy and have gift-orientated cultures – will have the time and inclination to buy treats for themselves and their families; it must therefore achieve the right quality and mix of retail to achieve satisfaction and high sales.

This information can be used to respond directly to specific customer groups: indeed, some retailers are already using it for this purpose. Within Heathrow, for instance, shoe stores change their sizing depending on the destination of some continental flights. (This approach is not new, and has instinctively been employed by such groups as Arcadia and Joseph in their London stores. For example, Joseph changes its clothes ranges around on Fridays and Saturdays because customers visiting on these days are usually from out of town and will spend more money on casual wear than on tailored, or structured clothes; the latter are therefore positioned to have less emphasis.)

Airports are in fact taking this philosophy a stage further, building on the characteristics of their terminals and on the passengers who use them to design new buildings and a series of new spaces which are complete lifestyle-branded environments. We will see leisure retailing developing new formats of entertainment branding, and the new retail environments will pull together all the brands to which aeroplane passengers are likely to be attracted in a lifestyle/leisure-store approach which incorporates both entertainment and food. In Heathrow's Terminal 3, which typically centres around short-haul travel for families going on holiday, this could mean taking the Nike World philosophy – a retail/entertainment mix which is like walking into a three-dimensional movie or advertisement for an active life – into an even bigger environment, so that a customer will enter the 'world' of the Terminal 3 passenger. This could mean developing a travel-based concept to give the passenger a virtual experience before he or she travels, listing what to buy for the trip, and all the sites to see and things to do once at the destination.

Below **This duty-free retail area is full of merchandise. Some attempt has been made to disguise the volume by creating a circular plan for ease of flow. With the abolition of European duty-free goods the focus is now on the retail experience rather than discount prices.**

In Terminal 1, the high-profile, director-level European business traveller, with very little luggage, may wish to buy gifts for his or her family, having spent time away from them. This could translate into retail concepts which will allow that passenger to order his or her goods on the outward journey, and either to collect them, or have them delivered, on the way back. The aim is to speed people on their way efficiently, while giving them an experience or service associated with their own travel objectives.

Railway stations

Below **Shell petrol is developing a new convenience store format in its petrol forecourts. These large images show exciting, colourful illustrations of fresh produce to entice the captive customers into the store.**

In just the same way that BAA realized that it had to change its approach in order to bring in more income, Railtrack in the UK identified major retail opportunities in a number of its railway stations, particularly in and around London. As part of the same process, supermarkets also woke up to the opportunities offered by large numbers of passengers.

Petrol-station forecourts

The value of travel-related retailing is also evident in the development of motorway service stations, many of which now offer a wider range of shopping facilities. Granada, for example, Britain's largest operator, piloted Boots and Tie Rack stores in the Hilton Park service station on the M6. Forecourt retailing has also been a major factor in the petrol stations' fightback against competition from supermarket chains, through convenience shopping. According to the Institute of Grocery Distribution, by 1998 forecourts had won 20 per cent of the convenience-food market in the UK.

Experiments continue in extending the versatility of forecourts, such as a tie-up between major supermarkets and fast food chains. In the USA, Chevron petrol stations in San Remo and Modesto, California, are currently trying out a new convenience-food format, the Foodini Fresh Meal Market, in which only ready meals are sold.

Niche retailing

One consequence of the expansion by multiple retailers into previously unfamiliar sites, and of the liaisons they have made with other operators for mutual gain, has been a sense of sameness in high streets and malls. As multiple retailers seek to drive down prices and refine the numbers of products they offer, opportunities have emerged for niche retailers to fill the public's demand for new products.

The beauty industry has long been dominated by large, traditional cosmetics and fragrance companies which control sales and distribution around the world. It is a luxury market selling dreams and fantasies with a low-cost product at very high prices. However, exciting alternatives are appearing, offering existing and new products in innovative formats which are challenging traditional department-store selling formats. Lush, for example, presents fresh beauty products like food. Perfumery has been another opportunity for niche retailer Sephora in France and the USA. In its huge, dimly lit shop in Paris, every fragrance imaginable is on sale. Beautifully presented bottles, individually illuminated like precious jewels, reveal the design and colour of what is on display. Showing the product clearly in this way is very important, as every bottle is designed to be distinct and recognizable. The company also has a good source philosophy, with trained employees who are knowledgeable.

Another area in which niche retailers can establish a significant difference is in service (this also applies in particular to traditional retailers, for whom service is a part of their point of difference). Niche retailers such as patisseries will

Above **Swatch Timeship, New York, designed by Pentagram. Niche and specialist manufacturers are developing their own retail sites. This enables them to create brand awareness campaigns, often around a single product. Swatch is a large and colourful brand with many of the watch characteristics reflected in their store designs.**

offer quality gift wrapping, a florist will deliver, many fashion retailers will offer alteration as part of the service, and a specialist camera retailer will have staff who are knowledgeable photographers. Service for a niche retailer therefore encompasses expertise, accommodation of customers' needs and a sense of personal attention which other retailers are often unable to provide.

Outdoor goods

The great success stories of the 1990s have been retailers who capitalized on how fashionable sports clothing had become. The often quoted example of Nike Town, which extended the brand into a marketing phenomenon, demonstrates the 'cutting edge' quality of sports retail. The theatricality of the Manhattan store and the manipulation of the brand through media advertising has made the Nike 'swoosh' one of the most sought-after symbols on clothes. However, there are signs that sports retailers may have to work harder to sell their products in the future since as the competition increases so do the features and gimmicks.

Children's goods

Fantasy is indisputably the most important element in the new concepts developed to sell children's toys and clothes. For example, Toys 'Я' Us in the USA has its new 'Concept 2000' design which features an interactive video games area; to visit FAO Schwartz at Caesar's Palace in Las Vegas, customers enter via a 15-metre (48-ft) wooden Trojan horse. This store also has interactive floors where pressure pads create sound effects when they are walked upon. The store is also filled with sound – the theory being that toy shops have to compete with the imaginative lure of cinema, video games and theme-park rides.

*Left **Wade Smith, Liverpool, designed by Davis Baron. This entertainment feature provides a climbing wall that is built into a sports shop. The wall is used both as a dramatic focal point and also to allow customers to try out the range of sports equipment that is sold within the store.***

Cars

Cars have traditionally not been regarded as part of mainstream retailing. Daewoo is credited with changing this attitude, with its emphasis on service, non-pushy sales people and comfortable environments which include cafés and children's play areas. Car showrooms and dealerships are becoming closer to retail outlets, with associated products also merchandised. Another factor which has helped to change the way in which cars are sold in the UK is the impact of deregulation in Europe on pricing.

The second-hand dealer, CarLand, opened its first UK superstore at Lakeside retail park in Essex in January 1998. Customers shop by using a touch-screen kiosk, selecting their chosen price, make, type of car and model. The cars are grouped by category such as estates, small cars, prestige cars and so on, rather than by manufacturer.

Home entertainment

While car dealerships illustrate the way in which a long-established market can change, the retail opportunities in convergence technology come from a truly new market. Such is the complexity of much interactive technology for the home – from camcorders to televisions and computers – that there is a clear demand for a retailer who can sell all of that technology together. Comet's I.T. Works in Reading, Berkshire, claims to be the first 'total technology centre' in the UK. It sells equipment for video conferencing, Internet/Intranet, e-mail and paging. Customers can try before they buy, and computers can be assembled to order in-house. There is a coffee bar, an impulse-buy section, a training facility and an area for accessing the Internet.

DIY

The DIY sector suffered major blows during 1997 and 1998 – in Asia from the currency crisis and weak consumer confidence, and in Europe as a result of preparation for the introduction of the Euro. International expansion did, however, provide an opportunity for a number of DIY retailers to grow. The US-based Home Depot, one of the world's largest retailers, opened its first international store

in Chile in 1998, while German retailers, Praktiker, Bauhaus and Austrian bauMax also prepared to move overseas. Home Depot has been expanding its new concept Expo Design Centre stores in the USA, while bauMax has been experimenting with expanding its consumer base by devoting space to areas such as pets and pet products.

Large store formats have continued to predominate worldwide, and DIY retailers generally have been exploring how to improve their offer: either by expanding garden products, or by featuring more fashionable showrooms, as Superbois has done in Belgium. In France, Castorama stores have concentrated on project-orientated purchasing, and each is organized into six 'universes': bath, garden, home décor, tools, building materials and kitchens. Top German retailer, OBI, runs in-store demonstrations about building projects. Within Germany, DIY retailers are offering a much wider assortments of products, from prefabricated homes to office supplies, books and videos. A few have even attempted to sell motorbikes and computers.

Above **Ingredients is an activity store where customers are actively encouraged to participate. The store sells ingredients for home baking, and produces freshly baked goods for sale. This activity within stores is a growing trend – it provides entertainment and a stimulus for people to gain a skill or make new friends.**

practical
implications

Programming a new concept and installation is a highly skilled part of the fast-moving world of retailing. The retailer has to take advantage of seasonal trading patterns and the designer must work within them, delivering the designs to a tight schedule. Speed is essential – to design an environment that takes too long to build could have a major financial effect on the retailer's trade.

Various fundamental design principles are common to all retailing activity: visibility, access, circulation, presentation and service, even though individual retailers may have vastly different stylistic approaches – from theatrical ostentation to monastic austerity. Sir Terence Conran has described the interior-design process as creating a lasting and reliable skeleton: ensuring that flooring, wall fittings, lighting and air conditioning are all appropriate and working together for an overall effect. The flesh of the design – incorporating aspects such as display, merchandising, graphics, signage and point of sale – is where the excitement comes into play. An effective new design will quickly be quantifiable in terms of sales turnover, but in the longer term could add value in many other ways such as increasing brand-awareness, confirming brand values and developing new markets.

The first image is important, since the shopfront design, signage and window displays will project a distinct look that defines the retail identity. A shopfront sends subliminal signals to shoppers about whether or not they will be welcome inside.

Engineering consumer desires

Above **Egg, Kinerton Street, Knightsbridge, London by Maureen Docherty and Asha Sarebei. The trend towards authenticity is exemplified in this simple but sophisticated shop. Natural materials and dyes are used to make these clothes, which are produced in small-scale batches.**

Previous page **Bazaar in Yemen.**

When buying goods for survival no longer becomes the prime motivation, retailers have to develop more sophisticated techniques in order to tempt customers to buy. The role of design in marketing relies on successfully eliciting their desires in the same way that street markets exploit and excite the senses of touch, vision, smell, hearing and taste. Many retailers use the intrinsic qualities of their products to make the impact. Bargains are prominently positioned, and products are theatrically displayed with ostentatious precision in terms of colour and form.

The 1990s' trends towards authenticity – as witnessed in the re-emergence of hand-made crafts goods, natural materials, organic foods, grass-roots political movements and environmental concerns – illustrates a move back to basic instincts, which is well understood by the world's leading designers and buyers as they search for new ideas. Retailers must also constantly adapt to consumer trends.

Some big 'brand' designers in the textile and clothes industries today seek out the genuine and authentic experience because this is where they find inspiration and is what their customers expect. The element of 'search' is an important factor for the London retailer Egg, tucked away in a Knightsbridge back street, which never advertises and yet is visited by virtually every fashion editor and stylist in the world. The store is unique, selling traditionally inspired garments made by a community of skilled women in India. The items are sold for high prices, but customers know that they are buying a genuine artefact, an experience and, most importantly, an element of exclusivity. Such customers have gone beyond the basic needs of the typical shopper: as educated consumers, they are paying for an extension to their lifestyle and for the reassurance of authenticity.

Moods

The creation of an atmosphere is difficult to define. Modern design can be devoid of warmth and character and may be misinterpreted as lacking in personality. The atmosphere in a store needs to reflect an understanding of the product, and is built up by a number of design features which have a subliminal effect on the consumer.

The retail environment is a physical manifestation of social and consumer trends, and the world of financial services is a striking contemporary example. The changes in banking, insurance and brokering, combined with political trends encouraging greater home and share ownership, have led to consumers who no longer bank for life at one institution, but who shop around for mortgages and financial advice. Traditional financial institutions are under attack by new players such as supermarket banking and direct telephone services. Businesses have changed emphasis from dealing with money to dealing with people; interiors have moved on from high security environments to encouraging people to browse, with open areas, comfortable seating and personal contact. Their visual imagery and atmosphere have thus fallen more into line with that of travel agents or shops, where service and access to information are of prime importance.

This is a stark example of how design can help to determine a change of perception, and it is achieved by ensuring that different elements work together. In any retail environment, the aim is primarily to direct the customer around the whole space, presenting opportunities and information at different points to touch, view and experience. At this level a designer becomes an engineer, formulating an environment to control desires and impulses. The aim is to trigger a range of different moods – impulsive, contemplative, meandering, positive – which will affect the consumer's behaviour. In a department store, for instance, it is no accident that the cosmetics hall is generally the first department. A customer will be encouraged to forget the reality of the daily routine, and will be overcome by a purely escapist landscape of exciting colours, tactile products and sensuous aromas. The traditional department store is in the business of selling dreams; luxurious finishes of marble and glass enhanced by soft, glamorous lighting will create an image of luxury and the illusion of being pampered.

In a supermarket the response that the retailer wishes to promote is one of freshness and quality (and, more recently, convenience), so the first things the customer will see and smell are flowers, fruit and vegetables, and a selection of ready made meals. In a DIY store, there will be equipment and gadgets to make life easier and to save time and money. In a fashion store, accessories and furnishings are sold at the entrance as an introduction to the more expensive clothing lines. Buying into some brands may take many visits before consumers feel totally at ease, and they should not be discouraged or made to feel insecure.

Sensory retailing

'Sensory retailing' is a term that explains the effect of a total consumer experience: to create an atmosphere which has a subconscious effect on the consumer by appealing to the senses. The sense of smell has a powerful influence on behaviour. Flowers placed at the fronts of shops, perfumery departments positioned at the entrances of stores and in-store bakeries all emit smells which are powerful, instantly recognizable and tempt the consumer to buy.

In some retail environments today, scented candles, joss sticks and aromatherapy oils are used in a much more spiritual context, encouraging an instant feeling of well-being and relaxation – these are all-important factors in the world of leisure retailing. The sense of smell encourages consumers more than anything else to be impulsive; they know that the scent of fresh flowers and the smell of fresh fruit and vegetables are signs of goodness which will not last. In Japan, aromas have been used in the financial services industry: lavender (calming) in customer areas and citrus (stimulating) where bank tellers sit. Some retailers have now recognized the potential value of artificially dispersing pleasant smells into stores: for example, to suggest an environment which suits a particular product, or to evoke a seasonal atmosphere.

In-store television, video walls and music are more established ways of seeking to excite customers' interest, particularly during special promotions.

Below **This highly seductive area of Harvey Nichols on the fifth floor is full of tempting goodies. Beautiful plants, foods and packaging create an exciting market buzz – the antithesis of the cool sophisticated fashion floors below. Designed by Wickham and Associates.**

First impressions

Anglomania
by Vivienne Westwood on 3

All retailers want to be noticed: they need to be different and to stand out from the competition. For a consumer, the shopfront is the first point of communication with a retailer: its design, layout and materials will convey an immediate message. Today there is a full range of dramatically different styles in most high streets, from the highly contemporary to the reassuringly traditional. Good window displays will enhance communication of the products and brand values of the store, and will encourage browsing as well as giving many new or reticent customers a reason to enter the store. Equally, a window display can communicate a viewpoint or trigger an emotional response at a glance. Some retailers use their windows as an art form, to promote an attitude or a political statement. The Body Shop of the UK, for example, promotes political statements worldwide in its windows. While some of its campaigns may not run in certain countries, as an international retailer the shop still has to be conscious of choosing campaigning messages which will translate across cultures.

Harvey Nichols in London, on the other hand, has used its windows to promote the work of new artists and, by association, to enhance the quality of its merchandise. The store's former head of display, Mary Portas (now of Yellow Door consultancy), has said that retailers should use windows as advertisers would use newspapers: making better use of colour and creative techniques. She points out that when the shop is closed the window is all that the retailer has at his disposal. Such is the importance of promotion on the street – i.e. before the customer even gets through the door – that retailers are experimenting with new kinds of technology to express their stores' style and content, such as pavement video screens, L.E.D. displays and three-dimensional icons.

Left **Harvey Nichols has always been synonymous with outstanding window promotions. This particular window features fashion designers' clothes, worn by mannequins, being sprayed with jets of water, creating a water-theme world by the in-store creative team headed by Janet Wardley.**

Left **Bluewater Shopping Mall, Kent, designed by architect Eric Kuhne. Glass façades, buildings and natural features combine to create a memorable, dramatic view of this commercial centre.**

Once the initial impressions have been made, the next step is to build upon them. There is an opportunity to influence the customers even before they enter the store – for example, by how products are placed within the space, by which backdrops or props are used, and by whether the prices of goods are displayed or not. The display approach can reveal, and convey, the overall attitude of the retailer.

Façades and shopfronts

First impressions are, therefore, critical. The shopfront and façade communicate brand values; the location of the store suggests the market level and likely cost of goods inside. The shopfront is a defining image which will persist in the consumer's consciousness, so the design solution must be memorable and clearly define identity and brand values.

Exterior and interior images must also be consistent and this applies to all signage, materials and lighting. The choice of materials and design of any shopfront must also be synchronized with the way products are displayed in the window: for example, high-class, expensive materials used for fixtures and fittings will reflect a high-quality product, while inside the store such products will demand appropriate merchandising displays to reflect their worth. For small objects, the shopfront should be focused at eye level; for large objects such as furniture, it needs to be big and spacious for maximum impact, and to suggest the end use.

Above **Ultimo, Dallas, USA, designed by architects Michael Gabellini. This colourful street façade for Ultimo has uncluttered views right into the store. The sculptural composition of form and colour combine to create an intricate retail interior of eminent style.**

Above **This purpose-built shopping mall designed by New York architect Peter Marino establishes a clear façade treatment. Shape and form create a soft circular panorama.**

Opposite **Space NK is a cosmetic company specializing in health and beauty products. This store in the Bluewater Shopping Mall has used a reversed sign which, when illuminated from above, creates the shadow sign reading Space NK. The store was designed by Virgile & Stone.**

The location and layout of a shopfront are also extremely important – for instance, the best position is usually on a corner site because it has multiple windows – and will raise a number of issues. The designer will have to consider carefully the options presented by the size and position of the windows in terms of sight lines: i.e. which windows will be most prominent from pedestrian and car viewpoints? Will the position of the door interfere with the sight lines? If so, it should perhaps be replaced with a shutter or with glazed doors. There can also be situations where windows are too big, and the designer must decide on the merits of an open or closed format to the window backs. Window backs have the advantage of creating internal wall perimeters and giving a complete, controllable environment to the window display team.

Furthermore, if the store is part of a chain, there may be common themes or design considerations for all the properties in the portfolio. Location will also determine whether there are local planning restrictions. For example, the shopfront may be listed in a conservation area which will have more onerous regulations relating to any alterations and the type of signage which may be used. There may also be local architectural pressure groups such as The

Georgian Society in the UK. There are many groups set up to advise on buildings of special interest or merit; their aim is to ensure that such buildings are protected and respected, so as not to damage or alter their character.

The retailer and designer need to decide how open the shopfront should be: will it, for instance, mirror the substantial exteriors found on London's Oxford Street, which allow large numbers of people access without obstruction? These open frontages are also seen in many shopping malls and in covered protected areas. By virtue of the size of the opening they communicate a more inviting and accessible feel but can be anonymous and, unless the designer is able to make a large statement, can make it difficult to establish the retailer's identity.

A closed frontage is more exclusive and allows more of the physical structure to communicate the values of the brand. Recessed fronts offer protection from the weather and work well in exposed streets. They also invite shoppers into the space without commitment: psychologically it is easier for shoppers to cross the threshold once they are in a recessed front. This can be aided with floor finishes which can stretch from the store on to the street, blurring the demarcation of the interior and exterior.

Signage

The retailer's logo and the typeface that is used on the front of the store immediately communicate that particular retailer's identity, and will often dictate the format of the signage used. Projecting signs are important to all retailers, since they are positioned at 90 degrees to the frontage and are therefore seen face-on by all passers-by. However, they should be used sparingly because, if misused or overused, they can appear to be cheap and downmarket. A number of materials are available for internally illuminated signs: extruded metal, plastic and cast materials can all be used to great effect. Signs can be made to order from a wide range of materials, or otherwise may be bought ready-made from manufacturers. Internally, there are statutory obligations for the size and prominence of particular signs, such as fire exits.

Historically, signs have been used to aid communication non-verbally. The pawnbroker's three gold balls, the red-and-white barber's pole and today the internationally accepted green cross to denote a pharmacy, can all be recognized without need of explanation. Similarly the logos and symbols of individual shops or brands are recognised on street signs, therefore reassuring the customer that the shopping experience in that venue and the products inside are familiar and associated with a certain brand and quality.

Awnings and canopies

These were traditionally functional items only, being used by many retailers to protect pedestrians from inclement weather, while also reducing the sun's glare and heat on the shop windows, especially when perishable goods – such as meat in butchers' shops – were on display. Today, canopies are used more decoratively as a further development of a company logo or name. Many materials are used; canvas is the most traditional, but increasingly, glass is used with illumination. Nicole Farhi on London's Bond Street has a sandblasted, stainless-steel shopfront with an etched-glass canopy. The whole is integrated into the shopfront façade and door treatment to give emphasis to the entrance of an otherwise flat, unobtrusive façade.

Windows

Windows are the most important factor within the shopfront, communicating style, context and price point. They can be seductive and exciting, based on emotional stimulus, or price-based (when they clearly emphasize value for money with easy and obvious ticketing).The window is one of a retailer's most controllable elements in relation to image and to what is happening inside a store, but there are a number of decisions to be made about how these effects are achieved. One of the first issues to consider is whether a window should be open into the store within, or closed. For department stores there is little choice, since the ground-floor perimeter wall which extends right up to the window will be the most expensive space on the site. Windows, therefore, must be closed in order to avoid losing valuable space where there are the greatest number of customers and sales. For many other retailers, however,

opening the backs of windows can work in their favour: by keeping the sight lines open to the customer, the store becomes part of the window, with the display acting as a 'taster' to the interior.

The open/closed option applies also to the backs of windows. If a store is small, it can be useful to leave the back open to allow daylight in. As a general rule, if a window is closed, then it gives complete control of the display environment; in department stores, this is essential, as it often has thousands of product lines to present in a very small space. Closed windows require good display teams to expose the brand and store values on a continually changing basis.

The best store windows can generate great excitement and a talking point for an entire city. They contribute to the environment by entertaining pedestrians, while simultaneously communicating the products and services on offer.

Below **Pleats Please by Issey Miyake, designed by Toshiko Mori, is located in SoHo, New York. This store has a fascinating visual effect; films are applied to the surface which give an optical illusion that alters from clear to distorted as you walk across the shopfront. This creates colourful shadows and an unusual kinetic effect.**

Some stores – such as the jeweller Tiffany – combine closed and open windows to create a stage set in which they have complete control of the environment. When the windows are open, a store can use the activity within the store as part of this 'street' theatre; this shows that the store is busy and will attract more people.

For a retailer willing to exploit the full potential that a window gives, the image-building process can be exciting and have enormous potential. A fashion retailer, for instance, will often change a window weekly to show the latest items on offer. As Ted Baker, a specialist shirt retailer in London, shows, a window display is also an opportunity to challenge perceived notions. Even a staid product can be displayed in a way which makes it exciting – in fact, window displays can often be more fashionable than the shops themselves because of their constantly changing nature and the incessant demand for sensation and new ideas. Shop windows are also a barometer of seasonal and social events. A glance into a shop's windows by a passer-by establishes the time of year and, very likely, a timely contemporary event. It might be a film release; it might combine seasonal points of the year such as Christmas, Valentine's Day, Easter or Mother's Day. At other times the propping may be based on colour schemes, materials or cultural themes – the possibilities for innovative ideas around such themes are endless.

Window displays are changed often: some, such as those at Harvey Nichols, are famous and have won an inter-national reputation and numerous awards. Various retail associations give such awards, including those for retail display and art direction. Harvey Nichols in London won a Design and Art Director's award for its windows in 1997. Selfridges, too, has established a reputation for window displays such as art installations, interactive media and 'living' windows which communicate an entire *Wallpaper* magazine-type lifestyle for fashions and the home.

Every department store has trained and highly skilled display teams which design and install window schemes. The teams may vary in size from five to 25 people, whose remit will cover windows, internal display areas, visual

merchandising, and the overall look and ambience of the store. Many chain stores also have mobile teams which produce schemes for all parts of the country; they will initiate a format which is then installed in sites nationwide.

Entrances

A good entrance should be easy to find, welcoming, and full of promise and seduction in order to invite the customer in. The doors should be appropriate: some designers would argue that solid wooden doors create a barrier, but during trading these might be left open. Doors can be used as devices in themselves, for display, punctuation (for example, the Next store in London's Oxford Street devised a door with an internal display, for jewellery and small items; when closed, it gave the impression of being an extension of the window promotion) or even within lobbies to create a sense of protection (the latter is mainly used within jewellery stores, with a high-security man-trap aimed at slowing down or barring any suspicious persons). Doors within lobbies evoke historical connections: before the invention of the air curtain, they were used to trap cold air and keep the shop interior warm. Today this arrangement

Above **Shu Uemura is a Japanese cosmetic company which creates sculptural illusions in its interiors. This store in SoHo, New York, designed by Yoshi Matsuyama, uses the illuminated forms to create interesting ceiling features. The display of the products is carefully stage managed to create impact and mirror images.**

Above *This Habitat store front is in an out-of-town shopping location. The standard format shed architecture is clad with a grid of clear and etched glass. Activity can be viewed through the façade which creates interest. The store, in Croydon, south London, was designed by Jeremy Taylor.*

reflects an ingrained value of exclusivity, by providing an obstruction and an opportunity to pause. For jewellers, the door also has a security function, allowing an air lock to be created before the customer is admitted.

There is a range of doors with differing functions: hinged, folding, bi-folding, curved, pivoting, full height, lobbied, revolving, automatic and concealed. Each has its particular uses:

▷ Folding doors can close off wide store openings; they can be concealed at either side of the opening.

▷ Bi-folding doors are double-hinged so that they are more compact.

▷ Curved doors can be softer and help to differentiate a door position or location in a façade.

▷ Pivoting doors are more of an architectural statement. The door is hung on pivot mechanisms instead of hinges or glides; this allows it to stand free, away from any framing, and this looks effective when glass is used.

▷ Lobbied doors are ideal for poor climatic conditions, such as in a wind- or rain-exposed corner site.

▷ Revolving doors are used for locations sited in poor climatic conditions and where lobbied doors are undesirable. They are often installed when large numbers of people are entering and leaving a store, as they regulate a disciplined flow while also aiding through movement. Many large supermarkets now have revolving doors through which customers with trolleys can walk unaided and unhindered by obstructions. These doors also provide the important function of keeping air-conditioned climates intact by acting as an air lock.

▷ Automatic doors are efficient in terms of space and are successful in achieving a fast and easy flow system into and out of a store.

▷ Arcades: open-ended arcades were very popular in the 1950s and 60s when deep, large windows were the norm. However, these were subsequently removed, as many shops increased their available sales space by using the front of the shop for merchandise. This area is the most productive part of any store and considered the highest yielding in terms of value.

As a town or city's planning policies change, different access points to a store may become more prominent. For instance, main access points might change from one side of the store to another, influenced perhaps by a newly pedestrianized street or a resited bus stop. The whole focus of a store may change over the years as a result, and many stores need to be aware of any planning changes that may affect their layout and sales.

Storefront materials

The materials chosen for a store front will be central to the retailer's image. Traditional materials such as stone, marble and bronze suggest a strong, established image, conveying quality, longevity and old-fashioned values. Wood – long used for all shopfronts and window frames – was easy to shape, mould, transport and fix, but was not easy to maintain since it needs regularly to be painted and protected from the elements. In more recent years it has been protected by wrapping in metal (either stainless steel or a bronze veneer).

A more contemporary feel can be achieved by using various metals. Modern aluminium drawn sections (extruded metals) can be manufactured and moulded to almost any shape or size; aluminium also has the advantage that it can be coloured or anodized with a metallic finish. On the other hand, its disadvantage is that it looks cheap – this material is overused by many shopfitters, and so it has no prestige value. Stainless steel, bronze and brass are alternatives which can be as flexible as aluminium but these are more expensive. These metals can be finished to a much higher degree than aluminium; polishing, matt-finishing and sand-blasting with different textures can all be used to create a contemporary look.

Glass, the qualities of which are obvious for retailers' purposes, is the most essential material in all shop fronts. Glass finishes can be varied from transparent to translucent, and glass can now be produced in very large sizes over very large areas. An example is Pilkington's Planner system, an architectural glazing system which gives a continuous and seamless viewing plane. The system has a patented

fixing device which allows glass to be fixed edge-to-edge over huge areas, and over more than one floor, creating a 'doll's house' sectional view into the store.

Information technology

All retailers should realise that the site of a store, often in a public area, gives unlimited potential for marketing and promotional opportunities. Information technology is now being developed in this way, and its use within store fronts and windows is increasing daily. Options available to retailers include large video screens that are visible from the pavement to interactive kiosks which, significantly, remain open for business when the store or bank is closed. Levis' touch-sensitive windows at its Regent Street store in London created a special interactive window, allowing shoppers to gain information about products even when the store was closed. ATM machines are also now incorporated within many retail lobbies and at the entrances to shopping areas, stores and supermarkets, allowing 24-hour access to money and information.

Above **The Wild at Heart building in Ledbury Avenue, Notting Hill Gate. This was created for the owner by the architectural practice Future Systems. The façade is clad in etched glass with a clear ovaloid form and is bridged over the pavement light with a steel ramp.**

Consumer circulation patterns

Below **Jil Sander stores are
characterized by being severe
minimalist abstractions of retail spaces.
They suggest exploration with enticing
views of staircases, walkways and high
level ramps, and circulation is induced
by temptation. This store in Munich was
designed by Michael Gabellini.**

The objective of planning and circulation is to guide customers around every area of the store, to expose them to all the products available. This can be done efficiently, formally or directly; or indirectly and subtly, using more meandering or suggested routes. The circulation pattern should aid the customers through the retail experience, but also fit into the overall style and reflect the brand values.

A traditional department store will have a defined walkway. This will often lead customers to vertical circulation routes (escalators, stairs and lifts) while creating a promenade from which to view the various departments and products. This formal and efficient system allows the largest number of people access through the store and reassures them that they will not lose their way – a real threat in a very big store. Smaller shops and stores need only to suggest a circulation route. This allows a more meandering, informal approach. A supermarket is the exact opposite, where customers are encouraged to be disciplined about their route for safety, efficiency and maximum exposure.

Good visibility is a prerequisite: from the moment of entering the store, customers must have a clear image of where they are going. Depending on the size of the outlet, this can be achieved with a store directory or, more effectively, by opening up the store to suggest an obvious route. If the store is multi-level it will also help to create visibility into other floors, either by the use of voids or glass floors, or with scenic lifts to suggest access and movement.

Circulation patterns are particularly important in department stores in which there is a structured route based on a walkway. In a supermarket the route is structured by shelving and by barriers created through the positioning of merchandise. In a smaller store there is no defined route; customers are simply guided by what they see.

Circulation can be vertical as well as horizontal, and it is essential that the customer can easily identify the positioning of lifts, stairs and/or escalators for access to all floors. Indeed, the importance of vertical access has resulted in many department stores being forced to rethink out-of-date circulation routes. In such cases, new escalators and lifts may have to be fitted into existing voids, and may subsequently become features in their own right (an example is the Egyptian escalator in Harrods).

The cost of such developments should not be underestimated. Selfridges in London, for example, invested £40 million on development of the store, which included opening up voids in the building for new circulation routes. This was achieved mainly through improving visibility by opening up huge 'vistas' across and through the store to link horizontal with vertical circulation. New glass-sided escalators were lowered from above into the pre-prepared voids, producing fast and easy access to all floors.

The rules of circulation

Circulation within stores is infinite. Both a multi-level store or a single-floor outlet will only work if the circulation route is obvious. There are certain 'rules' which most retailers have observed and witnessed over the years.

▷ Visibility means access – people like to know where they are going, and where they have been.

▷ Good signage is reassuring to the customer.

▷ Landmarks can create points of reference.

▷ Circulation in larger stores needs to be clear and easily accessible, particularly with escalators, stairs and lifts.

▷ Walkways help to penetrate the full depth of larger stores.

▷ Walkways should not continue in a straight line for too long, as they will appear never-ending and therefore tiring.

▷ Departments and product areas must not be too deep from the walkway to the back wall as this will deter customers from leaving the walkway.

▷ Dead ends should be avoided: customers like to flow from one area to another.

▷ Product areas should entice, and not be too large, deep or overwhelming, or customers may feel trapped.

▷ Bottlenecks must be avoided, especially around cash desks, fitting rooms, lifts and stairs.

▷ Points of relaxation should be included.

Circulation plan types

Most smaller shops and stores require only a minimal or a singular circulation route, whereas department stores need a more sophisticated and interconnected series of routes – some primary and some secondary – which allow circulation throughout the whole store. The basic types of circulation plans are as follows.

Racetrack or walkway

This type of plan is often used in department stores and in other complex retail spaces. It can provide an efficient way of moving people around large spaces, although this can be monotonous and must be interspersed with interest such as changes of direction and display, and special promotions. These will challenge the shopper to leave the route.

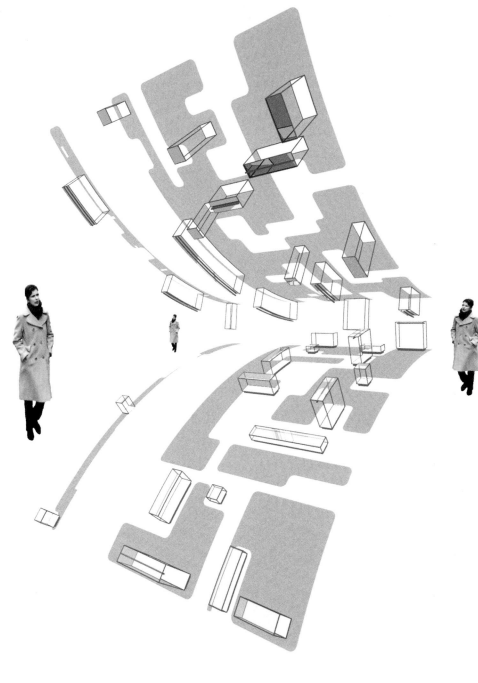

Curved circulation

The shapes produced by this type of route are interesting to the eye and 'softer', giving a more feminine quality. Curved forms involve more complex shapes and are seen to be more complex and costly. However, gentle curves can be incorporated within any design, as long as product bays are faceted to make shopfitting easier to manufacture.

Square or rectilinear

Often used in supermarkets and warehouse retailing, this type of floor plan makes the most efficient use of space since it generally follows the form of the structure, but can be inflexible. The sales and circulation spaces are uniform but can be boring because of the rigid grid-like modular system. This layout lacks stimulation, but has been adopted by many out-of-town shed environments, because it suggests efficiency and value for money.

Above **This store layout, designed by Mike Tonkin for a Hong Kong department store is fascinating. The circulation route is mirrored in the ceiling, thereby creating abstract forms, overlaid and defined by hard and soft surfaces on the floor.**

Free-flow areas

This circulation option allows more variety and flexibility in spacial volume. Routes are suggested in an informal way, but are varied in shape and direction to allow departments to become islands without barriers, and therefore inviting.

Planning

Store planning and layout must reflect the size and type of retail outlet. Since every building is unique, physical access must be studied in detail: storage of stock and deliveries, collection points for purchases, and pedestrian and car-park access must all be determined in terms of number, location and size. So too must the architectural layout of the space: planning of large areas must be discussed closely with the retailer, as this is a complex exercise involving many variables. A designer must assess the given architectural features, and decide whether to exploit, ignore or rearrange them. There are many retail spaces, built in the nineteenth century, which are really beautiful and offer wonderful

opportunities for the visionary designer. In contrast many American malls and new purpose-built units today are repetitive and built to modular systems with little or no individual character. However these structures represent an increasing proportion of retail spaces and present a real challenge to the designer.

Early design thinking and planning is clearly based on customer behaviour and social interaction. The designer and retailer must continually reassess their planning criteria, so that new layouts suit the customer's needs, contribute to the effective use of his or her time, and enable the retailer to exploit maximum sales potential from each customer. Before detailed planning begins, the designer must have a clear understanding of the following:

▷ The building's type, age and construction.

▷ Brand values, image and identity.

▷ A detailed breakdown of the customer profiles.

▷ The client's philosophy and objectives.

▷ Product information by category.

Below **Stairwell at Dickens and Jones, London. Planning and circulation should be clearly understood by the shopper. This circular void acts as a focal point, but also creates a mental store directory in the consumer's mind. It can seduce customers into exploration mode, whilst leaving them with an impressive image which they will remember having left the store.**

With these factors in mind, the planning of the layout must take into consideration not only the basic issues of visibility, access, customer flow and circulation, but also the positioning of merchandise. The layout will also incorporate the views and effect of visual merchandising, and display and promotional areas, service areas, lighting, security and storage. Other influences on store planning will be the type of merchandise, staffing policy, number of customers and the customer flow at peak trading times.

Any well-planned store should create three fundamental space divisions, based on impulse, convenience, and considered goods.

Impulse goods

These are 'luxury' items or 'treats', such as perfume, cosmetics, jewellery and confectionery. Sales rely on good positioning, effective display, clever marketing and accessibility. It is important to stimulate impulse buying, as most stores could not survive on considered purchases alone.

Convenience goods

This covers staple items of merchandise which are popular and often need replenishment, such as milk, bread, tobacco and newspapers, but also food, drugs, hosiery and accessories. Corner shops and garage forecourts are obvious examples of convenience outlets.

Considered goods

The purchase of these items merits longer and more considered thought. Typical examples are furniture, white goods and expensive items of clothing, jewellery or equipment.

Retailers will vary in their expertise at selling these different goods, and may specialize in one or more of the three categories. Some products may fall into more than one category, depending on a customer's requirements and mood at the time of purchase. For example, cosmetics and perfumery can be both impulse-treat items, which may be replenished often, or considered purchases for a special occasion. As a result, some stores now have dual-location sites, both in the traditional departments and within a

considered-purchase zone such as a dress department. Large department stores were traditionally designed as destination stores, intended to keep customers inside for hours. Modern department stores are planned so that the shopper can enter, locate a department, buy, and then leave or move on to the next department efficiently. Location and juxtaposition of products are critical, since most weekday shoppers have limited time.

Brands and considered-purchase items are usually located where they can be given a total identity environment, such as a corner. A retailer will generally locate impulse and convenience items at the front of the store so that people are doubly exposed to this merchandise. Different products should be clearly defined in each category and all retailers will tend to display a cross-section of products for consideration. Shopfittings generally should support and display the product to its best advantage. Each product group should have its own identity display or promotion area where possible. Added to this will be related merchandise which extends the offer and sales opportunities. For example, shirts will always be located with ties and cufflinks; in a car showroom, alloy wheels, stereos and other accessories will be displayed alongside the vehicles.

Above **This Habitat shed environment in Croydon, south London was designed by Jeremy Taylor. It has utilized vertical space for the purpose of circulation and product merchandising. Maximum use is made of all perimeter areas giving an impression of assortment and depth.**

Small stores

A common mistake with small stores is to put too much into a limited space. The main objectives here are to keep things simple and focused, to maximize available floorspace, and to make visual statements without obstructing the view or complicating the offer. Services such as air-conditioning, heating and lighting can cause problems in smaller stores; it is better to integrate them within the ceiling or to conceal them behind structures such as bulkheads and soffits. This will create a cleaner line and focus the customer's eye on the product rather than on distracting details.

As with most aspects of retail, however, an acceptable style can contradict these rules. For example, there are smaller stores which are complicated in design and express their image and style through a multi-layering of products, such as Lush, Paperchase and Jerry's Home Stores. To some this type of approach might be confusing and overpowering, but to others it can be a delightful experience. The retailer should decide on the product density, but the designer must understand the philosophy to accommodate the merchandise and the customers successfully within the store.

Visual merchandising

Visual merchandising can make a huge difference to any product area, transforming products and departments into an entirely new experience for the consumer. The visual-merchandising arena must be allowed to change and adapt over time; by its nature it is transient and must reflect the latest trends as well as the retailer's brand values.

Product adjacencies are particularly important and there should be natural associations made between products which do not surprise or confuse the consumer. Merchandise which can be touched and handled will excite, while products which are inaccessible or locked away will be harder to sell. These products will need to be service-assisted for best results. (For more detailed information on merchandising, see pages 112–15.)

Visual merchandising provides an opportunity for retailers to indulge in theatre, but for multiple retailers it is also used to convey a consistency of image. It can also create a sense of commitment to customers visiting the store by making them feel special – demonstrating that the retailer has made an effort with the store environment.

Visual merchandising incorporates windows and in-store environments. Interestingly, Andy Warhol, one of the twentieth century's most influential artists, had previously worked as a window dresser in the USA. A specialist visual merchandiser will work alongside the retail designer on a new concept for a store, to ensure that the latter's approach can accommodate visual-merchandising strategies.

Nick Grossmark, a UK-based retail consultant says that the importance of visual merchandising is for a retailer to create a standard for general presentation of the product. Grossmark, who has worked for Tommy Hilfiger UK, Joseph, Next and Debenhams, says that windows are as important as store interiors, but points out that retailers often make the mistake of concentrating on a window concept that is not followed through within the store.

A critical aspect of visual merchandising, he maintains, is the constant change necessary to ensure that customers remain interested in the products. 'You need to reinvent a place constantly – but people also need to feel comfortable within a store.' Grossmark's view is that a visual merchandiser must put himself in the position of the customer. He emphasizes, however, that visual merchandising is essentially a team effort which must therefore incorporate store staff. Retailers such as Gap, and Eddie Bauer from the USA, also aim to make each store – wherever it is in the world – look the same. As Grossmark comments: 'It is a standard of excellence that they want to achieve. They don't want one store looking like a poor relation, so there is this standardization.'

He particularly admires the approach taken by Colette in Paris. Here, the visual merchandising communicates the ethos of quality, taste and careful selection, with key garments from a range of designers brought together using objects – perhaps co-ordinating vases, or even CDs – which themselves communicate a lifestyle approach. Grossmark says that, in the UK, the concept of standardization was established by Next in the 1980s, and was then continued in the 1990s by Debenhams. However, he stresses that the visual merchandising of a store can never be taken for granted, but needs to keep continually evolving.

Display and promotional areas

Display takes place predominantly within the windows of large department stores. These are generally fully enclosed, offering the display artist total control of the environment. Window display as a promotional tool can elicit international acclaim and even notoriety, as has been shown by Harvey Nichols, Barneys and Tiffany in New York, whose windows are a talking point among the entire city for their inventiveness and minimalistic beauty. Clever displays manage to create a spectacle as well as providing information.

Promotional areas may be in the form of in-store mini exhibitions or demonstration areas which are continually changing depending on the season or on the product being promoted. Siting is important, and should be planned for a central location that is visible to most customers. An ideal site is by an entrance or at the base of an escalator, which is big enough to attract spontaneous attention, yet not so large as to create an obstruction.

Below **Gap for many years has led the way in merchandising. Stores pride themselves on simple stacks of clothes laid out with military precision. The use of layering and bust forms creates the pyramid shape which has become synonymous with Gap and influenced many retailers throughout the world.**

Service areas

The service areas of a store may appear to be a secondary consideration in the design process, but they can in fact be central to the success of a store. These areas can include cash desks, fitting rooms, waiting areas, repairs desks, sales desks and customer-services areas. In the back-of-house areas, they may incorporate stockrooms, ticketing areas, staff rooms, offices and space for tailoring or alterations.

The positioning of cash desks, fitting rooms, storage areas and service points must be carefully thought out. With a cash desk, a designer should avoid the negative psychological effect created when too close to the front door, but must also consider that if it is too far back it may create a security problem. Facilities at cash desks are important to allow space for packaging, customer service and storage, as well as for card-swipe machines and telephones.

Fitting rooms always leave a lasting impression on the customer. At the lower end of the market they were once communal with little privacy. At the top end, however, the emphasis will be on individual privacy, space and comfort. The fitting rooms in the new Top Shop store in London's Oxford Street show how glamorous and comfortable the fitting room has become even at this most popular of stores. Internal fittings should be considered as an extension of the brand. Retailers also need to consider the location of fitting rooms, whether concealed, or opening on to the retail space, to create visible activity. Some retailers may wish to encourage customers to go deeper into the store during the trying-on process; this has the advantage of privacy but also exposes the customer to new products.

Stockrooms and deliveries

Any product not on the sales floor is dead. With point-of-sale systems, stock information can now be reordered automatically (see page 46). The need for large stockrooms on-site is therefore diminishing. Deliveries to the store constitute another practical consideration. Many city-centre stores have restrictions on times and sizes of deliveries. However, using instant computerized information tills, retailers can be specific about stocking and replenishment, allowing smaller daily deliveries. Shopping malls are planned for continuous access, from the rear or at differing levels, with stock coming into the stores unseen.

Air-conditioning

In some parts of the world, there is no choice but for retailers to install air-conditioning in a retail outlet. In the UK and northern Europe, however, this is still an issue.

Right **The position, design and location of service desks and customer changing rooms is very important. They can differ enormously and create strong statements about brands. These fitting rooms have solid doors for privacy and a wider than average access space.**

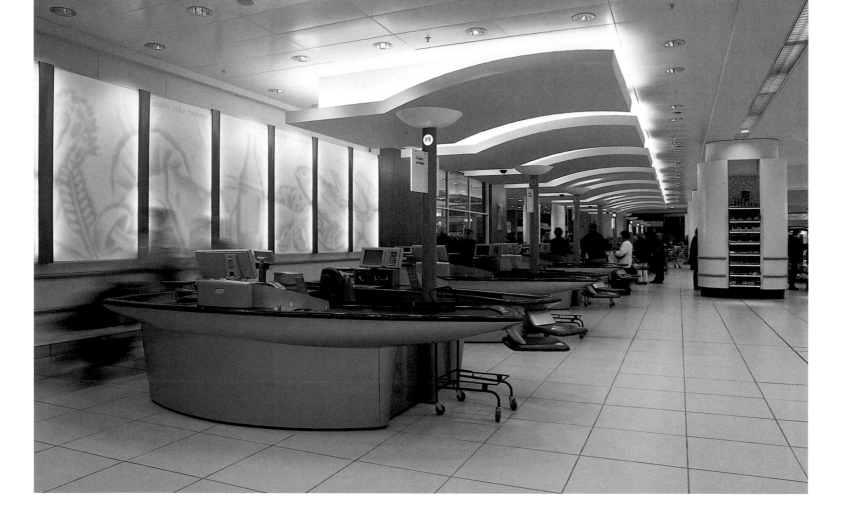

Most UK retailers are happy with comfort cooling (a secondary form of cooling) but many have begun to insist on full air-conditioning, and now build it into their capital expenditure. This has a number of implications for designers, including power requirements, where to position the condenser unit, and whether to use a cassette or full ducted system (which reduces the ceiling height and requires no small degree of invention to conceal). If ceilings are particularly low, the installation of air-conditioning may even require false walls or bulkheads, reducing floorspace.

Lighting

Lighting must highlight and accentuate the product while allowing enough ambient light to enable the customer to circulate. Lighting can be used to direct customers along a particular route, or to create intensity of light to gain attention. It can also direct customers and inform them through illuminated signage. (See also page 85.)

Security

Good security can be expressed by clear, open vistas between sales staff and customers. Technology helps to combat theft in stores, and devices available range from closed-circuit television installations to ticketing devices.

Safety and access

All designers should be aware of current fire-legislation requirements for water sprinklers, means of escape, staff rooms, fitting rooms and delivery areas. This ensures the safety of the public and personnel in stores, all of which has implications for design. A designer who creates a dramatically large window, for instance, must be responsible for its design safety in terms of its installation by the builder, and of its use by the public, by the window dresser, and by the person who cleans it.

Access and planning for people with special needs should form part of the retailer's philosophy. Criteria should include the provision of access to all areas of the store, and to WCs, for both customers and employees. Designers need to be aware that legal requirements vary in different countries. Knowledge of the laws relating to access must be an essential part of a designer's initial research. Issues which could affect a retail interior are the store entrance and use of automatic or manual doors, the availability of lifts and alternatives to internal stairs, increased lighting and the use of tactile materials to denote circulation for the partially sighted, the height of shelving, and any sharp corners. Many organizations exist to represent the needs of disabled and elderly people, and some publish guidelines.

Above **Check-out cash tills are becoming faster and more efficient. These check-outs in Marks and Spencers in Bluewater Shopping Mall, Kent, designed by RTKL UK Ltd, are streamlined and look very efficient. Speed and convenience are essential to process sales quickly. Lighting is indirect and the environment is invigorated by abstract illustrations.**

Shopfitting trends

Traditionally, shopfitters were artists, craftsmen and tradesmen who created store interiors from concept to completion. A post-war period of systemization and flexible modularization resulted in many shopfitters becoming manufacturers, producing systems which were sold on the open market. Today, however, the demand by retailers for individuality has caused manufacturers to rethink their products. The shopfitter's role today has become primarily a technical one, to build design concepts.

A wholly individual approach only applies to specialist retailers, however: many use manufactured shopfittings and systems, but still seek innovative ways of displaying products. Euroshop in Dusseldorf, Germany, is an international exhibition which specializes in the retail trades and distribution sectors. Staged every four years, it brings together the best new products in shopfitting and lighting.

A shopfit in the high street typically has a three to five-year lifespan. Exclusive retailers will often spend far more per square foot for quality materials that will obviously look good and last longer. The more fashionable high-street retailers will need to shopfit more regularly because this sector of the market is highly competitive, with a more fickle customer base.

Below left **This store, No Concept But Good Sense, in Tokyo, Japan, has exaggerated its shopfitting elements to suggest automation and an urban traffic chic. Designed by Japanese architects H Design Associates, it creates a distinctive interior.**

Below right **A watch shop called Watch to Watch in London's Kings Road. This detail shows a watch held on a plastic bracelet that hinges so the customer can try it out on his wrist. The store is designed by Cobalt Design.**

Shopfittings, fixtures and equipment

A modular system is flexible and cost-effective. Flexibility is important for presenting the product in different ways over several seasons. However, it is essential that the system does not overshadow the product. Fashion stores or products with a high style content require an invisible flexibility or one that does not appear over-systemized. A designer may need to put in two or three different systems, or create differing features such as niches, display walls and graphics walls, to break up the environment to achieve the illusion of space and specialization.

Some retailers choose an approach that is more akin to an art installation, with little or no flexibility; examples include Calvin Klein New York, Katherine Hamnett, Rei Kawakubo and Comme des Garçons. Others, however, such as Banana Republic and Reis, cannot afford this approach. Their priority is to create a shopfit that allows for variation in merchandising layouts, and therefore the creation of different moods, throughout the season.

Fittings can help to convey moods in a number of ways. In upmarket fashion stores, a contemporary atmosphere is achieved with a minimal approach by a one-shelf,

one-rail formula, with the product side-hung at the same level around the whole shop. This gives a clean, simple line, and needs little variation. This formula is possible because customers identify with the minimalist approach and are not intimidated. At the lower end of the market, in contrast, where customers are likely to be drawn from a much larger catchment area, there is even more choice of product and colours. At this end of the market, design is less about finesse and more about volume. The furniture needs to be robust to withstand the abuse it suffers from heavy weights.

Flexibility in fittings applies also to displaying electrical or household goods. When Habitat decided to adapt their stores in the early 90s, they chose fittings which would have a degree of change: for example, shelves used to accommodate homeware and cookware were flexible.

As will be discussed in greater detail on pages 112–15, understanding how a product is sold is an important part of store design. Habitat evolved a bazaar-type environment with lots of products on display, by studying the traditions of ancient bazaars in India and the Far East. In essence, the ability to re-create the activity, hustle and bustle within a modern setting was the objective, producing a cosier, friendlier environment.

In the area of fixturing, there are three basic directions available to the designer: off-the-shelf (stock) fixtures; customized fixtures to suit the client; and fixtures which are specifically designed for each client.

Off-the-shelf fixtures

The systems available directly from shopfitting manufacturers vary enormously in style and quality. The advantage is that many will be 'tried and tested' in terms of engineering, and carry guarantees. Another advantage is they will be standard items and therefore probably available from stock, making them easier and quicker to order and fit. The disadvantage is that retailers lose their individuality. Stock shopfitting items may look the same as those used by the competition, and no retailer wants that.

Shopfitting-equipment specialists work hard, however, to create standardized equipment which can be customized to suit individual retailers with different colours and textures. The use of standardized equipment may be more acceptable to larger retailers who can negotiate good discounts on substantial orders and are reassured by using highly reputable equipment suppliers who can supply both quality and quantity, such as Vitra in Germany.

Below left Calvin Klein Jeans in Bluewater Park, designed by John Pawson Architects. This new concept is imaginative in its use of shopfitting elements. Translucent screens are held in place with hanging rails and backed with translucent pigeon holes to take folded garments.

Below right Joseph's men's store in Brompton Road, London. Simple forms in wenge, a dark grained hard wood, are juxtaposed to create a merchandise story for each designer brand represented in the store. The store is designed by David Chipperfield with fixtures by Christian Liaigre.

Customized fixtures

Customization can be used so that the basic engineering and flexibility of a system (i.e. the slotted-strip mechanism) are not altered but the cosmetic look is totally restyled. One example was a Next frame which used the standard profile taken from an existing cabinet fixture. When attached to a steel frame a distinctive look was created with all the same components and dimensional modules.

Specially designed fixtures

Many retailers and brands invest generously in image and on the development of their own identity. For them, it is essential to have a unique style which cannot be confused with that of another retailer. Much time, energy and money are spent in creating fixturing and merchandising units which support the retailer's brand values and market

position. This type of investment does enable the retailer to copyright an environment in totality, although in reality it is almost impossible to guard a design internationally.

Some existing and new products on the market – such as hi-fi and information-technology equipment – require specifically designed equipment for in-store support and display. Much of this groundwork will be done by the manufacturer, but often it is the work of the retail designer to develop appropriate systems.

Achieving flexibility

Most of the systems and equipment used in shopfitting are modular in design. Some retailers who seek individuality are badly advised by inexperienced designers to produce custom-fitted units in all sizes, only to find later that it is impossible even to interchange a shelf and a hanging rail without ordering another special piece of equipment. Smaller, specialist shops and boutiques may need fewer options, but there will always be the need to present the store's merchandise differently from time to time.

Modular systems vary depending on the product and on the merchandising policy. Such systems need to be changed vertically and horizontally by department stores, although they are more likely now to have some fixed elements within an adaptable framework. Retailers who insist on total flexibility should be treated by designers with caution, as this desire may be a reaction to past experiences. It is far better to produce a prototype system with which a designer and retailer can work until they find an optimum level of flexibility within the merchandising brief, as flexibility is expensive.

The prototyping of systems and equipment is important, in order that the retailer understands the concept and becomes used to the new image. The system should be simple to use by untrained staff, and easy to carry, assemble and adjust.

Fixturing systems

Fixturing systems may be wall-mounted on the perimeter, or floor-mounted within the retail space as mid-floor units. These are the two basic types of system, on which many variations can be made. Most retailers combine perimeter and mid-floor units in order to define a space. These can be textured and layered (as in the case of Ralph Lauren), or minimal (as in the case of Jil Sander).

The perimeter system is the most effective plan, as it can present product and image to great effect. In the USA in particular, the floor-to-ceiling heights in some stores are enormous. These can be 4–6 metres (13–19½ feet), which means that the designer has a large area – approximately 2 metres (6½ feet) above the product line – to use for marketing, visual merchandise and display. Some retailers choose to minimize this space by lowering the ceiling line, but among more retailers it is fashionable to maximize the volume of space because, if handled correctly, space is associated with quality and impact.

Types of fixtures

Slattwall is a versatile and cost-effective system of horizontal slats made mainly from MDF (medium-density fibreboard) as well as from extruded metal. The horizontal slats have inset channels, into which brackets may be inserted to support a variety of products. It does have its uses, but can lack a strong visual identity.

Panel, posts and brackets are the most popular perimeter system, in which slatted channel inserts are fitted into posts or into the wall. The posts can be made of steel or wood, and they may be left exposed, or alternatively infilled with panels in various materials and finishes. This system has infinite design variations and can therefore be extremely sophisticated.

Both slattwall and post-and-panel systems are flexible and popular with larger retailers, being simple, cheap and quick to fit. The disadvantage is they can look too modular, have no character and look like any other shop with the same format.

Certain styles of retailing have started a trend which others have been quick to mimic. Benetton introduced the use of folded product, stacking from floor to ceiling colour-coordinated separates. Although the design changed, it was instantly recognizable because of its revolutionary merchandise layout. In its early days (1982/3) Next also achieved the reputation of being a coordinated retailer, using a mixture of hanging rails, pigeon holes and shelving. The Gap is an up-to-date coordinated retailer which has mastered the art of colour-coordinated fashionable separates. It has created a big impact with its mid-floor table fixtures which have been adopted all over the world.

Mid-floor units, from cabinets to gondolas (mid-floor shelving units) enable customers to walk among the product – a good device to encourage sales. They vary from secure glazed cabinets to open display units with products hanging from every surface. The use of antique or reconstituted fittings is popular with retailers such as Polo Ralph Lauren and Banana Republic in the USA. Many retailers have fixtures and fittings made to replicate historic shop interiors, which give an impression of tradition and establishment.

Above **This DKNY shop and showroom, designed by Marino and Associates, uses low-tech imagery to create a warehouse feel. Balustrades and glazing are therefore crude and industrially detailed. Natural daylight is diffused through obscured glass panelling.**

Menswear retailing tends to be more classic and makes wide use of this type of cabinetry, constructed to resemble wardrobes or closets from a bygone era. The use of several mid-floor units designed as a 'family' gives the appearance of a shopfitted solution rather than an ad-hoc collection of individual pieces of furniture. This is the result of a product category – such as knitwear or shirts – being merchandised in units specifically designed for that item.

Lighting

Lighting is seen by most designers to be a necessary technical element, yet in most cases it is rarely exploited or developed beyond the basic requirements. In the hands of a skilled designer, however, lighting can be used as a narrative, to create atmosphere, focus attention and

influence moods. It can create excitement, rhythm and anticipation – in short, it is an essential tool that designers should learn to exploit.

In recent years there has been a revolution in lighting technology, the biggest change since the early 1980s being the move to low-voltage tungsten-halogen systems. Lights today are smaller, more energy efficient and are housed in more attractive fittings. More retailers are now able to make a feature of lighting in their stores, and the options include creative effects using colours, kinetics, strobes, gobos, fire optics, lighting sculptures and resin. Specialist lighting consultants are usually commissioned for flagship stores or to design layouts for large, complex spaces such as shopping malls. The revival of interest in retail architecture also means that a designer may choose to emphasize existing features such as skylights, glass-paved areas, voids, staircases or even decorative details on ceilings, which previously may have been covered over. Many older retail buildings are rediscovering their architectural heritage and are using this as part of their brand values. Liberty in London's Regent Street, has begun to expose the original Arts and Crafts detail of its building, and Concord Sylvania has been asked to produce ambient and directional lighting for the building structure and the merchandise.

"Lighting today is a field in which technology and innovation never stop." says Janet Turner of Concord Sylvania. New product developments are being researched, tried and tested, and markets overwhelmed by the number of new developments. Understanding how to make a good selection is becoming very difficult. There are many practical responsibilities of which the designer must be aware, relating to set-up and running costs, flexibility, ease of maintenance, access, and the environmental concerns to do with energy wastage and light pollution.

In her book *Retail Lighting*, Janet Turner says "The correct source of lighting is essential for good colour rendition, and this can be made more effective by using a combination of light sources: metal halide for coolness, and tungsten for warmth." The choice of fitting should never be based solely on its outward appearance: in many cases, the type of lamp and reflector will be more important to the effect of the light. Fluorescent, incandescent and discharge are the main categories of lamp available.

▷ Fluorescent lamps have the advantage of being economical, and give a good colour rendition. New fluorescents are very small and can be incorporated within compact fittings.

▷ Incandescent lamps are the traditional lamp used in most households. They are inexpensive and inefficient, as most of the power is used to generate heat rather than light. Tungsten-halogen lamps and PAR lamps come into this category, and both give a better light quality as well as a longer lamp life. Low-voltage tungsten-halogen lamps offer the most seductive light, excellent colour rendition and miniature sizes. However, these need transformers either integral to the fitting or fitted close by.

▷ Discharge lamps are highly efficient but require large control gears to support their use. They have limited indoor use and often have to be used in combination with incandescent lights to improve their colour rendition.

When thinking about a lighting scheme for an interior, most stores fit into two basic categories: the first is ambient lighting, used for maximum overall visibility, as in supermarkets, pharmacies, DIY centres and out-of-town stores; the second is accent lighting, fitted where detail and illusion need to be exploited. More often than not, lighting schemes reflect the circulation plan and layout of the stores in which they are used. Ambient light is used along walkways and circulation routes, as well as in service areas such as lifts and escalators; accent lighting is preferred within product, merchandise and display areas to create atmosphere and enhance mood. With the correct use of light, merchandise can be made to look beautiful and full of life; lighting can also highlight and shadow to create visual effects and render even a dull product interesting.

Light fittings

These can broadly be divided into downlighters, uplighters, spotlights, suspended or ceiling-mounted fittings and recessed fittings. In many light fittings, differing effects can be achieved by using alternative lamps, to give a range of beams, from small and intense pinspots to wide and soft beams. By adding other features such as colour filters or moving parts, a designer can achieve a theatrical spectrum of effects to 'frame' products or, as in the case of jewellery where the lighting is essential, to highlight the cutting lines of the gem stones to dramatic effect.

Output, efficiency and cost

The output of lamps in Europe is measured in lumens whereas in the USA it is measured in candelas. The efficiency of a lamp refers to the amount of energy it uses against the amount of light put out. Modern lamps are becoming more efficient and consuming less energy. The expense is calculated two-fold: firstly the capital cost of installation, to include the price of the light fittings, transformers, cabling and lamps; and secondly the general running costs (such as electrical power, the cost of new lamps and general maintenance).

Below **This simple but highly effective lighting detail expresses the soffit while uplighting the ceiling and the structural elements. The eye is made to rest on the underside of the soffit which suggests a ceiling plane, without obscuring the structure. Designed by H Design Associates.**

Above **This impressive shop front for Calvin Klein Jeans has a translucent sign on the windows. The logo CKJ is structural and backlit, making it highly effective in terms of size and placement. This store was designed by John Pawson architects and is located in the Bluewater shopping mall.**

Exteriors/interiors

There are two ways in which lighting plays a major part in retail design. One is in the general exterior lighting and illuminated signage; the other relates to window displays. Much of the theatre of retail is achieved after hours, so that when the store is closed, or when the daylight has gone, the designer must encourage continued interest in the store. It is at these times that lighting brings the store to life.

The lighting must illuminate the product and project the right image for the retailer, whether it is bright and colourful, busy and exuberant or discreet, cool and sophisticated. Illuminated signage is important for brand identity, and illuminating the building makes a strong visual statement about the solidity of a brand, its value and its history. This is especially true if the building is seen as part of the brand in terms of its logo – for example, Harrods and Liberty in London.

Natural light

Whatever the exciting and innovative options coming on to the lighting market, designers should not neglect the cheapest and most obvious light source of all – natural daylight. It costs nothing, is accurate in colour rendition and, if well directed, can create dramatic spatial effects. By using skylights, windows and atriums, designers and architects can create a fresh feeling of well-being. There has been a growing trend of bringing daylight back into department stores, as has been done at Peek and Clopenburg in Germany. The introduction of daylight into a store allows some contact with the outside world, ensuring that a shopper does not feel claustrophobic or too cocooned by the building. Computerized systems can automatically alter the light levels inside a building, according to the level of daylight, whereas in the past there would have been a dramatic difference between light levels outside and inside. Such systems can also alter the light levels in shop windows, to boost the amount of light during the day in order to counteract the reflection caused by daylight, and to reduce it at night.

Natural light has disadvantages, such as heat gain and ultraviolet rays which fade fabrics, but modern building materials and techniques are reducing the effects of these by incorporating protective films and ultraviolet glass. However, natural sunlight in Eastern countries is frowned upon: sunlight can burn and darker skin tone is not desirable since it is a social pointer of lower class. The use of daylight is discouraged in stores, as many consumers prefer to avoid its direct contact.

Graphics

A graphics package within a store can be extensive, and can operate as a continuous development of the brand and its core message. Basic elements of this package are the labels, swing tickets, pricing, carrier bags and all aspects of signage. Many retailers still need persuading about the importance of this area of their business. Yet to most consumers it is the introduction to the brand, and it therefore needs to make an impact by being thought-provoking and eye-catching.

Ian Hutchings, graphics director at Din Associates, says that graphics provide the medium through which retail designers can respond quickly to trends. Graphics draw on a diverse range of influences, from television to ephemera and, at the opposite end of the spectrum, even on fine art. Hutchings feels that the importance of graphics is their ability to change the feel of a store easily and cheaply by telling a story. However, the way in which they are used will differ depending on the retailer: upmarket retailers such as Prada, for example, use graphics in a more sophisticated and understated way than less affluent stores would do.

Graphics will enhance the product by operating more as a quality endorsement or seal of approval. Prada's logo, for example, resembles a crest. In contrast, Gucci has shown an innovative use of graphics in its store windows: using images in huge lit boxes, rather than mannequins, to dramatic effect. Graphics used in this way bring advertising images to the front of the store, creating an impression of street photography. DKNY uses representations of New York scenes in its graphics, picking a different theme per season, each of which reinforces the message that its clothes belong to the streets. The Gap also uses in-store graphics to back up its advertising images: it does this by integrating the typography and pictures of the product to the extent that its window displays operate like advertisements, and even using text on the windows themselves to create a three-dimensional effect. Hutchings also believes, however, that the constantly changing nature and versatility of graphics are influencing how retailers approach branding. Nike's five dots, for instance, which are replacing the all-too-familiar swoosh logo, create a more layered and subtle brand image.

Graphics are becoming a strong medium for repeating an advertising slogan, logo or image. Huge-scale, almost abstract, blow-ups, can be used in certain retail spaces to make big statements about a brand. It is the initial cost of advertising images – often running into thousands of pounds – which is one of the reasons why their use has been extended into stores. Designers like to repeat these images to reassure customers that they have identified an image or brand that they have seen elsewhere in magazines, on billboards or perhaps on television. The same images will be used for decoration, point-of-sale material, packaging and brochures, thus operating as reassurance advertising. Consumers who are repeatedly bombarded with the same images cannot help but be influenced by them.

This holistic approach to graphics has been assimilated by retailers such as Esprit and Benetton. Esprit had a successful period when the graphics and interiors unified to create a wonderful concept that was full of life, and was carried through from swing tickets to carrier bags. Benetton developed a complex and controversial campaign which, while questionable, certainly was memorable; with the result that their green logo is instantly recognizable.

Below **This colourful window screen is a backdrop for text and images within the window of The Source (now renamed The Inventory), a home furnishing store designed by the Conran Design Group in Kensington High Street, London. The text on the window pane and internally on the screen create a striking layered image.**

Materials

Below **This Jil Sander store in Paris has a simple material palette with fixtures that are positioned like pieces of furniture. The light fittings suggest circulation routes and a steel spiral staircase winds itself without support through the space.**

The retail designer's choice of materials with which to create an image is almost infinite. Specific materials create their own language, whether it is historic, natural, industrial, organic or technical. For some designers the selection of materials for projects is an important part of their stylistic signature, and the choices that they make can destroy or enhance a good concept.

Most designers will spend a great deal of time going through product and material libraries for new ideas. Many like myself will make a collection of samples which they find inspiring, ready for use on future projects or to inspire a total concept which may emerge from a specific material. There is often great excitement when a designer discovers a new product, especially one that is versatile, durable and cost-effective. It is also significant if a material has not been used by other designers: certain new materials generate extra cachet if they are unique, can claim to have been discovered or are being used in an innovative way. One such new material, developed from a student project, is reconstituted plastic, made from waste plastics, and manufactured with ecological zeal by the UK company Made of Waste. It fits all the above criteria and was used extensively by Ben Kelly at the Science Museum in London.

The past ten years have seen a fashion for the use of natural materials in retail design, which has grown largely from concerns about destruction of the environment. Manufacturers and designers celebrated the development of MDF (medium-density fibreboard) in the early 1980s, which had many of the advantages of timber, could be moulded and was extremely versatile. However, it has since been revealed that MDF may in fact be causing much more damage to the environment as a result of its manufacturing process than the use of trees and raw materials; when worked on, it also produces a very fine dust which is potentially carcinogenic, making proper precautions essential for anyone using it. There is a new development of a material called MDF light, which is a much-improved product.

The choice of materials for specific tasks will be based on three factors: image, cost and practicality. All materials have an integral quality which the designer seeks to project. Certain materials, especially natural ones, have differing qualities; when crude they are basic and unattractive but, with varying degrees of cutting, cleaning and polishing, they can be transformed into a sophisticated and luxurious product (for example, stainless steel, marble, wood and stone). In various combinations, materials will project different values, while finishes may alter perceptions of quality, character and personality. Raw natural materials have an integrity and beauty of their own, while the same materials, honed and polished, develop a luxurious quality that can be brash. Choosing the right materials is therefore a critical aspect of successful design: the right materials will be a strong tool for a designer and, when skilfully deployed, will make a substantial impact on the overall effect that is achieved.

Practicality

Whatever the desired image, the materials chosen by a designer – in consultation with the retailer – must be practical, must not endanger life or well-being and must be fit for their purpose. In Britain there is strict legislation about the use of certain materials in particular conditions. Fire hazards and the surface spread of flame must be taken into consideration, and building controls take an increasing interest in the design and specification of buildings and interior finishes. The correct specification of materials – especially when dealing with historic buildings – is carefully considered. The use of glass in interiors has strict guidelines, and any other potentially hazardous surface or material can be questioned. Local authorities can examine the appropriateness of certain materials in some locations, such as glass staircases or balustrades. This was of particular concern during the threat of terrorist attacks in Manchester after the bomb blast of 1997, when retailers had great difficulty in persuading the authorities that glass was fit for its purpose. Materials should of course be considered for the image that they will create, but at the same time must be durable, low-maintenance and, when intended for international projects, consistently available worldwide.

Many of these points are self-explanatory, but safety will need to be researched and discussed with regulatory bodies to ensure that standards are met. This is often complex when dealing with international projects, but compromise may be necessary. A designer should be aware that safety regulations also extend to ensure that the correct materials are being used within the means of escape from a building. This includes ascertaining that the fire doors are

appropriate and they meet requirements on fire retardancy, and that the escape ironmongery is adequate, fully accessible and serviceable.

When considering durability and maintenance, the designer should understand the ageing process and the wearability of the materials being selected. Some designers specify the use of materials which will change in character over time, so that as they age they develop a different patina and personality. Retailers should be made aware of the value of good-quality materials and take into account that, in the long term, it will be more economical to use better, more costly materials that may last longer with minimum maintenance than to have to replace them, with the added cost of the effect on sales as a result of further disruption to the store.

Flooring

It is possible to tell a great deal about someone by looking at their shoes. By the same token, it is possible to tell a lot about a store by looking at the quality and maintenance of the floor. Flooring is an important element of any store design. It is easy to see when a retailer has skimped by settling for a cheaper option: the quality of finish should never be compromised, as the impact will run through the entire retail operation. The floor is a good way of formalizing and defining space. From outdoors to indoors, circulation routes, thresholds, public and private spaces: all can be defined by a flooring material. Harvey Nichols in Leeds has an interesting floor pattern, which is used to define space without physical boundaries.

The location and use of the floor will define the finish that is chosen. Floors can be neutral, bright and colourful, or incredibly detailed in design. High-quality flooring such as stone or marble will obviously be expensive, but these can be the most durable and easily maintained surfaces, and, over a number of years, will recoup their initial outlay by proving the most cost-effective and durable.

Thresholds, entrances, stairways and walkways will receive the most wear, and should be considered high-traffic, high-maintenance areas. For thresholds, a

Below left *The Japanese shop Pas de Calais, designed by Tsutomu Kurokawa of H Design Associates, has a reclaimed timber floor. The large simple planks, which are laid at an angle, suggest depth and warmth. The brick-clad, whitewashed walls also bring to mind the idea of a stripped-out, converted loft. The simple rails and an exposed structural column are further features within a classic, timeless location.*

Below right *This Hugo Boss showroom suggests a strict, high quality brand. Simple materials are incorporated on an extremely high-gloss floor, creating a strong reflection of the interior fittings. Designed by Dalzeil & Powell.*

good-quality mat should always be provided, especially from an external area. Grit and dirt can cause a great deal of damage to floors, so it is important to remove as much of this from shoppers' shoes as possible before they enter the mall or store. The mat used for this purpose could be coir (a natural material) or a combination rubber/fibre mix. This type of matting is available in many colours; it can also be made to measure and inset to any shape or form.

Carpet, or 'soft flooring', was a popular material with most retailers in the 1970s, and is still widely used today by department stores. The advantages of carpeting are its relatively low cost, low maintenance, durability and flexibility. There are many types of carpets on the market, from hand-made 100 per cent wool, to man-made 100 per cent nylon and every combination in between. Another advantage of 'soft flooring' is that shoppers like the feel of it underfoot. It is also more comfortable for sales staff, and in some situations can be perceived as luxurious. It reduces noise

and is essential for fitting rooms. A disadvantage, however, is that it may not be possible to alter the layout of furniture and fixtures without leaving obvious indents in the carpet pile, which can be difficult to remove.

When using carpets, designers and retailers must be aware of the type of underlay or fixing that is used on larger areas. Contemporary methods of fixing are to stick the material directly to a prepared screed: this will stop rucking and improve wear and tear. The disadvantage is that the carpet cannot then be replaced or patched in easily without looking obvious. Carpet tiles have the advantage that they can be replaced, but they will be difficult to match if the old ones have become faded or worn.

Advances in flooring-materials technology are enabling retail designers to order bespoke designs from companies such as the USA-based Milliken Carpet (which makes modular carpet) and the vinyl manufacturer Amtico. Examples include Milliken's recent creation of a carpet for

The Beatles memorabilia store in Liverpool, showing the faces of the four group members; and the flooring produced by Amtico for New York toy store, FAO Schwartz, in which shapes are cut into the floor from which sounds are emitted as customers step on them. Another material that is allowing designers to create stunning images underfoot is thin set Epoxy Terrazo, produced by the UK company Liquid Plastics, which has been used in the Los Angeles Convention Centre to create a map of the world and an interpretation of the Milky Way. Expona vinyl tiles, produced by Manchester company James Halstead, was used for the Meridian food court at Manchester Airport in the UK, in which the floor design was based on the different destinations which could be reached from the airport.

Hard flooring such as wood makes a natural, warm-looking and hard-wearing surface. Being a natural material, it also changes with wear and develops a character of its own. No two natural wooden floors are alike and they can be laid in a variety of decorative patterns which will add character to the retail environment. Many patterns can be achieved, but the designer should bear in mind, however, that the more complex the pattern, the more expensive it will be to lay. Single planks laid in the direction of circulation aid the flow and movement in a store, while planks laid across a store can help to create the illusion of width. Boards are available in a variety of sizes and types. Hardwood floors – generally made of maple, oak or beech – are favoured in retail environments for their ability to withstand harsh treatment. Each has its own colour and grain and can be stained to look darker. Fumed oak, left in a kiln-type oven and smoked, turns a deep brown colour which can look extremely effective. The more exclusive the timber, the more costly the product. A combination of carpet and wood is used in most shops and stores, and can create pleasing effects. Other types of materials to consider include stone, marble, granite and slate, all of which can

Below left **This Kenar store in New York designed by Warren Bohn has an intriguing mix of wood and glass materials. The suspended glass floor has an illuminated colour grid which adds a contemporary edge.**

Below right **Calvin Klein in Paris gives an impression of minimal chic. The limited palette of materials often uses little or no colour. A limestone floor with oversized slabs gives a strong angular grid to the space, and is perfectly complemented by the large carved stone bath. The floor-to-ceiling glass-etched room divider has no visible structural frame. Designed by London based architect Claudio Sylvestrin.**

Above **Paperchase, located in the Trafford Centre shopping mall in Manchester, makes dramatic use of this wall of paper, designed to give quick and easy access to the large flat sheets of specialist papers. The drawers are set deep into the wall for maximum effect. Designed by Wingate and Moon.**

create wonderful floors but are more costly to lay than conventional sheeted materials such as carpet, vinyl and ceramics. Other hard-wearing materials include ceramic, terracotta and mosaic tiles. While these are easy to lay, they can feel cold and be noisy to walk on. Natural carpets such as sisal and jute, although reasonably priced, were found to be unsuitable for commercial retail stores due to their loose construction, colour and lack of strength.

Contemporary and modern flooring such as poured liquid-concrete compounds have recently begun to be transferred from architectural use into the retail environment. Calvin Klein and Nicole Farhi have both used this system in the UK, Europe and the USA. Many manufacturers are also experimenting with methods of transforming natural materials and by-products into innovative new products, such as conglomerate marble, stone-ceramic tiles, flooring-grade laminates, and rubber and glass mosaics.

Walls

The options for wall finishes are many and varied. The majority of designers take the architecturally driven view that walls should look as though they are supportive and therefore structurally essential to the building. This design perspective has led to an increased use of the wall in order to establish a coherent design parameter. Walls are used to conceal, divide, support and as sculpture to provide interest and focus to the space. Finishes can be applied to the wall as decoration, or alternatively can be added to support the monolithic forms. Specialist plaster finishes are popular: for instance, the craft techniques of applying mixes of plaster and marble dust to create texture and finish are being widely used, and such techniques were employed to spectacular effect in the Donna Karan flagship stores worldwide. These are then protected with wax to give a matt or polished finish.

Paint is commonly used to create planes of colour for sculptural effect, for decorative finishes or to simulate stone, plaster and marble. Beyond the basic finishes, walls can be lined with boards, fixturing systems or in an endless variety of materials. The minimalist approach is to create a seamless flow of material from wall to floor, which creates a continuous environment in which structures take on a sculptural quality, and space and volume combine to create effects with light, shape and form.

Colour can add drama and excitement to a space, or be used to promote a specific association with a brand. For example, Prada has used a pistachio green shade in all its stores internationally, which has defined the colour as a brand identity. In its simplest form, colour can heighten space or conceal it. It can add warmth or be used to create the ultimate cool statement. Certain colours – such as red – are very popular with most people, and it is no coincidence that brands such as Coca-Cola, Virgin and Nike use red logos. Generally speaking, there are few colour rules that cannot be broken or tested by new concepts and strong wills. Essentially, if it works for the retailer, then it can be considered.

Ceilings

Ceilings are the most technically used plane, or surface, of the interior dimension. They are essential for concealing a large number of the technical applications and services which are essential in the running of any retail environment, such as lighting, electrical trunking, ducting, fixings, security, fire alarms, smoke detectors, sound systems, sprinklers and telecommunications. In addition, ceilings must appear attractive and their treatment should form a part of the overall design. A ceiling should not be a focal point, yet it remains an essential design consideration within any concept. Materially, ceilings can be monolithic, giving the image of solidity rather than hollowness. Such ceilings still need access panels, but the idea is to keep them clean and uncluttered, therefore drawing the eye down to floor level and therefore towards all the tempting products which are there to attract the consumer.

Ceilings can be decorated, whether using cornices and plaster mouldings – as at the Polo Ralph Lauren store in Madison Avenue, New York – or with inset light wells and contours, which provide relief in a large expanse of flatness. Quick and immediate access is essential for department stores and large retailers, which have a considerable amount of technical equipment concealed within the ceiling. In these situations, the suspended ceiling can be treated with a variety of finishes including mineral fibre, textured plaster or open-grid ceilings of louvred and metallic sections. Each has its own advantages, but all share the same function of allowing speedy access at low cost.

There are also many examples of open ceilings where all the services are left exposed. This cancels the cost of supplying a ceiling, but will incur costs of cleaning up the services left on show. The effect is a high-tech resolution which increases the sense of height.

Above **This unusual ceiling design is located in the Private I hair salon in Wan Chai, Hong Kong. The strips of rice paper hang from the ceiling like hair ringlets, providing an organic, shifting mass. Creating texture, the papers also act as room dividers. Designed by Mike Tonkin Architects, Hong Kong.**

Merchandising

Below and opposite **Brand messages and values can be extended across all manner of surfaces and objects. They are used to reinforce the identity of the brand which remains constant, while at the same time allowing the imagery to change and develop to create fresh ideas and to move in new directions.**

Camper, the Spanish footwear specialist, has developed a lively approach to their range of products. Humour plays a significant contribution to their brand, as well as heritage issues, family values and cultural idiosyncrasies. Their range of retail graphics includes signage, bags, boxes, posters, books and brochures – the design potential and the possible extensions of these ideas have almost limitless potential.

The product planning and merchandising of a store are crucial to the image and efficiency of the retailer. Most retailers employ experienced visual merchandisers who are responsible for the product and will influence the way in which it is presented. The visual merchandiser must consider each product individually and decide how best to present it. Products can be isolated for impact, but most are sold in groups for comparison or to achieve add-on sales. The visual merchandiser will decide on which products sit best together: this could be part of an overall theme for a store promotion, or be a smaller departmental theme such as a shirt and tie promotion. The story may be seasonal or based on colour, and the products may be linked through the display narrative or be part of a grouping of products which are lifestyle-linked.

Other considerations for the merchandiser/designer will be size, quantity, access, security and service, depending on product and price. Fixturing design and the merchandise philosophy must be sympathetic, and the product layout must represent the retailer's brand values.

Brand awareness

The merchandising of a product cannot be separated from the brand awareness developed by a retailer in conjunction with marketing directors and advertising agencies. In the case of a new product, a retailer may seek out a designer who can inject new ideas, or a new type of media with which to promote it. Some retailers may wish to launch a new product, or to kick-start an existing one from a different marketing viewpoint, and it is important to decide how best this might be done. Usually technology plays a part, or it could mean using a new photographer or type of model. It may incorporate employing new stylists or advertising agencies to give a different slant to a product or brand.

The term merchandising means creating a three-dimensional model, using the product and developing the tone of the brand using advertising and point-of-sale/purchase material. The product's image and the atmosphere within the store each evolve to support the brand awareness. Packaging design will also often be followed through for point-of-sale material.

Packaging can transform perceptions about the quality of a product, and increase sales as a consequence. Public acknowledgement of retailers as brands in their own right has also increased their confidence in creating packaging which asserts its own identity.

The speed with which consumers make decisions in supermarkets is another determining factor in assessing the importance of packaging design. The repackaging of Harvey's Bristol Cream sherry in a blue-glass bottle, for instance, recovered the product's status as a premium brand and ensured that it stood out from competitors in green or brown bottles; the new design also extended the sherry's appeal to younger drinkers. Packaging design will often be undertaken by specialist consultancies although, as the Biba case study illustrates (see pages 118–21), it can be central to the effective communication of a retailer's corporate identity and to a brand's ability to extend.

Exactly how consumers make up their minds may not be universally agreed, but there is no doubt that the influences at work are by no means strictly logical. The designer and/or merchandiser must, therefore, be aware of the intuitive and impulsive nature of buying and be prepared to create appropriate eye-catching and evocative store images to encourage interest. Technology now helps visual merchandisers to promote new products. It enables them to integrate audio, visual and interactive media within their environments, bringing to life vivid images of the product.

Fundamentally, however, in-store merchandising needs to be focused in order to keep a brand and its image alive. In this respect, retail designers have become brand protectors. Inevitably brands will evolve but, in the worst scenarios, their impact will become dissipated, with this weakening invariably being reflected in performance. A good example of this was Tommy Hilfiger in the 1980s, whose first entry into the UK market was confused and unsuccessful. There were many reasons for this initial failure, but a subsequent lack of management and financial control caused the ensuing problems. Today, however, Tommy Hilfiger is a huge, well-controlled conglomerate company of international repute, with a strong brand identity.

In his research about how brands have taken change on board, entitled 'Brand Strategies in the Information Age' (1997) and published by the *Financial Times* Retail and Consumer division, retail analyst Alan Mitchell looked at how one of the world's best-known brands, Coca-Cola, has reinvented its marketing, based on the phrase 'Always Connect'. Mitchell pointed out that the company's marketing strategy has been centred on this slogan since 1994, and explained how the phrase is used: '"Connect" means connecting at every possible level, from satisfying one of the most basic of human physiological needs – thirst – to connecting literally, by being within an arm's reach of desire, to connecting emotionally, so much so that the brand somehow becomes embedded in individuals' most heartfelt memories. "Always" means always appeal to every possible consumer, of every age and social grouping, at every time, at every place, in a way that is relevant to them.'

Fashion brands such as Gucci, Prada and Vuitton have retained their up-market image while managing to change sufficiently to attract younger consumers. Gucci, the Florence shoe and leather goods maker, was a byword for style in the 1970s but became blighted by internal problems during the 1980s and early 90s. However, it stormed back into fashion in the late 90s. In 1994 its fortunes turned with the employment of Tom Ford, the designer responsible for building on to and extending the business into a desirable brand with a youthful edge. Gucci's ensuing fashion collections caught the imagination of the existing clientele and, more importantly, of their children. It encapsulated the qualities of luxury, style, uniqueness and desirability, thus continuing the brand values yet presenting them in a revolutionary way. Gucci went on to become one of the most fashionable must-have brands in the world.

With the development of brand image, the natural progression is then to evolve the new directions into the store environments which sell the products. This has been achieved in many cases, creating a focus for particular brands and their products. Long-established fashion houses have also achieved this by importing new designers: among them John Galliano at Dior, Alexander McQueen at Givenchy and Alber Elbaz at Yves St Laurent.

Motivating customers to buy

If a designer is working on a new-concept store, it is often easier to bring in an external merchandising consultant, as an existing in-house team may be too locked in to old philosophies to be able to stand back and assess what needs to be done. The merchandiser can help to plan a store opening, develop a merchandising strategy and initiate campaigns; he or she will also take over the role of communicator, once the retail designer has finished the job.

Merchandising covers many aspects of how products are displayed and presented within a store. Skilful merchandising ensures the right products are in the right place at the right time. Visual merchandisers ensure that consumers are stimulated by constantly updated in-store imagery.

Below **This perfumery department in a Debenhams department store in Leeds shows an imaginative approach. The merchandise is duplicated for impact and the use of illuminated pigeon holes allows the perfume bottles to stand out against the background. Designed by Carte Blanche, London.**

Signage

Many retailers have realized the limitations of traditional signage, and the greater impact and communicative quality of visual merchandising and graphics. Research conducted in 1997 by Design Age – a specialist unit at London's Royal College of Art, examining the particular design-related issues of ageing – pointed to the need for signage in future to become subliminal and multi-sensory to meet the needs of an ageing population. The needs of older people will also require the revision of shelf-edge ticketing and use of colour, to take into account limitations in sight.

Grocery retailers are also beginning to understand that, in food megastores, the amount of time customers may take simply to locate the products required can ultimately cut down on the time they are willing to spend browsing. Some supermarkets are now using three-dimensional symbols to indicate where product areas are, making their location easier. A trial of this approach by Tesco in Sheffield resulted in innovative use of non-verbal imagery to indicate the location of particular parts of the store: there were penguins above frozen food, Friesan cows above dairy produce, and a fish head and tail poking out of the wall indicated the location of the fresh-fish counter.

Achieving retail success

The contemporary retail designer's skill is truly evident when it comes to the marriage of a design blueprint and the practical considerations of that blueprint. Design is, after all, functional – whether its aim is to create an environment which is theatrical, fun and feeds the senses, or one which is classically minimalist. Each polarity will generate its own practical implications, and the designer needs to be aware of a wide range of legal obligations, as well as of the importance of the functional items in the store such as doors, flooring and awnings.

Materials, and combinations of them, will contain messages for consumers about the status of a retailer, as will the arrangement of space and the quality of the fittings. Whether a retailer wishes to be clearly identifiable as part of a specific community – such as high fashion – or to set himself apart, the designer will follow the same process of interpreting the retailer's vision and making it a reality through a unique combination of practical decisions. All designers have to be aware of new opportunities offered by technological advances but, above all, must adhere to the retailers' basic principle: to make the best use of whatever space is available, and to make it pay.

Above **This highly intriguing façade denotes an out-of-town shed site for home furnishing lifestyle store MIKASA in New Jersey USA. The building is designed by Haigh Architects.**

new models

The following case studies cover a wide range of retail spaces which together represent a spectrum of activity worldwide. They range from an historic brand which launched lifestyle retailing, to exclusive high fashion, a mall with regeneration and public art, an accessible homeware store and new generation of food outlet.

A common factor of the case studies is the strength of vision they represent – Rei Kawakubo of Comme des Garçons, for example, is unrelenting in her approach and her style verges on the anti-commercial. Corso Como in Milan is the retailers' retailer and this store illustrates the seductiveness of space transformed into a series of galleries, while Selfridges department store in London is an impressive exercise in the management of brands while promoting the store's own unique style. Fashion retailer, Jigsaw, uses design to make architectural and artistic statements as well as to ensure its stores remain true to their locations by reflecting local character.

Biba was probably the first commercial synthesis of artistic sensibility and style, creating the first successful retail brands. Other case studies show how social change has influenced and structured the development of retail for specific markets and how design has become an egalitarian requirement in retail at all levels. Many of the studies considered illustrate that the public is more design aware than ever and that good design is a necessity. The final case study, Bluewater Park, shows how remaining true to a vision can lead to high quality public architecture and attract new groups of consumers to mall shopping.

Biba

London, England

Biba revolutionized retailing by introducing the concept of style into every aspect of consumer goods, from clothes to baked beans. It became the polar opposite of the trendy Quant and Conran look; a place where girls could attain a dramatically glamorous image. Its camp, 'glam' style aligned with contemporary rock stars and had the decadent roots of the 1920s, with the additional influences of Garbo, Dietrich and other Hollywood stars.

The first store opened in 1964 and Biba creator Barbara Hulanicki relocated to Kensington Church Street in 1966. Designers Steve Thomas and Tim Whitmore started working with Hulanicki in 1968. They worked on the children's department and subsequently on Biba stores at Au Printemps in Paris, Fiorucci in Milan, and Bloomingdales and Bergdorf Goodman in New York.

Previous page **Opaque, Tokyo, Japan.**

Right **This Biba cosmetics poster from 1974 won the British Council of Design Award in 1968, but was criticised by one of the judges as being "far too visual". The typically soft-focus, doll-like face was synonymous with Biba's glamorous image.**

Opposite **The Rainbow Room restaurant was located on the top floor of the Derry and Toms building. This room was completely remoulded and redesigned and was noted for its highly original ceiling details. The recessed lighting inset into the cornices varied in colour giving the rainbow effect. The Rainbow Room was unique for providing live music and in-store entertainment.**

BIBA COSMETICS

PROFILE

CLIENT: Barbara Hulanicki

FUNCTION: Lifestyle

CONSULTANTS: Whitmore Thomas

When Biba opened its doors at the London department store Derry and Toms in 1973, it was guaranteed a place in design history. The original Derry and Toms building in Kensington High Street was designed by French architect Marcel Hennequet under Bernard George and was received ecstatically when it opened in 1933. A striking art deco building, its stunning Rainbow Room fitted perfectly with the Biba look. In 1971, Whitmore Thomas were invited to design two floors of the Derry and Toms building. Thomas pitched for the whole building, graphics and advertising as a package and won it. At just 27 years old and a painter by training, Thomas admits he learned the practicalities of interior design as he went along.

With few retail designers to emulate, Whitmore Thomas had complete freedom. Ideas and inspiration for colour came from Hulanicki, 'Our task in life was to reflect her', and the two designers employed around 30 draughtsmen to make detail drawings from their sketches. Square footage was determined by Stephen Fitz-Simon, Biba's managing director and Hulanicki's husband, who also installed the first computerized till system in the building.

Some concessions were made to commercialism. Once cosmetics emerged as the store's bestseller, doubling expected sales, the cosmetics section was doubled in size and moved to a larger space. Cosmetics and women's clothes were the most successful parts of the store with one lipstick sold every 30 seconds. The food hall, initially, was also highly successful because customers bought goods for their stylish packaging. Thomas recalls: 'The sales figures for the first six months were extraordinary. Then the three-day week came along with the miners' strike and the store was lit by candles. People were walking out with armfuls of clothes because security controls were non-existent.'

All the areas in the store were originated from a variety of different influences. The accessories floor, featuring dark brown and cream marble, had a carpet based on a piece of moquette found by Thomas. The jewellery display unit was made of 900 pieces of pink and silver mirror. Records and magazines were also sold on this floor, using a replica

record turntable for vinyl records. Comfortable armchairs and listening booths were provided for customers as well as a library and reading area.

The first floor was a stylistic mixture of Hollywood and Egyptiana. The food hall had a Rennie Mackintosh-inspired skyscraper for displaying slimming foods, with a giant Warhol-inspired Campbells food can for soup, a churn and dovecotes for dairy food, a barge for fish and barrows for fruit. The children's floor contained a play area themed around West Side Story, a children's restaurant featuring oversized toadstools and a fairy-tale castle for books. The men's section even had a 'mistress room' where customers could buy underwear for their lovers.

Each floor of the shop had its own logo, notepaper and gift vouchers. The control which Whitmore Thomas exercised over the whole design package extended from shopfitting to graphics, including swing tickets, food

Above **Part of the accessories floor, this giant record deck with a roundabout turntable was styled on an original manual Dansette portable record player. The principle instrument of audio entertainment for teenagers in the 1960s, the steps are made to look like stacks of old vinyl records.**

Right **Located on the first floor, the mistress room sold a variety of lingerie, fluffy toys, soft play things and art nouveau exotica with beaded curtains, tassels and leopard skin. Its style is a fascinating reflection of the times.**

packaging and perfume bottles. Thomas acknowledges that Biba was his introduction to the overwhelming power of branding and the impressive range of its potential. Thomas says that 'Barbara found that people were buying into a lifestyle with an item for £1.'

Hulanicki is remembered as an instinctive retailer and designer. She organized in-store displays intuitively and designed clothes herself with a team of assistants and pattern cutters. Circulation in the store was a problem because there was only one lift but upbeat music in the stairwells was used to encourage people to circulate. At the store launch the floor plan was printed in a special newspaper which showed that customers went up by the stairs and down in the lift! The Rainbow Room, open until 1 a.m., was also radically new as it featured live music, after the store was closed.

Given the sheer size of the building, it is no surprise that at the time it was converted, the store was the most expensive shop-fit ever. The budget for the fit-out, which covered eight floors, was £1.8 million.

Further indications of how visionary the project was are evident from the list of what was originally conceived for the building, but left out, including: a 70-seater cinema and an ice rink and tennis court on the Roof Garden.

Biba was a landmark in retail design. *The Sunday Times*, featuring the opening of Biba in September 1973, said it 'merits comparison only with Harrods in this country or Macy's in New York'. It added...'the new Biba will remain a classic monument to 1973'.

Above right **Some of the 300 items of own brand Biba food packaging. Everything from baked beans to mascara was presented within the Biba house style. Whitmore Thomas designed the logos and packaging for every item in the store.**

Right **Cruciform cosmetics unit in black vitrolite with pink mirror. Biba made cosmetics fun and fashionable and their cosmetics counters were phenomenally successful. It is estimated that a single lipstick was sold every 30 seconds.**

World of Joyce
Nathan Road, Hong Kong and Bangkok, Thailand

Opposite **The women's shoe department features these Chinese lanterns, a nineteenth-century French Chauffeuse, a custom-covered velvet pouffe and a 1940s' bronze table.**

Below **The jewellery section in Thailand is very important. The display fits within the overall concept in terms of colours and yet is accessible with the minimum amount of obstruction. The custom-made utilities are in teak.**

Joyce Ma heads the World of Joyce empire and is a formidable talent. Interviewing her was quite an education and it was refreshing to speak with someone who has such clarity and vision in the complex world of retail. Through her ability to spot trends and develop talent, and her unswerving dedication to perfection, Joyce Ma has built an empire of global designer stores that have become household names on most continents.

The World of Joyce has been operating since 1972 and has imported almost every well-known European fashion brand into Asia: Giorgio Armani, Jil Sander, Dolce & Gabanna, Yves St Laurent, Costume National, Comme des Garcons and Issey Miyake, to name but a few. Many designers have trusted their brand to this Chinese-born businesswoman and worked closely with her to develop their presence and profile within the pan-Pacific regions. For many the relationship has been successful and, once established, designers have gone on to become a formidable force in their own right. Similarly, for many local consumers Joyce stands for quality and luxury, and reinforces new brands by her association. The World of Joyce today has many different facets; the original stores are individual shops offering luxury branded products, while other developments have included emporiums, and speciality stores offering a wider range of products including beauty and home goods and even a gallery showing objets d'art in Paris.

During the 80s' and 90s' the World of Joyce grew in terms of product and popularity, and the need to consolidate some of the lines into one environment became a necessity. An increasing number of product lines also meant it was essential to have larger spaces in which to show them. Over this period many retailers were beginning to create more spacious environments. The purpose of this trend was not only to show their products, but also to heighten the impact of the retailers' style ethos by immersing their customers in a total lifestyle environment, which communicated their philosophy in both a direct and subliminal way.

The World of Joyce reflects the individual style, taste and interests of Joyce Ma who is involved in every aspect of her business. She employed an American architectural practice, Tsao & McKown, to help devise and implement her strategy. According to a spokesperson for Calvin Tsao, who is himself of Chinese origin, "This was an instant meeting of minds. He and Joyce share a quest to discover a new Chinese aesthetic which is an amalgamation of East and West." A collaborative relationship was formed between them and their respective companies which went beyond a working relationship and became a creative amalgam, where style and development successfully meshed to create a new design aesthetic.

PROFILE

CLIENT: Joyce Ma

FUNCTION: Lifestyle stores

CONSULTANTS: Tsao & McKown

spacial forms by the inventive use of space, light and circulation patterns.

Joyce Bangkok and Nathan Road are concept stores where many of the elements of Joyce boutiques come together. Joyce discovered the Bangkok building and fell in love with the space. She had planned to rent part of the space but she knew immediately that she wanted to rent the whole building. It was planned and built as an exclusive shopping mall, with individual branded boutiques facing onto the street with names such as Armani, Hermes, Dolce & Gabanna and Issey Miyake. These brands act as the drawing influence and utilize the major part of the ground floor. It is a two-storey building and, as with all the Joyce stores, light and space are essential elements, adding clarity and definition to all the departments. Views are open across the floors and up through the atrium, with transparent boundaries created with the extensive use of glass-etched panels, and linen-draped fabric walls. Transparent images seen through the screens create a sense of movement as people are glimpsed through gently swaying gauze, giving a sense of luxury without grandeur.

Circulation routes in the Joyce stores tend to be undefined, allowing individuals to follow their own path of interest, but objects are placed in locations to entice and encourage exploration. In the Bangkok store, the clever use of floor markings loosely indicates zones, which is a refreshing departure from the rigidity found in many large stores. Discreet departments are located away from the main space where furniture and product placement define the different areas. The space divides into comfortable dimensions which allow the consumer to take in simple snapshots of beautiful merchandise.

The retail competency exists for the professionals to see, but by embedding this specialist formula within sensual images the whole store becomes a seductive and calculated strategy. The design of the store has made the physical fact of being there its own reward and it is a pleasurable experience just to walk around. To achieve this is not easy; at first glance the stores seem to have a variety of

Above **The restaurant is a service that contributes to the overall experience of the store. The chairs are custom made and the woodwork is stained mahogany. The wall sconces and lanterns create a powerful light effect.**

The underlying concept behind all of the Joyce stores is pure seduction. The items for sale represent the worlds of fashion and design, with products selected and redefined to create a seamless transition for the consumer from visual temptation to delivery of product. The architects and designers have created an environment that makes shopping a highly intimate experience where the styles within the store are aspirational and life-affirming. The stores themselves are a fusion of architecture, design and theatre. Sensuality is an integral part of the interior retail strategy and the customer is encouraged to discover new experiences and products that promise new horizons. The

Left *This area for shoes is reminiscent of a gentlemen's club in a 1940s colonial style. The leather-buttoned furniture and dark stained teak create the mood of this masculine boutique.*

Below *The men's furnishings area is made of antique library fixtures and fittings, which were re-worked and replicated to form this department. The look is eclectic, with Thai art deco chairs in the foreground.*

different decorative styles but the overall guiding factor is the highly skilled manipulation of space, light, procession and atmosphere.

The displays of the clothes are grouped in terms of intellectual or sensual expression; shoes are displayed as art. Fashion and imagination converge beneath a collection of silk lanterns surrounded by antiques. The flow of room spaces suggests individual boutiques which present differing snapshots of individuality, style and attitude.

The merchandisers and designers work closely together so that the detail creates a cohesive whole. Display sets and groupings of furniture or fixtures act as focal points within the departments. The menswear areas have a club-like atmosphere, with old leather furniture and accessories and filtered light through louvered wooden screens, reminiscent of the colonial style of South-east Asia. There are also interesting mixes of old and new which, when combined, create a delicate balance between comfortable and accessible but

have a contemporary edge. Much of the furniture and many of the old fixtures are bought during the early design stages and planned as the building process takes shape. Spaces are sometimes left for particular items still to be sourced, or if an important feature is located then departments are reworked around it. This process establishes a look which is eclectic and unforced. The selection of individual items is subjective, but when chosen to a specific criteria they have a cohesive look without predictability or repetition.

The furniture is often found in flea markets and antiques stores around the world, from New York to Paris. The pieces can be in a terrible state of repair, needing complete rebuilding, and sometimes are copied to create several identical units. These pieces are carefully selected for their design style and function, and are unsigned so there is no copyright infringement. Pieces are also commissioned from contemporary designers to sit beside old items, therefore injecting a highly distinctive individual

Above **The shoe and accessory departments in Nathan Road have an European influence. Signature furniture pieces are used to create a timeless quality, with strong colour punctuation.**

Right **In the women's contemporary department of Nathan Road the displays are almost incidental to the product. Teak flooring is used with multi-layer laser-cut acrylic screens by Proctor-Rihl studios, London.**

atmosphere. The silk lanterns in the Bangkok store were commissioned from the designer Thomas Boog. These have the effect of softening and controlling light, but add important form and colour statements throughout the store.

The range of materials used is simple, yet effective, with travertine marble flooring combined with ebonized teak, glass and bronze detailing on the furnishings. Often the same materials are used in different areas creating an important unified approach to the whole concept.

Colour is a powerful element in these large stores and is used to create either a bold or subtle statement. Particular colour combinations are used to evoke moods or reinforce references, whether it be through furnishings or fashion products or a combination of both. Lighting is carefully integrated, enhancing the products without distracting attention from them. It is used as a focal point only through the special lantern fittings, other lighting is concealed wherever possible. The combination of colour and highlights works well together to create an exciting focus with backlit and spotlit surfaces.

The main differences between the stores is cultural, says architect Calvin Tsao. Retailers are bullish about inter-nationalism but we are all aware that something is lost in the application of globalism. Hong Kong is a city where money and achievement equal power. This is a city where people are not ashamed to show what they have, therefore the store reflects this confidence by being a promenade or catwalk for people to show off.

Bangkok is very different. Thais are more discreet, says Tsao, so a soft palette of colours and materials was used to create a much more classical interior. Thais love jewellery so there are small boutiques scattered around the store as well as in displays. The store is large, cool and tranquil, and spaces flow from private to discreet.

The simple, easy layouts are delightful to experience and the East-meets-West motif is cleverly created in a chic urban environment. Style is not an easy concept to sell to a retail consumer, and yet the clearly defined sense of style within the Joyce stores bewitches the customer and evokes a sense of real pleasure.

Above **Colour plays a significant role in the presentation of the Joyce stores. As well as providing a fashionable counterpoint, it helps to set the scene and can also contribute to the evocation of a particular period. The choice of furniture and finish will play similar roles; this area features silver-leaf woodwork and custom-made tables.**

Io Corso Como

Milan, Italy

Opposite **A large skylight over the home furnishing gallery ensures that it is beautifully lit with natural daylight. The triangulated chandelier is a central feature and the interior also has a number of exotic light fittings made from moulded polycarbonate forms.**

Below **The concealed courtyard entrance is a cool oasis from the busy streets of Milan. The store surrounds the courtyard on three sides.**

Shopping nowadays can become monotonous for the international shopper; New York, London, Paris and Tokyo sell the same brands from the same store image. Much of this global branding is influenced by huge marketing budgets that eliminate originality and allow the same products to be bought through airports, mail order, department stores, and now on line. Variety is no longer available, leaving the consumer with fewer choices. Due to the ease and speed of reproduction, many products are so similar that some retailers have reacted against this formulaic style and are instead developing a personalized approach based on a highly individual vision.

Carla Sozzani is a former journalist for Italian *Vogue* who opened Io Corso Como in 1991: 'I wanted a shop I could treat like a magazine – instead of pages I would have shelves and rails, and instead of readers I would have customers.' Its off-pitch location in Milan is far removed from the typical Eastern bazaars from which it draws inspiration, and yet this venue has all the vibrancy, colour and excitement of a Moroccan souk.

Although difficult to find, the location will not disappoint. Set within a courtyard, it has no conventional shopfront and, set back from the main thoroughfare, tends to attract only the most informed and seasoned shoppers. Housed in an old building that was once a mechanic's garage, the rather dull exterior gives no clue to the store's inner treasures. The courtyard garden is an ideal transition point between the street and the private interior; café bars surround it and each gallery has its own entrance overlooking the courtyard. This area acts as a central point of reference for all the various activities that take place within the building and it has a life of its own, offering a quiet respite for weary shoppers, or creating a 'buzz' for an opening night reception.

Sozzani has assembled a personal range of her own favourite products in fashion, accessories and furniture. Over the years the store has grown into a series of gallery spaces which link from one to the next. She sees her role not as shop manager but instead as art director; the space is treated like a musical score, with Carla as conductor, weaving in and out of a central theme with little detours and discoveries along the way.

As you enter the ladies' fashion store through the large wrought-iron gates, prepare to be overwhelmed by the imagery and the range of products. There are beautiful fabrics and racks of clothes, interspersed with scented candles and accessories, and yet everything is beautifully balanced within the overall framework. The walls, floors and ceilings are treated as a canvas for artworks, screens, wallhangings and sculptural light fittings, adding colour and movement within the vast open spaces.

PROFILE

CLIENT: Carla Sozzani

FUNCTION: Lifestyle

CONSULTANTS: Kris Ruhs

Circulation routes throughout the store are suggested, although not compulsory. There are no demarcation lines for products or merchandise, and yet there are defined areas which feel comfortable in scale. There is no single point of view; the story here revolves around personal expression with brands juxtaposed to create unexpected individual statements. There are many focal points and junctions as the customers make their way around the store discovering new items in every corner.

Ladies' fashion leads through to home products and in this area there is a huge skylight over the central space. The surfaces on the wall and ceiling are decorated with primitive illustrations. The centrepiece here is a large 1970s' style pyramid-shaped light fitting and the geometry of this fitting has an unusual effect within this simple interior. The floor has the sort of highly polished concrete surface which feels industrial and yet also reflects the variety of light patterns and the many forms that are hanging above it.

Above **A spectacular circular stainless-steel bar sits in the centre of one of the ground-floor galleries. The illuminated windows have interwoven mesh screens which filter out unwanted daylight and offer privacy within.**

Right **The first floor gallery space displays an exhibition of Couregges, a fashion designer's work from the 1960s. The galleries at Io Corso Como produce several exhibitions each year.**

The menswear fashion area is more austere in terms of colour, yet with an unusual mix of prints and photographs of icons from the 1960s and 1970s. A huge table with a large glass top acts as the cash desk. Racks are suspended from the ceiling, creating small clothing bays with wrought-iron floor-standing rails in between. Much of the geometry and traditional symbolism in this section originates from an American artist, Kris Ruhs, with whom Sozzani has lived and worked for many years.

On the upper floors overlooking the courtyard the bookshop sells a select range of highly illustrated and sophisticated books, often displayed flat for easy browsing, covering art, design, fashion and architecture. Adjoining the bookshop, the music and design rooms show an eclectic range of furniture from different decades and continents. These rooms blend together harmoniously and are comfortable and welcoming. Shop assistants do not impose and this unthreatening atmosphere is described by Sozzani as 'taking the idea of a bazaar and adding to it the warm feeling of a home'. The final space on this upper floor is a gallery which is transformed for each new show. This also reflects Sozzani's perspective, allowing her to promote ideas, designers, and artists from the past and future.

In the simplest language Io Corso Como is a large, flexible white box. Sozzani focuses on a concept and then redefines it in a way that to her customers feels integral to their own lifestyle and aspirations. Preferring to work intuitively, she decides what products to buy, and by doing so creates an individual look from a personal standpoint – the selection of products in the store is so intimate that it almost feels as if we are trespassing. This approach redefines the 'superbrand', global image into a local brand with a recognizable handwriting.

Right **This view of one of the upper galleries shows the eclectic range of furniture originating from different continents and decades, resulting in an interesting mix of contemporary pieces with older objects. All the pieces are specifically chosen and coordinated into a domestic setting.**

Nike Town
London, England

Opposite A central gauze cylinder is suspended over the town square, acting as a 360-degree projection screen where promotional videos are shown. Automated daylight blinds improve the ambient light levels before each show.

Below A view towards the front of the building showing the more contemporary architectural enclosure of the escalators. Bridges join the retail areas to the central information core.

Nike is one of the most influential global brands of the late twentieth century, spreading the aspirational slogan 'Just do it' to world-class sports stars and ghetto teenagers alike. The brand led the booming trend in active sportswear as informal and comfortable everyday clothing, transforming both lifestyle clothing and sports retail. The 'must-have' Nike logo became a powerful symbol of the crossover between the worlds of sport, entertainment and business.

The first Nike Town opened in 1990 in Portland, Oregon. Eleven others followed, but it was not until the summer of 1999 that the brand opened flagship stores outside the USA, in Berlin and London. Between the

opening of the first Nike Town and those in Europe, the brand suffered as a result of a shift in public attitudes. Towards the end of the nineties, athletes' reputations were tarnished by accusations of drug-enhanced performances, and repetitive-strain injuries caused by over-training became common. The emphasis shifted from obsessive, sweat-inducing work-outs to gentler, more controlled exercise. Instead of jogging and working out, media icons such as Madonna switched to yoga or Tai Chi. In tune with this Nike repositioned its image away from athletic power performance imagery and towards a softer, more accessible product that promoted health through fitness and exercise.

According to Nike, the London store, designed and built in collaboration with Building Design Partnership, is the largest in Europe at 6,500 square metres (70,000 square feet) and aims to rival the store in New York. The space in the London store was carved out of an existing structure, previously the flagship of London retail group Arcadia. The space was completely remodelled, creating a circular axis surrounded by retail and circulation areas.

Nike Town has a prime location at Oxford Circus, and incorporates a range of different design styles that reflect the city's architecture. It includes design references to the eighteenth-century window tax and custom-made man-hole covers, and these are integrated with more modern constructions, with a glass façade enclosing a bank of escalators that are illuminated by natural light.

The layout of the store covers three floors. It has a circular, central 'town square' just inside the entrance lobby and this acts as a meeting point or as a stage for events such as sports clinics. From the square upwards is the central focus of the store. There are circular display areas on the first and second floors around a centrepiece called the 'chandelier', composed of 750 sporting photographs from around the world. Surrounding this display area is a 360-degree projection screen where promotional films are shown every 20 minutes. In the same way as the Nike flagship store in New York, expectation is dramatically raised before each screening by lowering the light levels.

PROFILE

CLIENT: Nike

FUNCTION: Speciality

CONSULTANTS: Building Design Partnership

The store could be described as a town within a town with the first and second floors comprising of 10 different sports pavilions, each dedicated to a different consumer interest: football, rugby, tennis, training, running, basketball, golf, all conditions gear, women and children. Each pavilion is characterized by different designs, displays and products – from the football pavilion which has an exposed stadium-style roof and Astroturf floor plus a turnstile hatch, to the training pavilion designed to look and sound like a gym with pulleys and dumbbells built into the fixtures.

Circulation space is substantial. At the entrance to the store, a large semi-circular lobby directs customers towards a customer service desk, the meeting point and the first retail space. Up and down escalators are placed on the Great Portland Street side of the store, with a lift operating from the ground to the third floor. Viewing balconies are placed around the central area for watching the film shows. The third floor houses the stockroom, customer services, lavatories and the product transport system which delivers shoes to the different pavilions in just 90 seconds through four tubular automated carriers.

Above *The running pavilion highlights the familiar Nike themes of innovation and passion with two pillars; one is devoted to the story of waffle-soled running shoes, and the other zooms in on the London runner Ray Mouncey.*

Right *A view of the automated shoe rotational units. The acrylic tube encloses the shoe container, which travels between stock room and sales floor at a speed of 3mph. This method means that selected stock is delivered to the customer in just 90 seconds.*

Daylight is controlled by a computerized system that automates blinds to cut out natural light during projection times. Theatre spotlights and projectors are used to great effect in the central area, while most of the specialist areas have individual lighting schemes. Nike Town London is a high-volume experience; music fills every inch of the retail space. Within each pavilion there are also atmospheric sound effects ranging from the roar of crowds to the thud of tennis balls on racquets.

The history of sport, athletic performance and technical innovation dominate the graphics and displays. Nike graphics have always emphasized the emotional connection between performance and winning. However, in this store there is more focus on customers and activities, with images of children participating in sport, and 'street' sports such as rollerblading and boarding. The emphasis is heavily multi-cultural and urban, reflecting the youthful nature of sport in this country.

There are drawbacks, including a lack of customer facilities such as a café, and places to sit and take in all the visual stimuli. The store's momentum is based on movement, and there is a pressure to move on swiftly which feels unengaging. The retail spaces tend to be cramped, and while there is a huge number of graphic logos and messages there are few products to touch and feel.

The London store promotes itself as a centre of excellence within sports retail and yet it is more orientated towards circulation, information and tourist interest than towards products, retail activity or commercial awareness. It is undoubtedly a strong marketing tool, carrying the added bonus of product sales, and an excellent example of excess – a venue that is over-designed and over-engineered at every conceivable level. It boasts 'more' of everything than any other store and yet it falls back on established structures and imagery rather than developing apace with patterns worldwide.

Above **This view shows the brick façades of a mock eighteenth-century terrace. The architects intended this to reflect the different architectural styles to be seen within the city. London street signage and manhole covers are also used to promote Nike's position as an authority in sports retailing.**

Shanghai Tang
Hong Kong

Opposite A customer seating area where tea is served while fabrics are selected for the bespoke items within the store. The floor is of dark rich mahogany to contrast with the vibrant coloured banquette seating.

Below The exterior of the Shanghai Tang store in the Peddar building in the central district of Hong Kong has tall elegant archways which are hung with sepia prints of beautiful oriental girls.

The concept of Shanghai Tang sets out to revitalize Chinese design by interweaving traditional Chinese culture with the dynamism of the twentieth century.

Shanghai Tang was founded in 1994 by Hong Kong businessman David Wing-Cheung Tang. This is a Hong Kong-based speciality store that sells everything from fine Chinese porcelain and silk clothes to kitsch wrist watches that sport images of Mao looking out from pop-art backgrounds. Despite its eclecticism, Shanghai Tang has been a great success. In its first year alone the Tang store attracted over a million visitors...by the end of 1997 this had risen to over two million.

Shanghai Tang offers an expanding range of products from fashion to home furnishing, leather goods, silverware, porcelain and novelty gifts, all of which extend the concept of revitalizing Chinese arts and crafts.

Shangai Tang clothes are based on traditional Chinese styles which continue to evolve but are given a modern twist by producing them in vibrant – some would say garish – colours and using beautifully made and woven silks and cashmeres from China. The colour selection and juxtaposition of fabrics is inventive and the use of Chinese motifs is distinctive. The aim of this brand is to produce the first global Chinese lifestyle brand.

Unique to Shanghai Tang is Imperial Tailors, an exclusive made-to-measure service which revives the diminishing art of Chinese *haute couture*. Tailors are housed in-store to craft from a selection of fabrics such as silk Jacquards, velvets and delicate linens.

Clients are invited to make appointments with the store and a car is provided to pick them up if required. The clients are measured by the tailor and then, whilst seated comfortably on a large overstuffed banquette, tea is served while the possibilities for fabrics and linings are discussed. Several fittings are made so that the clothes fit each client individually to their satisfaction.

The flagship store is housed in 1,400 square metres (15,000 sqare feet) of the historic Pedder Building in the central district of Hong Kong. The exterior of the store is beautifully lit with tall elegant archways hung with sepia printed images of beautiful oriental girls wearing traditional clothes. The central piece graphics logo is a framed picture of a building incorporating five stars, the symbol taken from the Chinese flag, and motifs of Chairman Mao.

The two floors are laid out in a comfortable low ceiling environment. There are many divisions within the space, that help create the warm sense of intimacy one feels immediately on entering. The overall impression is of a riot of vibrant colour, textures and materials not only from the products themselves but from the treatments of the floors, walls and ceilings.

PROFILE

CLIENT: David Tang

FUNCTION: Speciality

CONSULTANTS: David Tang

Above **This shows an elaborate cash desk in curved mahogany with a highly decorative metal caville detailing. Products for the home are set out on the table in the foreground and a selection of clothes is displayed on the plinths in the background with mirrors staggered behind.**

The flooring uses mahogany floor boards or is made up of thousands of tiny mosaics, laid out in detailed patterns that help to define walkways. All are articulated in Deco styles and patterns. A spiral staircase with a flowing butterfly-wing balustrade sweeps the customer downstairs. The walls are a riot of mirror glass panels with inlaid, illuminated, stained-glass details. Many are clad with wooden panelling and dado rails from which hang pictures and images of the Orient. Art deco lanterns and light fittings are suspended or wall mounted around the perimeter creating a domestic feel.

Ceilings and columns are vividly picked out with huge replica art deco-inspired stained-glass ceiling details, highlighting the raised cash desks. Small intimate gallery areas are sited to the sides of the main space. These give both privacy, and a sense of exclusivity to each product range. The store exudes the old world charm and ambience synonymous with the design style and art deco architecture that flourished in Shanghai pre-World War II. A mixture of European and Eastern hardwoods are lacquered and polished into a deep, rich, black-brown sheen. The fixturing and panelling is deeply carved with Chinese motifs.

There is a richness and theatricality rarely seen in Western stores in the twentieth century. The mix is heavily inspired by art deco 1920s' to 1930s' colonial style. Traditional Chinese forms are juxtaposed with contemporary Chinese art. It is this credible fusion that personifies Shanghai Tang's unique style: the old and the new – East meets West, the functional and the kitsch; contradictory themes creating an overpowering but exciting picture.

The furnishings are generally a mixture of antique and reproduction pieces which are used throughout the space for display and merchandising. Seating areas are provided for guests in velvet-covered armchairs with antimacassars.

Women's wear and the bespoke Imperial Tailors are located on the raised ground floor with home style, men's and children's wear situated on the lower ground floor.

This exciting interior is both individualistic and nostalgic. It charms and amuses with a good eye for detail and an enthusiasm that is infectious.

Visual merchandising is a mixture of still-life settings, with the occasional table set for tea showing homeware gift items, or a dressing table set with boudoir beauty accessories. Chinese lanterns are used as focal points throughout the store, which give a domestic scale to the environment

This interior charms and amuses and yet has discriminating detail and a rigorous enthusiasm. The enigmatic figure of David Tang is one of a diverse range of influences evident within this store. The total scene is individualistic, nostalgic, sumptuous and rich in colour and vibrancy.

Above **The imperial tailor works at his bench making bespoke tailored clothes for individual clients. A large selection of fabrics is available with a number of exclusive ones that are only available at this store.**

Right **This shows a view of the staircase in New York. This store is much larger than the Hong Kong venue but it does use many of the same features and materials – such as stained glass and mosaic flooring.**

Boots

Bluewater Park, Kent and Manchester, England

Opposite **The lipstick tower incorporates 800 different types to choose from. Such an enormous choice caters for most tastes and pockets. The big circular drum is internally illuminated for maximum impact.**

Below **The child and babycare centre advises parents on the best products and procedures. Soft curves and etched glass screens with attached hand prints are typical features within this area.**

Since Boots was established in the UK more than 125 years ago it has become recognized as the nation's chemist and has developed beyond this. Home products, clothing, snack foods, photography, children's wear and toys as well as a growing list of health-related services such as dentistry and chiropody have all been added to the Boots brand.

With the store offers changing so dramatically, it is necessary for the retailer to reassess its store image constantly. Boots' target customers are women aged 25 to 45, often with children, interested in health and beauty. The company is keen to maintain its strong reputation for trust and reliability, although at the same time its ambition

is to create a more up-front, dynamic and fun concept: 'Look Good, Feel Good' was a mission statement that set out a vision for the future.

The company has around 1,400 stores within the UK, as well as about 50 stores in Holland, Thailand and Japan. Its strategy is to continue with an internationalization programme and this is another reason for developing a new design in-store.

Four stores were chosen to test a new concept in 1999; two of them pop-in stores in Keynsham and New Malden, and two destination stores on major sites in Bluewater Park shopping mall and Manchester city centre.

The Boots' destination store concept is proving both popular and profitable. With such a departure from its origin as a purely health-care motivated retailer, it now competes on the high street with more aspirational competitors. The concept works by bringing together the primary healthcare image of clean environments with sophisticated materials and the use of concealed lighting and glamourous pictures. The overall image is that of a series of high-class continental boutiques. The use of space and the juxtaposition of circulation routes is suggestive, rather than dogmatic, so that consumers are encouraged to meander.

The open layout allows customers to discover products in an unregimentated format. The spaces are friendly and welcoming, and branded cosmetic counters are cleverly handled to project their own identity while maintaining the Boots' concept. This is one of the most difficult retail challenges and this store concept has managed to balance the diverse interests within it.

The design brief for the new concept was, 'to deliver a holistic design for the envelope that creates a flexible, internal backdrop for the specialisms'. The aim was to create a living magazine within the stores, with graphics showcasing particular themes, from health and wellbeing to seasonal beauty and fashion issues.

Boots The Chemists wanted a design which ensured that core specialisms were delivered without compromise and that also communicated experience and expertise. It

Baby & Childcare Advisor

PROFILE

CLIENT: Boots

FUNCTION: Speciality

CONSULTANTS: Pentagram; Marsh and Grochowski

Above *The beauty and cosmetic areas have been furnished with soft curved forms. Long lengths of straight gondolas have been superceded for smaller self-service areas, with adjacent products for follow-on sales. Systems are still modular and some incorporate interactive screens for news and information about new products.*

aimed to encourage customers to visit the store to seek products for health and beauty, cure and prevention but, in addition, to discover those that would enable spiritual and physical enhancement. The company wanted to switch a customer from 'needs' mode, meaning shopping quickly for known products with little thought, into 'indulgence' mode, meaning having an engaged perspective, seeking ideas and being open to the leisure aspects of shopping.

The first floor of the store at Bluewater features a shrine-like barrel vaulted ceiling, while on the ground floor where ceilings are higher, there is a pendentive vault. The dispensary has a revolving carousel carrying 700 prescription medicines, and this allows the majority of customers to be served while they wait. A queue point gives customers the opportunity to sign prescriptions before arriving at the counter. An Oral Health Advice Centre uses multi-media technology to offer personalized help. In addition, there is a chiropody practice featuring a waiting area, two consulting rooms and central preparation areas.

Areas displaying cosmetics include an eight-foot lip totem that features over 180 lipsticks by colour, along with a test and play area showing customers how to achieve a variety of make-up looks and a range of services from the on-site beauty consultants.

On the ground floor the men's fragrance and shave shop features a central totem incorporating a plasma screen showing sports images. Boots Opticians has a 200-metre store with three consulting rooms, an optical laboratory and a contact lens area.

The store in Manchester features a 23-metre full height glass wall which opens it on to the street. The central hall ceiling contains barrel vaults to depict the traditional market area, while the perimeter is more contemplative, with the ceiling dropping to a lower level, and finishes varying from aluminium to limed oak. On the first floor, a flat, high ceiling in the centre communicates the sense of a central shrine and barrel vaults have been used to create arcades. On the second floor, the Sandwich Café provides panoramic views over Manchester. Its interior includes a limestone floor, etched glass, maple wood and satin stainless steel finishes.

Lighting is used to create distinctions between different areas and floors. Purity, spirituality and beauty were concepts underlying the lighting in both Bluewater and Manchester. Light and colour levels are variable and change according to the time of day. Specially designed pendant and gimbal spotlights highlight merchandise, with accent lighting on key product areas. The ambient lighting level has been reduced. Pale cream terrazzo floor tiles containing blue and green glass chips also reflect light.

The rear wall of the Bluewater store comprises a series of glass panels lit by a fibre-optic system and slow moving colour wheel which changes during the day. This creates the effect of water moving over the surface, a design feature which links into the overall water theme of Bluewater Park.

Above **Children's clothing and other new products are incorporated within the new stores. Floors, walls and ceilings are clean with a minimum of detail and fuss. Large lifestyle graphics are incorporated in the ends of units to add a sense of fun.**

Left **Beauty treatment areas are incorporated within the department to provide advice, guidance and demonstrations. These semi-private areas help to break up the department and to create a personal zone where the customer can get individual service.**

Discovery Channel
Washington DC, USA

Opposite **The store, which is divided into four floors, reflects the layers of the earth. The ground floor features a cast of a** Tyrannosaurus rex **skeleton that represents a prehistoric world. Customers can also experience an archeological dig.**

Below **Dubbed Ocean Planet, this floor represents the inside of a ship. The floor features a shipwreck and a scale model of the** Titanic.

Discovery Communications Inc. is a cable channel that broadcasts in nearly 150 countries worldwide. It includes The Learning Channel, Animal Planet and Discovery Channel. It also offers publishing and Internet services. In 1995 it entered retail by buying a US chain of shops, Discovery, and subsequently another chain, Nature. Globalization is clearly an aim and airports have been identified as a basis for expansion. The company has experimented in translating the concept to smaller stores.

The Discovery store is uniquely in tune with interests in world culture, anthropology, scientific achievement, space exploration, the natural world and the desire for

expanding knowledge which greater access to information has generated at all ages and all levels of society worldwide. The popularity of museum retailing has been evident for at least a decade but large-scale commercial exploitation has so far been limited. Instead, the obvious links between retail and leisure have been concentrated on powerful brands such as Disney and Warner Brothers.

It begs the question – is the Discovery store a museum or a shop? It is in fact, more than just a crossover between education and retail. It is also a meeting of television and retail, not in the conventional sense of series merchandising, but in that it draws on the resources of a channel dedicated to the natural world and uses those stories to inform both merchandise and the interior.

The basis in broadcasting and education is behind another critical feature of the flagship – the stories it is telling. As the store layout shows, the earth and its position in the universe is one layer of the storytelling. Within each of the floors and specialist areas, the unlimited information on the natural world provides enormous potential for a range of associated stories, and, crucially, for these stories to be adapted through various media, including Discovery Channel, without altering the concept of the store.

The flexibility of the source material is a great benefit. It also ensures that unlike other media-related retail, there is potentially unlimited public interest, particularly if innovative product sourcing is maintained. Some examples currently on offer include a framed dinosaur tooth, An Ice Age skeleton of a bear, amber jewellery, sportswear and cards; this diversity aims to cater for all tastes and wallets.

In some instances, the flagship will be used as a basis for programme making. For example, speakers featured at the store will be filmed there for broadcast in other stores, and it can also be used as a set for television programmes.

However, it has not all been plain sailing for Discovery. One of the key problems has been ensuring it can compete with some of the world's best-stocked museums for customers. Opening hours are one solution; another is the range the store offers.

PROFILE

CLIENT: Discovery Channel

FUNCTION: Speciality

CONSULTANTS: Ron Pompei Associates

OLLOW WHERE THE PATH MAY LEAD.
STEAD WHERE THERE IS NO PATH.
AND LEAVE A TRAIL.

Anonymous

Above **The large curved service desk snakes through the space like an amorphous form. The walls are clad in metal, which give the space an aged look and the impression of being in various states of decay. Text is used against this with information and entertaining quotes. Large murals are also incorporated to suggest upper levels or strata.**

Designer Ron Pompei wanted to incorporate the experience of discovery and adventure. Another important design element has been the integration of other attractions such as graphics, interactive games, sound and vision – ensuring the shoppers' senses and intellect were equally stimulated by the store environment.

The Discovery Channel store covers 2,800 square metres (30,000 square feet) and is on four levels, reflecting the earth's layers. On the ground floor, Paleo World, there is a cast of a *Tyrannosaurus rex* skeleton and a kiosk which takes customers on an archaeological dig. A curved media wall promotes the Discovery Channel programming.

The mezzanine floor sells clothing, toys, games and accessories and is laid out like the inside of a ship. Dubbed Ocean Planet, it features famous shipwrecks and a scale model of the Titanic with associated footage of exploration of the wreck. On the second floor, Wild Discovery, is a giant ant colony, and World Cultures is an art gallery used for various exhibitions, for example the history of tea. A selection of world music is available to listen to and totem pole carvings can be explored. Travel goods, books, music, gardening equipment and home decorating products are available for sale.

The third floor, Sky and Space Science Frontiers, features a B52 bomber plane, a Hubble observatory with photos from the Hubble telescope and the Discovery Channel studio. Shoppers can view human skeletons and peer into microscopes. Finally, on the fourth floor, the history of Washington is told through murals and films, screened regularly in the Discovery Channel theatre.

Left **The third level represents sky, space and science. Features include a B52 bomber, Hubble Observatory and Discovery Channel studio.**

Below **Technology is a key feature of the store and a lift contains sound effects as it passes through the various floors. Other attractions include graphics, interactive games, sounds and visual devices ensuring that shoppers are stimulated at every level.**

Technology is a key feature of the store. Sound effects are transmitted from a lift which change according to the level it is passing through. Print, photography, video and other electronic devices such as games and tutorials are used to communicate the stories being told. On the third floor, where microscopes and telescopes are on sale, there are five kiosks explaining the products. Other kiosks include games such as how to make a pebble or dig your own *T. rex*. Other kiosks play mini-documentaries.

A second flagship store opened in 1999 in Sony's entertainment complex, Yerba Buena Gardens, San Francisco. This new store features an aquarium, bi-plane and a whale skeleton.

The Discovery store has been a phenomenon waiting to happen and the whole concept is totally in tune with the times. It is a meeting point of the turn of the century's commercial pre-occupations: media, retail and leisure as education and it is on this basis that it is part of a brand building exercise.

Jigsaw
London, England

Opposite **The shopfront has an impressive double height space allowing customers to absorb the overall style of the store quickly. This can also act as an intimidating barrier.**

Below **To the right-hand side of the store a narrow staircase takes staff up to the first floor. A view into the ground floor of the shop shows how the obscured acrylic screens divide the space into smaller areas.**

The Jigsaw flagship store in Bond Street, London was designed by the architect John Pawson and set up in 1996. It was a clear architectural statement about where the retailer wanted to position itself. Jigsaw has 50 to 60 stores worldwide. Its philosophy is to use different designers according to the size and location of its new stores. An in-house design team is responsible for smaller stores, while outside consultants are also employed.

It is a store that signals the shift away from theatre in retailing to the use of cleaner and more classical lines. Original artwork in its window, commissioned from Michael Craig Martin and shown during February and March 1997,

unusually linked a high-street retailer with contemporary fine art, to the extent that Jigsaw even invited customers to a private view, using the conventions of a gallery opening. The floor was created from metre square (three foot square) Irish granite tiles with sand-blasted stainless-steel fixtures, sanded acrylic dividing walls, wide Douglas fir floorboards in the basement and unique white plaster walls. This pared-down, minimalist interior aimed to send a clear message that as a retailer Jigsaw was not prepared to compromise on quality or design.

The Bond Street site is a one-off. It operates in the context of the other flagship stores within the locality as well as the private galleries that sit alongside them. In the tradition of flagship stores, it was never conceived as a 'roll-out' concept. Even if there had been plans to re-create the Bond Street interior, realistically it could not have been done – this is simply because its impact lies in its uniqueness, the quality of its materials and its classic design. Pawson's interior was formative at the time it was opened. His interpretation of minimalism was particularly influential during the 1990s. As one of the prime exponents of the style working at the time, whose philosophy extends throughout his work, Jigsaw's decision to use him was both radical and essential to the site. Although Jigsaw is a high street retailer, the choice of location in Bond Street demanded an approach which would ensure the interior reflected cutting edge high fashion. The decision was important too, to Jigsaw's other store interiors. As a result, Jigsaw has developed a philosophy for store design that challenges the uniformity of other multiple retailers. The company is probably more responsive to local context than any other UK high-street fashion retailer.

Jigsaw has always differentiated itself as a clothing retailer in its commitment to contemporary art. In terms of interior design, it is now distinguishing itself by fitting stores in dramatically different styles according to their architecture and location. This makes Jigsaw an interesting proposition for the discerning customer who is virtually guaranteed that the offer will never be identical either

PROFILE

CLIENT: Jigsaw

FUNCTION: Fashion

CONSULTANTS: John Pawson

Jigsaw's approach to design has resulted in an eclectic mixture of styles drawing on a number of influences. In the company's Oxford store, where the architecture of the university buildings was an important reference point, local reclaimed stone was used for the floor with floral curtains providing a more softened look for the changing rooms. In Manchester, a showcase touring exhibition of Royal College of Art graduates was launched at the shop in October 1997.

An illustration of this philosophy is to examine the radically different design approaches from the Bond Street store and the store in Westbourne Grove, London. While Bond Street was dramatically altered from its original state, Westbourne Grove has kept, and used as a feature, walls with flaking plaster. This design fits perfectly into the laid-back, fashionable, understated and elegant locality of the store itself. It sits among antiques shops, the showrooms of designers and specialist delicatessens, where there is a young and wealthy community that expects exclusivity. The shopfront is painted pink and restored to its original Victorian style. Inside, wooden furniture, old mirrors and distressed plasterwork convey the impression of an interior with history – a shop almost by accident, which has taken over a space and imported a few fittings in order to sell clothes. The fittings themselves are basic and the floor consists of stripped boards. The message from this interior is bohemian. Designer Andrew Martin says it is intended to communicate a sense of the eclectic while being friendlier to the customer: a fusion of white walls with the tactile. From a pragmatic point of view, this approach has also resulted in significantly lower-cost shopfitting than previously may have been expected. By contrast, stores at Bluewater Park in Kent and in Chester and Kingston, are closer to the minimalism of the Bond Street store.

'Jigsaw is about doing what feels right at the time, for different buildings' says Martin. The same design philosophy applies to fixtures. Where required, new fixtures will be commissioned, but equally designers are free to use those that have worked well in other stores. Martin points out that Jigsaw's direction is to work with a bare structure without making it too modern or pristine.

Above **In contrast to other locations, the Westbourne Grove store is a local store on a small scale. This individual approach reflects the brand values of Jigsaw, with interesting finishes and stylish but low-budget fit-out costs.**

nationwide or globally. The Jigsaw merchandising policy states key looks but its local store managers are given the responsibility for adapting these.

The company ventured into menswear but has subsequently sold off this side of the business. The commercial thinking behind this decision was clear; menswear attracted a younger customer than womenswear, but the latter was more established and had maintained loyalty from older customers as well as continuing to attract new shoppers.

Left **The double height space in the Bond Street store is also used for art installations. This installation by Michael Craig Martin was launched with a private view for Jigsaw customers.**

Below **The view into the store from the entrance shows the soft focus impression of clothes behind the etched acrylic screens. The staircase to the left is highlighted by low level illumination, and the walls are framed by light.**

Opaque
Tokyo, Japan

Opaque is a distinctive store with an unmistakable presence on the high street. It presents itself without pretension as a bold, brash retailer of young, fashionable products for the not so wealthy. Sited in the Ginza area of Tokyo, this traditional district is dominated by the Imperial Palace and the banks and business sectors. The area is the Japanese equivalent of the Champs Elysées where business people meet for lunch amidst the department stores and the surrounding shops of Seibu, Takashimaya, Mitsukoshi and Printemps. It is also an area with a great many chic and expensive designer boutiques such as Chanel, Celine, Luzia and Fendi.

The shopfront is designed as a huge lightbox making a strong visual statement although no heed is paid to the ecological concerns of light pollution and excessive energy consumption. This aside, it does effectively draw your attention to its location at night. The front of the store consists of a sandwich of glass, of double thickness, which when open has the sense of creating a series of lobbies. This space is used for lighting and adds depth to an otherwise flat façade, which in turn acts like a doll's house with clear views into the rear areas of the store.

The signage is subtle and is formed out of clear glass bonded to the inner skin of the façade. The store is easy to read and the consumer is left in no doubt about its size, location, layout and the products on offer. The store itself is beautifully laid out, with a choice of entrances that guide you into the interior or into a separate lobby with access to the lower ground floor pizzeria restaurant called Tanto. The entrance lobby is clearly defined with a cosmetics area. Visible from the street, it is subtly presented within simple glass midfloor fixtures set off by a low illuminated wall with a strong graphic image. Colour is the keynote here with fashion colours suggested without a need for garish branding or advertising imagery.

The overall impression within the store is one of clarity, yet this is tempered with glass divisions treated with coloured gels and translucent films. The effect is to give an almost ghostly feeling with movement and activity suggested but not obvious. The views are diluted through a milky white film. People come and go regularly, yet there is an ethereal quality to their movements. Similarly, decorative glazed screens are used to conceal the entrances to the staff areas and fitting rooms. These act as strong graphic images, which add to the almost colourless environment.

The merchandise is laid out clearly and this includes fashion and accessories. Reflected light, rather than direct spotlighting, is used to highlight the products. The lights are concealed and obscured behind pelmets and below fixturing, with uplit, mid-floor low-level tables creating a focus for the goods on offer. The circulation route is not

PROFILE

CLIENT: Opaque

FUNCTION: Fashion

CONSULTANTS: Casappo and Associates

Above **A view into the ground floor of the store reveals the cosmetics counters. The glass theme continues in this area with a large illuminated abstract graphic wall as a backdrop.**

Right **The Italian restaurant in the lower ground floor can be accessed either through the shop or directly from the street. Customers arrive at a raised level with views into the seating area.**

defined, yet the staircase is a central feature and is visible from all corners of the store. It acts as a point of reference and is accessible from two directions. A large void over the staircase allows visible access to the upper floor and a glass balustrade along its entire length heightens the stair form. Film is used on these plains so that from certain angles the image appears to change in an abstract display of light and transparency.

The choice and location of the staircase is well thought out; it is not central but positioned to one side so it does not divide the space into two equal parts. The movement of people throughout the space creates an effect rather like the ripples on water, that is difficult to record.

All services are elegantly controlled with little or no intrusion on the interior of the store. Materials are kept to a minimum. Glass is used extensively with limestone flooring throughout and inset carpets in the shoes areas. The same material palette is used on the upper floors. The cash desks are long, large and visible with rear counter displays of product stacked for maximum impact. Consumer comfort is not forgotten and there are a number of ottoman benches for weary customers.

The restaurant/pizzeria is accessible both from the store and directly from the street. Access to the restaurant is via a ramp and the simple space is divided through the centre. The restaurant can seat up to 104 people and its colour scheme is warmer in tone than the rest of the store.

Although the design of this store is simple, it is never boring. Inventive use of transparency and blurred views allow revealing glimpses into the interior that intrigue the customer and encourage him or her to explore further.

If I have any criticism of this store it would be directed at the representation of the product. The store lacks a clear product philosophy neither being selective enough nor passionate about the merchandise image. A minimalist approach will only work if each product is imbued with a special quality. Some of the products lack definition. The most successful area of the store is the cosmetics area where the relationship between customer and product is clear and immediate.

Above **This specialist undulating ribbon glass façade is an intricate and complex structure to reproduce. Created by the company Future Systems, the surface of the façade has a textured finish, which further distorts the translucency of the interior forms.**

Comme des Garçons

Tokyo, Japan

Comme des Garçons was founded in 1969 by Rei Kawakubo and the first boutique opened in Aoyama, Tokyo in 1975. The woman behind Japan's most admired fashion label is an intellectual who studied art and literature and whose ambition for her clothes goes far beyond fashion; she sees them as expressions of freedom and individuality.

Rei Kawakubo has described her work as architecturally inspired. Indeed, as well as fabric and garments, she regularly designs furniture and in 1983 she produced her first furniture line, winning many awards and much critical acclaim. Bold and inventive, Kawakubo's furniture is not designed as isolated pieces with a functional purpose, but as a backdrop for her stores. Her interest in architecture and furniture has nothing to do with the current trend for brand diversification, but stems from her desire to create the perfect environment for her clothes. It is therefore as much an expression of her creative aesthetic as her skill in designing garments: 'I've always tried to create as complete an environment as possible for my clothes, so furniture was a natural progression. Comme des Garçons has always been about a complete environment.'

The first shops were developed with the designer Takao Kawasaki, with whom she has continued to collaborate. These shops were as provocative as her early collections and created a great deal of attention. Notoriously one of them displayed no clothes at all, being entirely empty with the clothes only being shown upon request. Kawakubo explains that a principle of non-conformity runs throughout her designs; 'I want to express something new without the constraints of convention.'

Her two latest stores in New York and Tokyo follow these principles. The New York store, situated on West 22nd Street in the untested area of Chelsea, is the only store of its type in a neighbourhood of neglected buildings, artists' studios and galleries – spaces which are risky and uncompromising. A pioneer of unconventional spaces, Kawakubo's original New York store was sited in a challenging location, the once bohemian area of SoHo. This area has since become an upmarket shopping destination attracting brand names to every corner.

The exterior of the New York store has a modest and undistinguished first impression. At first glance it appears to be quite undeveloped, having retained the old signage 'Heavenly Body Works', which dates from its time as an auto repair shop. On closer inspection, however, the original drive-in entrance frames a new and dramatic architectural intervention; here a simple, prefabricated inner tube is formed with curved walls of steel, which have a scrubbed,

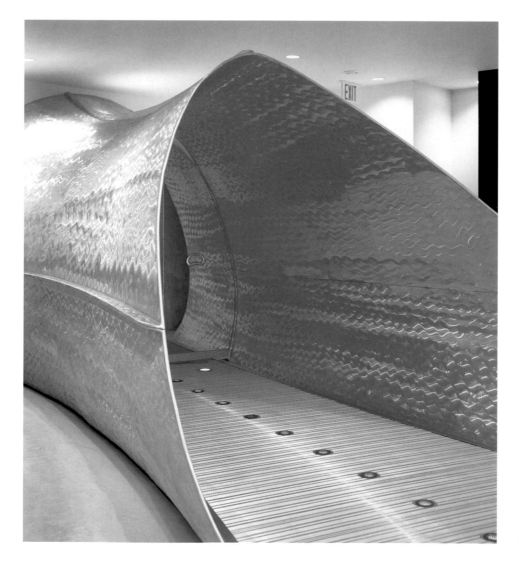

PROFILE

CLIENT: Rei Kawakubo

FUNCTION: Fashion

CONSULTANTS: Takao Kawasaki and Future Systems

Above **This specialist undulating glass façade is a complex structure. Created by Future Systems the surface has a textured surface which plays with the translucency of the interior forms.**

textured sheen and a slatted floor mat with recessed lighting that creates a rippled effect along the whole length of the tube. The aluminium tube's monocoque or single rigid structure was designed by a London architectural firm, Future Systems.

The entrance leads you out into a huge 465 square metre (5,000 square foot) white space that contains various volumes of sculptured white forms suggesting tiny buildings set within a larger one. The plan, shape and form do not speak within any conventional retailing vocabulary. At once inviting and challenging to the customer, the design encourages exploration with no guidance, tantalizing the viewer with glimpses of product without revealing the total story. Sometimes reminiscent of Richard Serra sculptures, the

shapes and forms seem arbitrary and yet play off one another in exercises of positive and negative tension. Instead of creating a chain store uniformity, Kawakubo has deliberately chosen to give her customers a highly personal shopping experience.

The original stores in the 1970s resembled little more than boxes where the clothes matched the architecture and formed part of a strong, minimal environment. However, from the late 1980s the stores began to change, each one starting to adopt its own identity, but sharing a consistent feeling of movement. Spaces were largely open plan where strong colour statements allowed space and light to interplay with the products. By contrast, the Comme des Garçons store that opened in Aoyama, Tokyo, in 1999 is a development and testament to a design philosophy that has grown from the confidence that comes with experience. The spaces are concentrated and undiluted, with no easily visible explanation. The pure will of the designer, as demonstrated here, is uncompromising. It is an interior that is a private, and ultimately personal, expression and will appeal to loyal customers of Comme des Garçons.

The exterior of the Tokyo store consists of an undulating glass façade constructed with continuous ribbon glass. Again created by Future Systems, the textured surface plays with the material's translucency and the reflection and refraction of images, products and movements. In the same way as the New York store, the interior forms are juxtaposed in an imaginative composition. The walls are by Christian Astrigueville and Sophie Smallhorn and there are many sculptural references to artists such as Richard Deacon. The flooring is a series of screeded grid patterns, which clash into each other within the space, adding to the sense of anarchy and discord.

The overall installation is more in tune with an art gallery than a retail area and this will, no doubt, be an inspiration for its imitators. This is not a space that complies with any defined retail formulae; in fact it flies in the face of convention and turns the rulebook on its head.

Above **The interior fixturing follows the contours and colour of the glazing and echoes its sinuous quality.**

Left **The featured structures shown here are mini installations of architectural proportion. They are integrated with selected products and also with works of art, in a seamless transition through the spaces.**

Vinegar Factory and E.A.T.

New York, USA

Opposite **This shows an interior shot of the Vinegar Factory check-out. The produce is at low level, while the stock is stored all around the perimeter at high level.**

Below **This shows Eli Zabar, the founder of the Vinegar Factory. He is pictured standing within the polytunnel structures on top of the roof where fresh produce is grown for his stores and restaurants below.**

Eli Zabar, born in 1943, is a scion of the family that created the landmark delicatessen on the upper west side of New York. The family deli Zabar's is the quintessential New York brunch venue famous for its smoked fish. Eli had a different vision – he was inspired by the food halls and markets of London and Paris, and developed his keen sensibility for food into a passion.

He established his first store, E.A.T., in 1973. This small upmarket gourmet store, directly across town on Madison Avenue, sells housewares and pre-packed foods. At first it was not a great success, but after a lot of hard work it became recognized for its quality.

Eli's Bread started in 1985, in the basement of E.A.T.. Unable to find the kind of bread he wanted for his sandwiches and bread baskets, Eli decided to bake his own but it was a struggle to get the ingredients right. Initially the shop only produced rolls, many of which he had to give away. Finally he gave them away long enough that people actually began to like them and demand grew. In 1987, once the demand was established, Eli began to sell bread wholesale. New doughs were created and more breads were added to his repertoire. He began to supply bread to many of New York's finest hotels, restaurants and retailers, and today Eli has his own bakery that can produce up to 500 loaves of bread per hour.

Eli's Vinegar Factory is Eli's think-tank. While E.A.T. is about perfection – the best sandwich and the perfect loaf of bread, the Factory is all about experimentation.

Eli's strengths lie in his ability to assess the market and his willingness to change direction according to his vision and the needs of his customers. When E.A.T. was first launched no one bought his pots and pans so he decided to put the idle pots and pans to use. Eli bought cookbooks and thought hard about food, whilst he taught himself to cook. He developed some very simple but definitive ideas and created a distinctive aesthetic which is still the hallmark of Eli's today.

When Eli bought the Vinegar Factory (the last working Vinegar Factory in Manhattan) it was instinctive. He did not have a clear idea of what he would do with it, but he moves intuitively, guided by his passions.

The Vinegar Factory opened in 1993 and maintains the integrity of the former factory by retaining many of its original features. This late eighteenth-early nineteenth century industrial warehouse has a rugged industrial aesthetic which has been left exposed. Eli and his architects have combined the building's structure with fixtures of rough wood and stainless steel. They have deconstructed the tall wooden silos originally used to distil vinegar and converted the aged wooden planks into display fixtures, islands and restaurant tables.

PROFILE

CLIENT: Eli Zabar

FUNCTION: Food

CONSULTANTS: Richard H Lewis

The mezzanine floor looks down into the food store below. The upper floor was specially created to lure customers into the store by producing a café area (which can also be hired for private parties) and a housewares department specializing in cookware and utensils which have the cheapest prices on the upper east side. Eli saw this as an ideal way of integrating the tools of cooking with the best ingredients.

The lightweight pine display trays are designed by Eli and made in the Vinegar Factory's own carpentry shop. Four full-time carpenters are constantly employed to build Eli's designs. All of the displays in the store, tables and staircase are built and maintained in the workshop. This hand-built quality is what gives the Vinegar Factory its charm. The handwritten signs are also fascinating as they give a market-style immediacy to the store which is endearing. The mixture of quality produce and informal but fastidious care and attention to detail are what make this environment so successful.

The store's layout reflects Eli's personal passions, consequently the store is constantly changing and growing. The concept for the Vinegar Factory was to get as close to the source of his ingredients as possible. By buying his vegetables direct from the farmer, curing his own beef and roasting his own coffee beans, his vision was for a unique market where everything for sale was made on the premises.

Not satisfied with buying produce, Eli began to grow his own. Three polytunnels (greenhouses) were built on the roof of his building to supply baby greens, tomatoes and beans directly to his market and restaurant 'Across the Street'. When Eli decided to sell organic produce he hand picked his suppliers by visiting up to 50 growers. On a visit to Paris he was so impressed with some tightly bound floral bouquets that he built a showcase flower department.

Every day a culinary team of 25 people prepare fresh salads with more than 70 dishes to choose from. Refrigerated cabinets display a tempting array of home-made soups, sandwiches and breads. There is also a hot food section where side dishes, pastries and cakes are prepared and sold.

Right **Handwritten signs taped to sticks show the goods and prices throughout the store. This casual approach is distinctive and indicates a refreshingly personal touch.**

Below **This is a picture of E.A.T., the upmarket gourmet store which opened in 1985. The store is streamlined with a variety of food highlights. The counters and cabinets are made of stainless steel and marble.**

Nothing goes to waste in the store; fresh fruit is squeezed into juices or churned into sorbets and ice creams. Bread is cubed and ground, seasoned and toasted for croutons. Ripe tomatoes are turned into sauces, potatoes are sliced and fried into potato chips and berries are turned into jams and preserves.

Service is also very important to Eli's customers and orders can be phoned or faxed to the 'Home Shopping Department' using a pre-printed list. Delivery is free of charge with large purchases. There is a regular newsletter/paper that is produced six times a year keeping customers updated and containing articles, stories and reviews by some of New York's finest food writers.

In addition to his vision Eli is an astute businessman with a head for what keeps his company healthy. All the businesses seem to have grown organically to form a cohesive whole. With his hand on the financial pulse he is able to achieve profitability without compromising quality. The business has evolved, and he pursues what interests him following his passions and his instincts.

*Above **A raised view of the Vinegar Factory from the mezzanine. The circulation routes are clear and the products are piled up abundantly. The environment is tactile with a much less sterile atmosphere than that seen in other larger supermarket multiples. The circular units add interest, and they are all designed by Eli himself and made on the premises.***

Let's Eat
Melbourne, Australia

Growing demands on our time have increased the importance of convenience, and the use of partially or fully prepared meals has made meal preparation easier.

A report, 'Food in Focus', looking at eating habits, social trends and food preferences, was commissioned in 1996 by Murdoch Magazines, Australia. It identified, not surprisingly, an increased demand for fresh food and discovered some food statistics which confirmed the changes affecting eating habits. The report showed that 97 per cent of the population had modified their diet in recent years. There was a marked increase in enjoyment of food and its emergence as a lifestyle interest.

This lifestyle aspect is now reflected in the advent of a 'Café Society' with a large increase in cafés, restaurants and speciality food outlets. Researchers noted that eating out and going to restaurants with friends is, to a degree, replacing home entertainment. Although cooking at home is decreasing, the gender distinction is blurring with one third of men claiming to be the main cook and six out of ten saying they are involved in cooking at home. A surprising 33 per cent claim to be the main grocery buyer. The report concludes that traditional cooking skills are being replaced by meal assemblage skills.

Let's Eat is a food and wine emporium, tailor-made for the time-poor professional with high expectations, or the adventurous housewife looking for something special. It is not a new idea but one which has increased in popularity within a specific market, which needs convenience without compromise to quality. H.M.R. (Home Meal Replacement) is today's jargon for ready-made meals but Let's Eat has developed the idea into a unique experience.

Let's Eat offers a selection of full or partially prepared meals using fresh ingredients, to take away or to eat within the store. It is located within a market area of Melbourne called Prahran Market and it is estimated that the market has 52,000 visitors each day. The emphasis in the store is on fresh food and wine integration says architect Mark Landini. Service is informed and welcoming, and imbues the store with a market atmosphere. Customers are encouraged to experiment with regular tastings and the chance to match meals and wine from around the world.

The concept is owned by the Coles Myers Group, a leading food supplier in Australia. Managing director Alan Williams said "The project aims to see top chefs in action, customer interaction, speciality foods and wines, delicious aromas, taste sensations, innovation and technology."

A large team of specialists was needed to produce this concept from its original idea. Each stage, in terms of products, packaging design and layout was reviewed by the design team which closely monitored each phase. The project has taken two years to develop.

PROFILE

CLIENT: Coles, Myers Group

FUNCTION: Food

CONSULTANTS: Landini Associates

Above **This view from the check-outs up to the mezzanine floor shows the demonstration and cookery school in the background. The specialist chocolate counter and refrigerated units are stocked to the brim with produce.**

At the heart of the store is an open-plan kitchen, where 60 chefs are employed to prepare customers' meals. Customers can select from a choice of 1,600 meal suggestions displayed on computer terminals around the store, or select from the daily specials cooked to order. All meals are prepared daily and are displayed in 100 linear metres (330 linear feet) of specially designed display cases, using only ingredients from the store shelves, all of which can be purchased by the customer.

The library is located on the mezzanine where cooking demonstrations and tastings are conducted. This space can also be booked for parties or functions. Meals can be ordered through their web-site and delivered to your home.

The store is 1,400 square metres (15,000 square feet) and is built on two floors. The shop circulation is kept tight, to create interest and the sense of a market place. Landini says that customers like finding things and this is encouraged. Walls of merchandise are presented for maximum impact. Landini Associates have designed all the units to be raised off the ground so that wine and other product

suggestions can be juxtaposed next to the main ingredients. The materials used throughout are white marble, stainless steel and an industrial polished concrete floor tile by Sadler.

A special point-of-sale system informs each purchase with a serving suggestion or recommendation of complimentary wines or desserts. The whole process is educational as one purchase informs another. Four interactive screens provide information on meals and cooking instructions or printouts of ingredients. Videos are also available free of charge to help with your food preparations.

There are over 1,300 product lines. The store is at once a fresh food market, florist, bakery, chocolatier, sushi bar, delicatessen, cheesemonger, butcher, greengrocer, classic wine cellar, wine bar, café, snack bar, kitchenware shop, cooking school, cookbook shop and general place to hang out. It has everything for the food enthusiast, even a home economist available for food and dietary advice.

Customers can eat in or take away and the store is fully licensed so you can drink a glass of wine whilst browsing. Your chosen ingredients can be handed to a chef and cooked in front of you, or, if you prefer, whilst you are shopping or resting – they can bleep you when your meal is ready to collect. Most of the meals are fully cooked during the week when customers are time pressured, but at weekends many more are partially prepared, and more ingredient shopping takes place when people have more time to cook their own meals.

Staff were recruited from the world of theatre, leisure and retail. The main criteria for employment had to be a real passion for food. Most of the staff successfully transmit this to the customers and with their various skills are able to help and assist sales. The store employs 150 people, including chefs, bakers, butchers and a fishmonger. The chefs are drawn from all over the world: Japan, Thailand, China, Morocco, Russia and India, each with his or her own specialization.

Staff are all fully trained and customer focused. They are flexible and multi-skilled to ensure customers receive excellent service and to make sure they make the most of the Let's Eat experience.

The overall effect is efficient and exciting, and certainly fulfils the client brief beyond expectation.

Above **The whole store is licensed for alcohol, so customers can drink from the bar, or even wander round the store with their glass of wine.**

Left **This shows the cookery school demonstration area. In the foreground is the cookery library with a refectory table. This area can also be used for tastings or eating whilst reading.**

Tesco

Peterborough, Kensington and Bishopsgate, England

Opposite **An external shot of the Tesco store in Kensington at night. The double height glazing allows clear views into the store from passing traffic and makes a striking feature when illuminated at night.**

Below **An artist's impression of the store and a prospective building above as yet unconstructed. This site is in a prominent position at a gateway into the City of London.**

Tesco is one of Europe's largest food retailers, with an increasingly international presence including developments in markets such as Eastern Europe and Thailand. Their retail strategy is to build a global market within the next 15 years and the 'hypermarket strategy' is a working format for this development. Stores will be set up in each country, with local management reflecting the local culture and buying patterns. Tesco's standard brand values will apply to these stores: the implementation of world-beating formats; stores that are easy, simple and enjoyable; the use of modern and innovative brands; and most importantly the communication of value, quality and service.

In the UK Tesco has introduced various formats selected and adapted to each store's location and demographics. Research is undertaken to ascertain the effectiveness of each format and the choice of products: Tesco Express, a petrol forecourt format; Tesco Metro, city stores in increasingly product-specific locations; Tesco Metro High Street, local stores aimed at the older generation; Radical Compact, standard-size supermarkets; Superstores, the most profitable size to date, sited on town perimeters with car-parking facilities; Tesco Extra, superstore, with non-food products, similar to the European hypermarket format.

The future strategy outlined by Tesco's design controller, Jeremy Lindley, incorporates a populist vision in order to answer consumer demands, a dynamic approach to embrace change, and a responsiveness to local issues to engage with the community. The corporate directives are clear: design requirements must have business justification and must result in improved efficiency. In fact the stores today cost 42 per cent less to build than four years ago. Such statistics would be the envy of most retailers but such a strategy always runs the risk of losing the essential dynamic that keeps bringing customers back.

In February 1999 Tesco opened a new format Tesco Extra shop in Peterborough. At 9,300 square metres (100,000 square feet), it is the impressive size of three football pitches. It also boasts the largest non-food area of any of the current Tesco stores, and this section accounts for some 50 per cent of the total linear footage. New departments were launched at this venue for sports, electrical goods and an opticians, and existing departments were updated and modernized.

For some years Tesco have been developing their non-food offer in order that it should command an equal status to their traditional grocery offer. In addition to this, the design also needed to meet other commercial and manufacturing objectives: to provide contemporary ranges underpinned by a value-for-money ethic; to improve the shopping experience for customers; to simplify the

PROFILE

CLIENT: Jeremy Lindley, Tesco Design Controller

FUNCTION: Primarily food, with non-food developments

CONSULTANTS: Two design teams

merchandising process; to create a flexible and modular merchandising system simple to use by all staff; and to reduce the fit-out cost by 10 per cent.

The design objectives for the Peterborough Tesco Extra wcrc based around the generic graphic and interior design blueprint created in 1996 for Tesco by Future Brand Davies Barron. The new features of the blueprint included a sense of style that was faithful to the Tesco brand, yet helped the group to alter customer perceptions. This design policy enables Tesco to achieve a high degree of style through

Left *A view of the interior of the Kensington store which provides a coffee bar and seating area for many shoppers and passers-by alike.*

Below *A view through the non-food areas at the Peterborough store. The home merchandise is co-ordinated with high-level graphics acting as landmarks. The prominent fixturing systems tend to dominate the area.*

good visual merchandising that echoes high-street values, while also recognizing the need for it to be easily maintained. It provided greater distinction between product categories with a flexible parts kit that could be incorporated according to space and location requirements, providing better accommodation for the new ranges.

Home Shop World, the Kensington Tesco Superstore, is one of the corner-store developments of the new non-food trading area, that also includes the Cookshop. Health and beauty, men's and women's departments have all received special treatments. Clarity of products on display, attention to detail, and noticeable changes in materials, lighting and graphics give each area a distinct identity.

Tesco has paid much attention to 'outfit-led' merchandising and coordination to create an appropriately robust high-street feel. However, the vastness of the retail shed environment is difficult to come to terms with. The lighting whilst efficient is not sensitive or evocative of a comfortable home shopping environment.

Tesco Metro, Bishopsgate, is the 'town and city centre' format of Tesco stores, selling a large range of fresh food, snacks and top-up shop product. These stores tend to be busy and handle heavy footfall in large surges at different times of the day. The main customers are young professionals, local workers, residents and tourists.

The Bishopgate store is a new building erected behind the façade of an old fire station. This project was intended to deliver a new format of Tesco Metro. Design objectives were 'brand led' with more specific requirements to tackle congestion and queuing problems; create an offer more suited to customer needs; encourage customers to shop the whole store; facilitate the operation and management of the store; and create a fun environment.

The overall focus of the store is visibility and access. Customers are usually short of time, yet will happily spend money on the right product, so stores are planned for total convenience. Wide side aisles encourage deeper penetration, and fixtures are used low at the front getting

Above **A view through the Kensington shopping arcade which is at the forefront of the store. A series of specialist counters and produce is presented in convenience style below the mezzanine floor. Illuminated signage clearly defines the offers and their location.**

Below **Store circulation need not be limited to convention. This striking helical staircase is used to connect the mezzanine non-food floor with the café and food area. Its glass balustrade and open treads make it a bold example of modern supermarket design. It is a dramatic statement for a Tesco store and yet it fits perfectly within the architectural transparency of the whole.**

progressively higher to the rear and perimeter. Produce is sold right up to the windows and all refrigerated cabinets are kept to the perimeter of the space to ensure store circulation is unobstructed.

Colourful signage and graphics add to the feeling of metropolitan freshness. Large graphics clearly signal the location of products around the perimeter, helping to attract customers further into the store. Smaller graphics are used to highlight more product specific areas. Lighting has been improved with a perimeter band and uplighting which highlights the signage.

Visual devices such as 'goal posting' and an information hierarchy help to define the product clearly. Impulse products such as CDs are found at queuing locations.

A new queuing management system was also incorporated in the operational layout with standard and express checkouts at the front of the store.

The store has proved successful, with higher trading figures than anticipated. The customers comment on the sense of space and freshness, while the layout eases access and queuing. More shoppers are using trolleys, signalling a higher spend than is normal in a Metro Store.

Left **A detail of the music, video, newspaper and magazine shop in a Tesco Metro. The location of these products is essential in encouraging shoppers to impulse purchase whilst waiting at the check-outs.**

Below **The transparency of the store is best appreciated in this illuminated exterior view at night.**

For the whole Tesco portfolio branding is essential. Whilst offering vastly different products to different customers with vastly different needs, Tesco has managed to make each proposition work well within the brand. The projects are easily identifiable as Tesco stores yet that is where the similarities end. It is a great advantage to Tesco to be able to identify and produce interesting formats that suit individual customers with similar buying patterns. The quality of these environments is remarkable when you consider the design restraints and the business directives imposed on such a well known brand.

Technology has played a major part in the ability of Tesco to react quickly to its customer needs. Computerized systems distribution is speedy and efficient, the right product can be replenished efficiently, chilled distribution of products means they arrive fresher to the consumer, and quicker than ever before. All this provides the best affordable quality, underpinned by value for money offers and Tesco's own loyalty card scheme.

Idée
Tokyo, Japan

Opposite **Workstation was designed by Astrid Klein and Mark Dytham to combine workshops and showrooms for young designers to work on the experimental side of the business.**

Below **The interior of the Idée store showing accessories on the ground floor of this double height entrance space. This store is influenced by Bauhaus and sells modern classics as well as more accessible pieces.**

Tervo Kurosaki is the mastermind behind the design and retail empire of Idée. Rather than a shop selling designed products, Idée demonstrates the fusion of the design process itself, by explaining and educating the consumer about the value and benefits of good design.

Creation and development form the cornerstone of Idée, combined with a discerning eye and an astute understanding of business. However, from Kurosaki's perspective, financial business concerns should be secondary to the pleasure of creating things that are provocative and useful. The Idée concept is evolutionary and over the last 18 years they have been involved in publishing books on art and design and have also recorded their own music CDs, but the main focus has always been on furnishings and accessories for the home and office.

The whole evolution of the design process is reflected in each of the Idée stores. On the roof of the stores sit two geodesic domes, which house and develop various product ideas from visiting designers. These designers are also offered manufacturing and financial assistance in their development. This area provides a hothouse of new and developing ideas that slowly make their way through the manufacturing and marketing cycle and may eventually end up two floors below in the retail outlet.

The retail areas consist of environments that are tailor-made for many tastes and styles. From the avant-garde to the classic, there is something to offer everyone, whether you are a connoisseur or have a more limited experience of design. Products include the latest imports of furniture from Europe, but the variety of pieces on display is also guaranteed to impress. There are three basic lines: Idée which is Bauhaus inspired; Frame which has a 1950s' and 1960s' retro style; and Paysan which has basic, ageless classics. There are other lines complementing these: Petit Mobilier offers children's and small-scale furniture; Wood Cabinetry has wooden fixtures and furniture; Idée Co-ordinates offers basic home and office accessories; Workshop is a design team that creates special items made to order, and also miscellaneous design projects which involve young or established designers on specific projects.

There is also the Idée Club, which has been set up to introduce its ideas and activities to the public, and to share skills and information in order to develop better ways of living. Customers can become members and are entitled to various benefits as well as discounts on all publications, products and activities. It even allows a trade-in service for old Idée furniture on new purchases.

The Idée Shop opened in 1995 and is the largest of the three outlets presently run by Kurosaki. It encompasses most of Idée's interests, and includes the Café Bar, Cigar Room, Flower Shop, Gallery and finally an interior design

PROFILE

CLIENT: Tervo Kurosaki

FUNCTION: Home and office wares

CONSULTANTS: Various designers (see main text)

consultancy. It covers most of the middle ground in terms of taste, style and accessibility. The store offers a one-stop shop for the home or office interior laid out on three floors of retailing spread over an amalgamation of three buildings. The staff are knowledgeable and friendly.

The original site developed over time into the neighbouring buildings and has an amiable, organic feel. At ground-floor level, there is an overstuffed flower shop spilling out into the foyer. This small lean-to shed building with a corrugated roof feels low tech and wholly appropriate to its surroundings. The store itself is packed with home furnishings that are well-selected design brands with the quality and high price tag you would expect from European imports. The whole shop is a rabbit warren of little rooms, each with a character and style to suit its pieces. All available surfaces are used to present the products in room set environments that help customers match products, furniture and accessories.

Highlights of the store include the Italian restaurant on the third floor with its terrace bar and view over the low buildings of its Tokyo neighbours. The Havana Room is also located at this level where customers congregate to chat, drink and smoke Havana cigars in a convivial atmosphere.

The Gallery is also located on the third floor and is used to launch new products and to introduce new designers to the Japanese market and Idée Club members. It incorporates a small bookshop specializing in art, architecture and design books.

In a side street some 180 metres (200 yards) from the main store, the Idée Shop 'Pacific' has a range of antique, modern and reproduction furniture, goods and tableware from all corners of the Asian sub-continent, particularly Indonesia, Thailand, China and the Philippine Islands. It acts as an antidote to all that is bold, brash and modern.

This small store is beautifully presented and is both traditional and modern, and natural and organic in its use of vernacular building materials. Surfaces are bamboo and cane, sisal and basket-weave, melting a modern viewpoint into the authentic Asian culture. It is an eclectic but unconfused mix. Colonial styles jostle with regional cultures that

balance and work together in dark, rich tones and yellow ochres. The imagery is rich East meets West and both are influential on the new products being designed. Most of the products are for sale, and there is a design advisory service available to source the objects and unusual materials from their countries of origin.

The basement contains Rojak, a gourmet restaurant serving organic and ethnic cuisine from the pan-Pacific areas. It has its own entrance yet feels at one with the whole store concept. Dark, hardwood benches and long refectory tables complement this exciting environment.

Above **Idée Pacific sells products and furniture influenced by the East. Many of these pieces are made by local craftsmen to new and modern designs and are able to fit into traditional Japanese homes alongside existing furnishings.**

Left **Avant-garde furniture is sold at Workstation by many leading international furniture designers. The work is cutting edge and attracts many forward-thinking customers.**

Right **The Havana room within Idée is a cigar smoking environment. This trend was imported from America and allows cigars to be bought and smoked after dinner without interruption or polluting the restaurant's atmosphere.**

Below **The kitchens at Idée are open view and the atmosphere is relaxed, sociable and pleasantly informal.**

Kurosaki's latest shop Idée Workstation in Shimjuma, is the product of another design partnership, Klein Dytham, to whom he has acted as patron. It is a design atelier designing and producing custom-made furniture.

The building provides workshops and prototyping facilities which deliver an essential learning experience for new designers in getting ideas manufactured, and into production. Idée is proactive about design and reinvests money back into ideas and new products whilst working with and encouraging young designers. The great success of the Idée design ambition is clear to see in designers such as Marc Newson, Matthew Hilton, Karim Rashid and Philippe Starck. Each of these designers was involved with Kurosaki in some way and are now established in the design world.

The Idée Workshop accommodates working space for specific technicians and specialist craftspeople whose work focuses on developing prototypes and architectural details for buildings. This forward-thinking approach definitively sets this retail venue apart from other retail outlets that work within more conventional boundaries, merely selling products through their shops.

British-trained architects Astrid Klein and Mark Dytham designed the Workshop building and associated offices. The building is constructed around a small kiosk, a space that originally housed the offices of a family petrol station. The Idée administration is now accommodated in this former kiosk. There are showrooms on the ground and first floors and a design studio on the second floor.

A fully glazed elevation at ground floor level allows dramatic and uninterrupted views into the store from the street. On the upper floors a large, curved polycarbonate screen protects the interior views from the chaos of a large road junction outside. In the daytime the screen allows natural light to filter into the upper parts of the building whilst at night the same screen is brought alive by the use of animated and projected images, creating images and shadows, both still and moving.

The interior structure of the Idée Workshop has been left fully exposed to reinforce the sense of it as a working area. The construction elements are visible and this acts as an industrial backdrop to the avant-garde furniture on display. Floors are left as concrete screed with resin- poured finishes that are polished to a high sheen. Coloured films have been stuck to the windows creating a two-way colour tone effect during the day and at night artificial light is projected forward onto the screen, continuing the effect. There is also a dramatic counterplay of forms from the sinuous lines of 1950s'-inspired furniture and the originality of the grid-based building that holds the structure together. Klein and Dytham are already working on their next Idée project: a five-storey showroom, café and micro-brewery in central Tokyo.

Below **This restaurant in the Pacific building is called Rojak. The dark wood furniture and fittings in the restaurant create a heavy and rich interior.**

Hema
Amsterdam, Holland

Opposite **This multi-level area is crowned by a huge skylight over the void. The steel window sections and roof structure add an industrial feel to the environment. Large colour illustrations are used to catch the eye and break up the wall surfaces.**

Below **Bright red walls are used to clearly define the cash desks whilst large photographs and illustrations clearly denote the products for sale.**

"Hema is a modern shop at the top of our customers' list. A healthy enterprise, where you enjoy working." This simple sentence taken from Hema's company brochure is what this company is all about. Hema is a chain of shops that combines convenience and accessibility with a dominant market position. The target market is women between 25 and 45 years of age with an average family income, who have a preference for modern styling. The stores are designed to appeal to the average consumer.

Hema is a 'price advantage chain' dedicated to offering added value. They have developed a handwriting which is organized, stylish, economical and eye catching. The company has established consumer awareness about its products and stores by informative communications in the media, the store and on packaging. It continually operates surprising visual promotions which keep the brand in the public eye and encourage return visits. Hema provides an assortment of everyday homewares, clothing and foods with modern contemporary styling at competitive prices.

The stores are purposely designed to create an upmarket feel. They are sensibly laid out, clearly identifiable and respectful of the architectural heritage of the building. The building is simply articulated, without fuss or over-detailing. There is a sensible thought process throughout these stores which, by defining the building, is giving clarity to the shopping experience. The shops are clean, functional and have an enjoyable atmosphere.

Visibility is important; the glazed atrium sited at the top of the Amsterdam store offers a fresh open environment. Columns act as defined elements within the store space. They are used to connect spaces – visibly – through the building to help identify the circulation routes. They are also used to act as graphic signposts to departments as well as to delineate specific areas.

Although large, this store has an approachable and accessible feel to it. The relaxed nature and social meeting points are key to the added-value destination of this area. Circulation routes are made easy through good communication and site lines. Hema supports its shop presentation with clear signposting so that customers can easily find their way around. Special offer displays and promotion sites increase the number of impulse purchases.

Architecture is also influential in the shopfitting elements, which are clearly developments of the same themes. Walls are inserted at certain points, which act as both commercial mid-floor perimeter units but also as graphic billboards or poster sites onto which colourful graphics and information are added. The graphics are controlled efficiently and effectively throughout the store. There is a hierarchy of information on the signage and a presentation style which is manifestly catalogue in essence

PROFILE

CLIENT: Hema

FUNCTION: Supercentre

CONSULTANTS: Merx and Girod

BETAALBARE
KWALITEIT

ECHT
HEMA

yet less contrived. Images and products work side by side, to be seen from a distance and yet also relate to each individual locality.

It is clear throughout the store that the Hema selection and assortment of products are largely exclusive to this brand. The brand values are consistently presented through quality, price and choice. Every item on sale has been carefully selected for the stores. The products, though not leading edge, are continuously influenced by current trends and are provided in volume to fulfil demand. Customers are presented with pieces at an affordable quality; whilst their assortment is brand led it does not offer a wide choice of product group. They sell only products that are frequently bought by consumers, and these tend to largely be sold in self-service environments where there is an obvious price advantage.

Hema also has an environmentally aware policy. The goods and packaging selected have 'a low visual impact pollution tax' and they use, wherever possible, recycled raw materials. The stores are set up to be customer friendly, but without the expensive use of sales staff. The stores are also designed to be easy to shop; and they focus on the desire of the customer to search, find and buy quickly. Hema also has a guaranteed money-back scheme, so that if the customer is not satisfied, the goods are replaced or refunded without discussion.

Space is important and Hema gives more space to the layout of the store so that customers feel more relaxed and less confined. Hema has a customer care policy, which focuses on being approachable to their customers beyond the norm. Attention and space is given to the service areas where customers spend time, which are designed to be stimulating, comfortable and efficient. Products and items

*Left **This fixturing is modular and cost effective. The product looks good because it is well presented and in some detail. High level pictures are used to signify to customers the various products available. This is particularly important in a self-service store such as this.***

that are heavily service assisted are discouraged. If service is required, it is provided effectively so that the continuation of the shopping experience is seamless.

Staff at the service till are highly trained. They are probably the only point of contact that a customer will have within the store, and are therefore skilled communicators.

There is a rigorous attention to detail and this is consistent and reassuring in a national chain. Yet the use of illustration, both on packaging and on large wall murals, is both amusing and idiosyncratic, suggesting a character that has warmth and understanding which this store image has successfully managed to harness without being self-conscious or precious.

The Hema concept is a combination of social values, good communication and clarity. The environment is clean and stylish. Colour graphics and illustration play a large part in its brand identity. The stores are well designed and exploit the architectural envelope in an intelligent way. Put all these components together, and you have an image that communicates at all levels to all people.

Above **Colour plays an important role in the Hema café where the terracotta coloured tabletops contrast with the blue walls. The columns are tiled with text messages running across the top whilst the lantern fittings and clock add a conventional flavour to the space.**

Left **Some foods and wines are also available to buy in-store. A change of materials and ceiling heights makes this space feel more domestic in scale.**

Selfridges
London, England

Opposite **Escalators were manufactured off site and lowered by crane into place. This central escalator was the last to be fitted. The bronze sculptural features are by Eduardo Paolozzi and the existing decorative columns have been restored to their original condition.**

Below **This circular wall with inset crystal glass rods defines the champagne bar. This is one of many leisure breaks around the store.**

Selfridges in London's Oxford Street has been the vanguard of a revival in department-store retailing within Europe. Under the leadership of Vittorio Radice, the store has positioned itself as a destination for brands, turning its back on the trend for own label and rekindling the original reputation of the store as 'the first with the new'. During 1999, Selfridges opened a second store at the new Trafford Centre mall in Manchester. This store reaffirms Selfridges' positioning as a design leader within UK retail.

Selfridges was founded in 1909 and is one of the most prestigious department stores in London. It has traditionally had a strong appeal to tourists but it was the effect on sales of an ageing customer base, as well as its maze-like interior which highlighted the need for a major refit. The battleground upon which Selfridges competes with other large London department stores such as Harrods, Harvey Nichols, Dickens and Jones and Liberty, is branded and designer clothing. Womenswear accounts for the largest floorspace in the store.

The London store's design strategy, its 'Masterplan', has been in place since 1993, when circulation was identified as a major problem. In 1994, a number of consultants were brought in to help reposition the store. Clean circulation patterns and clear vistas were critical to the Masterplan. Subsequent renovation included major structural work such as the introduction of central escalators, creation of central walkways on each floor and improvements to escalators on the eastern and western sides.

Service and leisure were also an important factor in the Masterplan, resulting in the incorporation of 13 restaurants and cafés within the store, each venue carefully designed to reflect the style of the departments in which they are placed. Restaurants include the popular Conran restaurant on the roof.

For Radice, a consistent environment is essential in order to convince customers to shop in the store. He says: 'The biggest thing is not so much about saying, "let me go after a customer;" it's about making sure that you do it with integrity and with your own style. The people with money will appreciate it and the people without money will appreciate it. We should sell a £10,000 dress the same way we sell a £5 T-shirt, with the same energy, the same smile, the same customer service, packaging, flooring, lighting. We need to be very accessible and easy, with a casuality, not like some department stores where you have to make an effort going in.

'The mistake which is sometimes made is to assume there should be a major difference in environment for classic and contemporary ranges. It doesn't mean because it's classic, there has to be carpet and dimmer lighting and for contemporary, a stone floor.'

PROFILE

CLIENT: Vittorio Radice

FUNCTION: Department store

CONSULTANTS: Six design teams (see main text)

LALIQUE

Lalique was a designer who in his
professional career spanned both Florid,
Art Nouveau & Rectilinear Art Deco
styles. He began his illustrious career
as a highly successful jeweller. When
René Lalique died in 1945, his son Marc
began designing for the company.
Today his grand-daughter, Marie-Claude,
continues.

SWAROVSKI

Above **The basement areas are gradually being refurbished on a phased programme. China, glass, giftware and tabletop were completed in 1998 and now incorporate illuminated cabinets and display plinths.**

Radice's vision for Selfridges is a store which is the destination for brands. He is not interested in the own brand route being taken by many other retailers. 'I would like the biggest offer of brands you can find in Britain or Europe. The ultimate aim I have is you buy any magazine and you open a page and see a brand and you think, Selfridges. This is what Selfridges is famous for. It was always the first place a new item was shown. I don't understand the need to create a private label when people are doing it much better than us. The world is dominated by brands. I want to be the first store where Armani decides to launch their first fragrance.'

The scale of the work undertaken by Selfridges has meant that various design companies have been involved in the project. Selfridges' in-store architect, Martin Illingworth, says six design companies have contributed to

the refurbishment, with Din Associates, Christian Liaigre and Vincent Van Duysen being of particular importance to the image of the store.

Each design company was selected for its particular strengths, to suit the product. Illingworth stresses the high quality of materials used, from dark stained oak and white carrera marble to fibrous plaster and stainless steel. 'There has also been innovation in the use of some materials,' says Illingworth, 'such as concrete flooring and resin being used in The Loft on the second floor.' Lighting throughout the store has been largely the responsibility of Isometrics.

Underlying the design philosophy, however, has been the desire to preserve the store's architectural heritage, while making no compromises on contemporary design practice: openness and light being at the core, as well as ensuring comfortable, well-fed customers.

In the basement, the sound and vision department uses different finishes, depending on product section, with carpeting, white ceilings and light wood fixtures for browsing, and black ceilings and timber flooring for computer and audio visual sections.

The china, glass and luggage departments, designed by Din Associates, were completed in 1998. The luggage department reflects London's two airports, Heathrow and Gatwick, and the different customer profile of each. Glass screening is designed to allow the beauty of each product to be displayed to the full, while communicating that the department is a destination for quality brands. Table-top china and glass is a Selfridges' speciality. The department has been totally redesigned using dark stained oak and glass with polished stainless-steel trims. Large timber-framed units are used to divide the department and act as open display dividers for the merchandise.

The ground floor was the crux of Selfridges' difficulties. Developed at various stages from 1906, through the 1920s to the 1930s, and in 1957 and 1971, the building had progressed piecemeal. Here, Selfridges' architectural history is particularly noticeable, and required sensitivity. A lower ceiling was introduced, the interior columns retained and cornicing was reproduced.

The cosmetics hall refurbishment was completed in 1998. It was designed by Christian Liaigre whom Selfridges chose because of his feel for contemporary classical interiors. The key was the emphasis on light, using glass and marble flooring. Clarity of line was maintained by ensuring concessions did not reach above a certain height. The new shopfit has increased turnover in cosmetics by 20 per cent in the first year.

Men's accessories, also designed by Christian Liaigre, continues the synthesis of contemporary and classical, with the emphasis on proportion and scale, while brands such as Hackett and Thomas Pink contribute highly traditional concessions in keeping with their products.

Spirit (formerly Miss Selfridge), designed by the John Herbert Partnership, is a young fashion department in the store's rear extension which was refurbished in 1996.

Ceilings were made higher, services exposed and gantries installed to support light fittings and projectors. Lighting inset in the stone flooring divides concessions.

On the first floor in men's fashion, refurbished in 1996, there is a clear progression from formal tailoring, through Polo Ralph Lauren to high design areas, such as Armani and street fashion. In some sections, traditional features of the store such as ceilings, columns and timber block flooring have been restored. Windows, too, have been opened. Selfridges is encouraging more concessions because of the popularity of brands.

Women's contemporary fashion, on the second floor, was designed by Vincent Van Duysen. Like men's fashion, it progresses from the contemporary to more formal wear

Below **The cosmetics hall was completed in 1999 and was designed by Christian Liaigre of France. Good lighting is particularly important in a cosmetics environment and these striking chandeliers were made in Italy in Murano glass.**

from east to west. Here, too, brands are being encouraged into the store. Concessions are allowed to bring in their own designs within constraints set by Selfridges. Illingworth says Van Duysen was selected for his distinct minimalist style which allows the clothes to speak for themselves. Designer brands such as Moschino and Miu Miu are given valuable freedom to express their high quality and recognizable image within the concessions.

Radice believes the most innovative move for Selfridges has been opening up contemporary menswear and womenswear. He comments: 'We didn't sell a pair of jeans for men four years ago. In general what we have done is made sure that Selfridges was not just the classic store. There was much more to offer.'

A third of the fourth floor is branded, with the rest furnished with generic fixturing. The bed and bath department has strong visual impact using the wall, floor and

product, and works by simplifying the buying process for the customer. Materials used here include glass mosaic, marble and polycarbonate laminates.

Selfridges' anchor store at the Trafford Centre in Manchester was the first satellite outside London and was promoted as focusing on design. It faced a challenge in the context of the Trafford Centre, with its Las Vegas-style references to much of the world's most important classical architecture spanning Roman, Egyptian, Moroccan, Chinese, New Orleans' French, as well as tropical rainforest. In addition, as Selfridges first store outside London, it was a flag bearer for the company's expansion plans.

The store consists of 18,600 square metres (200,000 square feet) and is at the centre of the mall. Its frontage within the mall is of Rosso Alicante marble, while the store's street exterior has a more manorial facade, with a fountain, lawn and shrubs.

Below **The luggage area is based on functional heavy-duty luggage and quality designer brands. Walls are maximised floor to ceiling with items of colourful products to create some life.**

The store was designed on two levels, focusing on a sense of space created by high ceilings, as well as emphasizing lightness through the use of materials such as natural stone and marble for flooring.

At the centre of the store is a Moleanos limestone staircase. The curved structure is reminiscent of the grand-style department store, Galeries Lafayette.

For younger shoppers, Selfridges' Spirit, so successful in London, is a unisex environment featuring industrial finishes and theatrical lighting rigs.

In the food hall, counters were designed by Italian craftsmen using glass, steel and timber, while flooring is in Portuguese grey stone. The hall has more than 60 metres (200 feet) of glass-covered display cabinets.

The perimeter walls of the cosmetics hall are curved and the circular, radial design of the hall is reflected in the cosmetics counters. The floor is in marble, with glass and marble used on the counter finishes. Light is key to the use of this space. The cosmetics hall, pivotal to the store, creates an antechamber to the Trafford Centre.

Above **The contemporary ladies' fashion floor features white carrera marble units and counters with white resin floors. Ceilings are exposed over walkways to give maximum height and are then lowered over product areas.**

Bluewater Park
Kent, England

*Opposite **A view into one of the glass turrets that form part of the glazed atrium at Bluewater. Colourful cones are suspended down from the centre of the turret to create interest and excitement.***

*Below **An exterior shot of one of the many restaurant terraces at night. This view highlights the illuminated fountains, lakes and cliffs which form the natural quarry into which the mall was built.***

Bluewater Park is a new generation shopping mall. A reclamation project using a 100-hectare (247-acre) former chalk quarry in Kent, it is the synthesis of the vision of a world-famous architect, Eric Kuhne, and of the desire of the developers, Lend Lease Corporation, to design a shopping centre that provides consumers with the highest-quality environment.

The structure of Bluewater Park trades on the power of three – with its triangular shape forming the basis for a village-style segmentation of retail and leisure areas. It ambitiously attempts to move beyond banal consumer categories by using art, literature and design to create the divisions. A visual experience on a grand scale, Bluewater is the most extensive park to be created in Kent during the twentieth century and it contains the largest greenhouse built in the UK over the same period. The landscape was designed and adapted to fit in with the ambitious project, and building the mall in a former quarry involved developing 20 hectares (50 acres) of parkland, along with the planting of millions of trees including 300,000 indigenous woodland species. Reed beds were incorporated into the six lakes, re-created beneath towering chalk cliffs, to aid water filtration. A nature trail was built, along with access for fishing and boating and 4 km (2½ miles) of cycle paths. A sensory garden was also created for children with disabilities. The scheme represents a major investment in public art with 50 original artworks commissioned for the centre, which include The Aviary, Fire Dragon, Water Clock, Whirlpool, Rose Trellis, Critter Clock and Standing Stones.

Architect Eric Kuhne has quoted influences as diverse as Blenheim Palace's water garden, Kew Gardens, artist John Singer Sargent and the English tradition of landscape architecture practised by Humphrey Renton and Capability Brown. From folksong to Shakespearean poetry, Kent wildlife to the River Thames and 'new age' imagery of sun, moon and stars, Bluewater attempts to re-create a community's history and the sense of belonging which is so often missing from commercial developments. For example, the rotating aluminium vents on the roofs that allow fresh air into the centre were based on the design of Kent oast houses. All this is evidence of the commitment to making an architectural statement, which, unusually, offers high-street consumers much more to look at than simply what is on display in the shop windows. Furthermore, as the trees at Bluewater mature, the quarry will be transformed into a forest, which will highlight the roof of the centre, the water and the avenues leading to its three anchor stores, thus giving the visitor an even greater sense of discovery.

Bluewater was conceived as a shopping centre for consumers who do not use shopping centres. In other words, it aims to attract those shoppers who are used to the

PROFILE

CLIENT: Lend Lease Corporation

FUNCTION: Shopping mall

CONSULTANTS: Eric Kuhne and Associates

exclusive and more visually stimulating environments of mid-market designer retail, small specialist shops in architecturally quirky locations and, perhaps most significantly, to shopping in town centres which have developed organically. Bluewater has attempted to emulate this organic style chiefly through the quality of its materials and design, while simultaneously promoting itself as an 'experience' that can compete with thousands of other potential days out. Up to 70 per cent of sales are expected to be delivered by three target consumer groups: young fashionables, county classics and young executives of whom, research revealed, 60 per cent hate shopping centres. Bluewater has estimated that it will receive 30 million visitors each year with a projected annual spend of £665 million.

Innovative store design was another criterion for retailers within the centre. A special design development team was set up to manage and promote the cause of good design throughout. Their role was to brief retailers and designers about what was expected from them in terms of quality and innovation. Retailers were requested not to repeat existing formats within this development, and were told that fundamentally they needed to expand their formats or create different and exciting new concepts. From Lend Lease's point of view, having invested heavily in a new architectural concept, the last thing they wanted were tired formats which customers could find on any high street.

A detailed design guidebook and visual references were given to each retailer to encourage new directions in store design and layout. This refers to shopfront layout and graphics which were sketched in detail. Many examples were given on the type of design innovation the design team were looking for: shopfronts that moved, were angled or curved – anything but the conventional. The retailers and

*Left **A view through one of the malls showing the vaulted ceiling and white sails suspended from the roof. An intricate pattern of light and shadow is created as these sails move and cast shadows throughout the day as the sunlight moves across the building.***

their designers were given all the assistance and co-operation they could to enable them to break normal conventions and restrictions that mall operators normally enforce. Of the 320 retailers in Bluewater, 200 used completely individual store designs. Once the store designs were complete, they were presented to the design management team for comment. Most were passed and some were encouraged to try harder. Some of the most notable concepts on view are Boots' new store which is a radical departure for them, introducing beauty and sensuality into their format. Jane Norman's cool trendy chocolate brown and burgundy scheme is reminiscent of 1970s' boutique style; Calvin Klein Jeans has an interesting use of graphics and pivoting screens. The Ted Baker store was an extravagant departure from the norm, a shop concept within a shop, where an inner skin was designed so that it stood away from the mall structure and gave the sense that it was raised with a moat around it. This was enhanced by a drawbridge door which is raised and lowered each day.

High fashion and shopping for men were of particular importance to the centre which has attracted 72 retailers with stores in Covent Garden, London, and 58 retailers with outlets in the King's Road, London.

Bluewater is divided into three distinct areas. First, the East Mall or Rose Gallery with a landscape theme is designed for family and high-street shopping. Secondly the West Mall or Guildhall with a townscape theme is designed for lifestyle, upmarket and aspirational shopping. Finally the South Mall or Thames Walk is designed for media and entertainment, and has a waterscape theme.

The East Mall is characterized by glass façades and friezes of rose trellisses and leaves that are mirrored in the floor and give a sense of open space. Its leisure area is the

Right A high level view looking down into the food court. The natural environment is the predominant influence in this design. A multi-level facility with sinuous forms bordered by rows of plants, it creates something reminiscent of water or the meandering line of a river bank.

Wintergarden, a huge lakeside glasshouse with eighteen-metre (sixty-feet) high trees, a grotto for children, seating zones and water features. It has 1,000 square metres (11,000 square feet) of glazing, and outside there is an adventure playground with rowing boats for hire.

The West Mall is designed to admit the least amount of daylight of all the three malls, and it features more formal shopfronts, timber detail and sophisticated seating. There are 106 impressive sculptural reliefs representing each of the traditional commercial guilds – this is the largest guildhall tableau in the world. The Village, representing its leisure area, is reached past a row of shops based on the style of London's Burlington Arcade. A central square features cafés, a caviar bar, restaurant and patisseries, while outside there is a rose garden, bandstand and performance amphitheatre.

The South Mall features a glazed ceiling that allows the entrance of natural light and uses sail-like canopies for shading. This mall is curved and the design themes revolve around the River Thames, which is represented on the floor. From Thames Walk, shoppers can take time out in the Water Circus, an entertainment centre complete with fountains and cascades, American-style diners, sports bar, climbing wall and, in winter, a skating rink. This area has

Above **The conical dome above the Star Court borrows from a stage set for Mozart's Magic Flute with a radiating geometry of fibre optic stars cascading from its peak. The constellations of the zodiac are sculpted out of stainless steel wire fabric. Above an obelisk in the centre of the room is an armillary sphere representing the geometric volumes of Bluewater (the sphere, tetrahedron and cube) surrounded by a ceremonial staircase.**

Right **This shows a detail from the dome of the Sun Court.**

been designed for day and night use, with a Virgin Megastore, cinema, terraced cafe, and a circular performance and exhibition space. It is decorated with theatrical drapes, illuminated nymphs and internally lit columns.

The three anchor stores, John Lewis, Marks and Spencer and House of Fraser, which are situated at each apex of the triangle, have astronomically themed 'courts' with seating and domed ceilings. John Lewis, whose court is the sun, features natural stone and precast panels in keeping with the chalk of the quarry. The sun's rays decorate the domed ceiling and in the floor is a world clock showing time zones and directions to major cities, while a day in the life of a Kent family is depicted in a frieze. Marks and Spencer, whose court is the moon, is characterized by its glass and green copper façade with a glass atrium allowing daylight to flood in. A frieze shows the tides, and glass balustrading is carefully etched with phases of the moon. The ceiling is asymmetrical and in the stone floor is a 10-metre (33-foot) high 'thamesometer' – a sculpture measuring the level of the River Thames. The actual cycle of the moon is shown by an orbiting sculpture in the frieze. House of Fraser, whose court is the star, is a distinct rotunda also built of masonry and precast concrete in keeping with the cliffs behind it where hundreds of optical-fibre lights are placed in the dome and floor. The frieze shows stainless-steel mesh sculptures of the signs of the zodiac and constellations are etched in the balustrade. A sculpture of a family group at the centre of the court holds an armillary sphere.

Bluewater is probably the best shopping mall of its type to be found in the UK and will act as a blueprint for retail design throughout the twenty-first century.

Right **Underneath the tipped cone of the Moon Court, radiating aluminium bands of 'moonlight' emanate from the conical oculus. A lunar sphere with the craters of the moon in fixed light revolves around the base of the cone every lunar cycle. In the centre of the court is a column that has a rotating globe of the earth, turning into the sun every 24 hours.**

the future
of retail

Writers or film-makers who anticipate the future present us with a world which is dehumanised and manipulated by technology. Our vision of how we will be living is therefore tinged with Luddite anxiety. The latter half of the 20th century has undoubtedly been dominated by the rapid development of technology. Generations of people have memories of the words spoken on the first moon walk and the television images accompanying them. Others have never known a time without PCs, mobile phones, fibre optics, colour television, the Internet, CDs, microwaves.

Everyone can expect major technological changes to occur throughout their lifetime which will affect how they work or socialise. This is why I believe we should revise how we see the future, because it is happening now. Certainly there are some projects currently being researched which may not have an impact for decades. But at the same time there are trends which will influence the emergence of a killer format (technology that becomes the standard) much sooner and can provide retailers with indicators of change. Retailers need only look around at the innovators, whether they are using the Internet or using their space to make aesthetic statements, to see the future. They need only talk to children or young employees to witness shifts in education, expectation and attitudes. The music world shows us that the future starts with the grassroots, somewhere in sweaty clubs or in wired-up bedrooms. To understand the future, retailers need to be in tune with the creative thinkers of the present and harness images which become old almost as quickly as they are seen.

Zero zero

I would not suggest that retailers face an easy task in understanding the future. There are enormous contradictions in contemporary trends. While multinational companies develop genetically modified foods the public is demanding organic produce. Against high technology stands the trend for simplicity as embodied by retailers such as Egg.

Retailers, however, have to express these trends and find ways of using technology to benefit the public while still providing experiences which they enjoy. Shopping has become inextricably linked with socializing with the increasingly blurred lines between retail and leisure. In simplistic terms, it has also polarized into the purchase of commodities and the purchase of items which give us pleasure.

There has been much commentary about retail and leisure, but few examples of truly radical attempts to satisfy a growing public desire for an all-round experience which is manifested in the success of occasions such as the annual UK Clothes Show live event, where the public has

the chance to see fashion shows, have makeovers and buy clothes under one roof. During the 1980s, I worked with Next to develop a range of retail formats which combined retail with experiences associated with the products on offer. One of them, a holiday format, for example, brought together a travel agency with the opportunity to go swimming, play golf and buy sportswear. It may be that the retailer, in order to accommodate new trends, needs to stretch its brand (see page 210). This is happening, not always successfully, but is another indicator of how businesses can respond. By contrast, other businesses may choose to consolidate by focusing more clearly on expertise and finding ways of becoming a centre of excellence.

The case study of Let's Eat shows how this Australian retailer is satisfying another important trend for customization. They allow consumers to decide the level of convenience they want: whether food is totally or partially cooked, whether the consumer is merely buying top-quality ingredients with a menu provided, and whether it is eaten in or taken away. It is recognized that busy couples with differing tastes want to be able to eat together but not necessarily the same food: one may want Indonesian, the other French cuisine. Let's Eat can provide them with that.

There are parallels in fashion. Consumers expect basic commodity clothing to be high quality wherever they may buy it. Other items need to be different and special. For retailers, the key is identifying what that special element is: is it luxury or difference, or a combination of both? What these trends indicate are that consumers are more selective while still wanting value for money.

Furthermore, while this trend may be starting at the top end of the market, it will inevitably move further down the scale, until, like strawberries at Christmas, it is expected by the general public.

However, these and undoubtedly many other trends will not be easy for retailers to translate into a manageable strategy. Large-scale retailing, incorporating new technology and improved customer information, has largely become an exercise in number crunching or software development. For these corporations, the view of the future may well contain

Previous page **Issey Miyake Making Things, exhibition at Fondation Cartier, Paris**

Below **The Twyfords industrial plant laboratory in England is responsible for cloning saplings.**

the scenario in which a supermarket retailer would know when a customer needs a specific item and could pre-empt sales or replenish items direct to that customer's kitchen. "Intelligent" refrigerators and waste bins designed to read discarded items could also be programmed to make repeat orders without the need to visit the supermarket.

It is the retailer's ability to humanize large scale and technologically sophisticated operations which is now more critical than ever. The challenge for the retailer of today and tomorrow lies in ensuring that the massive corporation behind the shopfront or website does not inadvertently alienate customers by losing sight of their requirements. The decline in sales experienced by world-famous brand, Marks and Spencer in 1998 proved no retailer, however large, can be complacent. Edward Whitefield, managing director of the international retailing consultancy Management Horizons Europe, believes that the improvements made in tracking individual customers and store sales, and in identifying bestsellers on a regular (even on an hourly) basis are bringing the retailer closer to the position of a market trader – giving him local, isolated, individual knowledge of consumer demands. Such technological developments benefit both retailer and designer: the retailer may need to provide less merchandise than in the past by being more customer-and/or product-specific, thus being able to leave more space for the designer to create an experience, or simply to reduce the size of his operation.

The role of the designer, therefore, becomes far greater than that of simply removing potential barriers. Furthermore, says Whitefield, customer experience – both environmentally and in terms of service in its broadest sense – is becoming critical. In his view, the customer's definition of what constitutes retail has changed radically to incorporate health and financial services, as well as holidays and travel in general. In addition, the new geography of retailing incorporates all the existing and new channels available to modern retailers, from mail-order catalogues to direct telephone, as well as the Internet, electronic retailing and the future of on-line digital services to the home and office environments.

Top **The Asda Internet website offers information on products, stores and job vacancies. This feature is a computer promotion for local schools called 'The Checkout Challenge'.**

Above **The website of American shoe designer Kenneth Cole is one which extends the visual ethos of the brand.**

The designer as strategist

The impact of these changes on retail design contributes significantly to the shift in approach required by designers. Retail design made an enormous leap when it branched away from shopfitting and became a discipline in its own right. Although this seemed revolutionary, it was in fact a gradual process over a number of years from the mid-1970s. Retailing in the 1990s demanded of designers another leap into strategic brand management. The integration of design with strategy is particularly important when considering brand extension (see page 211), as well as for businesses attempting to sell to consumers through different channels.

In order to meet a retailer's demands, the designer must be informed and aware of how social and technological change can be synthesized into three-dimensional reality. A good example is the Virgin Megastore, which opened stores in London, Paris, New York and Berlin. Based on the successful London prototype, they became the benchmark for the company's international programme of development. Another successful example is the Gap clothing company. Founder Don Fisher opened the first Gap store in 1969, on Ocean Avenue in San Francisco. The store, which sold jeans and records, was named after a cultural phenomenon that was the talk of the times: the

generation gap. In 1991 Gap again focused on that era with its campaign: 'For every generation there's a Gap.' Today the company has stores all over the world.

The development of international brands, of communications media, and the increasing ownership of mobile phones all point to better-informed and much more mobile consumers. Internationally, communities and businesses have greater access than ever to highly localized and global information, while new markets – such as China and Russia – continue to emerge as a result of political and social changes. The growth in the Asian market is expected to be larger than the American market by the year 2010.

The management of knowledge is one of the major differentiators between a designer working now and one who was in business 20 years ago. Large-scale investment in technology during the 1990s enabled design companies to speed up their working methods and be better attuned to the ways in which retailers present them with information. Within minutes they can all be discussing the same image or text between client, designer, printer or builder, taking advantage of local skills and costs internationally. More significantly, however, retailers are now using designers more than ever to establish the focus for a new concept or brand development. Designers have thus become a creative

Below left **In the late 1970s Conran Design Associates were involved in the launch of the womenswear chain Next which was the beginning of a British retail phenomenon.**

Below right **By the early 1980s Next had developed menswear and began to create combined stores.**

Opposite **The Department X stores rode the tide of lifestyle branding in the late 1980s. This store designed by Din Associates launched the brand on Oxford Street, London in 1988.**

resource in a more strategic sense. Creating a new identity for a retailer becomes a yardstick with which to measure the overall management and performance of the business. By acting as the eyes and ears of the retailer, the designer is closer to the consumer. They must also speak the same language as the retailer, have an equal grasp of information tabout target consumers, business and social trends and combine this with specific design objectives to give the information visual meaning. A designer might also give the client insight into new markets, by suggesting alternative routes for exploration. In this way the designer is not only fulfilling his brief, but is developing its potential.

Today's design company is more likely to buy in the skills of other specialists, such as market analysts, packaging technologists and cost consultants, requiring the dextrous co-ordination of new working partnerships. The senior designer must develop new abilities, enabling him or her to manage all these different elements as well as utilizing the core skills of the company. Design companies are more likely now to be expected to forecast or speculate knowledgably upon future trends. As a result, the companies are more likely to specialize in retail, and to employ strategists.

In the 70s retail shopfitting was about modular, flexible systems which were characterless and essentially about survival; while in the 80s retail design was dominated by career and professional lifestyles. This resulted in slick, masculine design styles such as matt black or high-tech. In the 90s the power of brands brought design into a new era of awareness: distance and time seemed unimportant to the ambitions of the global players. In the new millennium, it is likely that brand diversification, consumer mobility and new digital media will lead to a new retail language to appeal across generations and continents.

Predicting the future

Trends agencies, such as those mentioned later (see page 209), are also likely to become more important to retailers and will become more focused on particular groups of consumers. The value of good agencies is that they are dedicated to understanding their target group. They operate more instinctively than focus groups but, nevertheless, act as a link between advertising agencies or brands, communicating imagery, values, attitudes and tastes. It is well understood that any underground movement will eventually become assimilated into mainstream culture. Combat trousers, for example, made their way out of punk's slipstream in the 70s to Gucci in the 90s. Flares were worn in Manchester clubs in the 80s, prompting column inches of analysis on their revival. A decade later, four year olds were kitted out in them for the first time from high street retailers. But young people, in particular, are well-attuned to any attempt to trespass on their territory. They are sophisticated enough readers of the media and advertising to spot a gauche marketing ploy and those who are actively involved in a contemporary movement will demand authenticity.

Below **These huge tubular gauzes hang from the ceiling, highlighting the CDFA accessories exhibition designed by Michael Gabellini. The lighting is used here to impressively dramatic effect.**

It is this expectation of authenticity and precision which illustrates another dynamic shift in power – the demarcation between expert and consumer is no longer as clear as it used to be. Trends agencies are set up to understand this blurring of division and, as a result, their influence can only increase.

Creative reinvention

As UK advertising expert, author and television producer David Bernstein has eloquently pointed out, true creativity comes from showing well-understood truths in a new light. There is, after all, only a limited number of stories and plots available. Great writers and visual artists, musicians, comedians, mathematicians and engineers the world over understand this, and consequently some of the most compelling creative work comes from engaging everyday human concerns. Retail in its purest sense is one of the oldest activities in the world. Whether they were bartering with cattle or with the rarest Etruscan coins, our ancestors engaged in the same simple process as Wal-Mart, Harrods and Amazon.com have institutionalized today.

The fact that trading links opened up the world is as much a truism as that both history and the future are about reinvention. John Hegarty, founder of London-based advertising agency Bartle Bogle Hegarty, is well placed to understand this concept, and asserts another simple truth: that information goes in through the heart. Using the triangle of need – desire, function and form – he includes among products created in this way the revolutionary Dyson cleaner and Apple's IMac and the Volkswagen Beetle. 'If information goes in through the heart,' British industrialist Michael Frye also asserts, 'true creativity takes place there.' It is the task of the designer to overcome the blockages which act as barriers to understanding.

Increased consumer demands

As has already been discussed, retailers are learning that customers are much more complex than the marketeers would once have led us to believe. Just as a president or prime minister might display the 'ordinary' side of his or

her life by revealing an obsession with saxophone or guitar, the woman with three children trailing behind her in the supermarket is more than likely to have at least one other 'life'. Retailers have slowly begun to acknowledge that their mass of customers resists and resents simple categorization. Customers may be becoming more tribal – in the sense of defining themselves by interests and activities, rather than by social status – but a side-effect of mechanization and the disintegration of traditional family structures is that people will demand to be seen as individuals by institutions such as supermarkets, which have risen in importance by laying claim to the title of community leaders. The challenge for these institutions is to reflect the diversity of the individuals in the way they run their businesses and present their merchandise.

Vittorio Radice, chief executive of Selfridges department store in London, believes that one of the key drivers of the future will be a retailer's ability to satisfy this diversity by customizing the products on offer (for example, by including different colours and/or sizing). Radice's vision

is based on democracy: that is, to provide all customers with the same level of service, regardless of the amount of money they are spending. He can do this because of new technology and the options that it gives for individual service. As he explains: 'The confidence of the customer is getting bigger by the minute. Instead of accepting what is on sale, he or she will say: "Can you do the alteration? Can I have it in red or yellow?" The future is in these questions, which state: "I want to personalize my life." If you can accommodate them it makes the difference. Special orders are our life. That is what makes us different.'

Marian Salzman, head of brand futures group at advertising agency Young & Rubicam, believes consumers will increasingly demand purity in products and more peaceful, harmonious home environments which are flexible enough for a number of uses. Elderly people and children are becoming more important target markets for those selling products and services. Salzman says, 'The primary goal is not to predict the future, but to uncover images of possible, probable and preferable futures.'

Below left **This is a retrofit music studio situated in Idée. The whole studio has been individually designed to meet a client's specific requirement.**

Below right **A detail of the Challenge of Materials exhibition at the Thomas Heatherwick Studio Science Museum. This exhibition was designed by the studio to exemplify the nature of materials and their composition.**

Global media

Vittorio Radice is, however, also conscious of the new context in which retail now finds itself. The elements that influence consumers emanate from the media – including high-quality magazine images, massive billboard advertising, fast-moving television – and the driving force of each of these is novelty. As a result, a new cosmetics product, for instance, has a best-selling lifespan of around three weeks. As Radice emphasizes: 'You need to renew yourself much faster, because of the communication available to people. They get tired very quickly of the same product.' For Radice, the retailer of the future will be 'the one who starts tomorrow. The person who recognizes that this is a very fast-moving industry. The one who wants to progress and be a leader, not a follower.'

In addition, just as Radice argues that the most influential brand in recent years has been not a fashion business but a computer company, Microsoft ('because it changed the way we think'), Bernard Dooling of the London-based design company 20/20 believes that 'the real powerbrokers on this planet today are the media people'. The increasingly blurred boundaries between print, broadcast and new interactive media present yet another challenge to the retailers of the future. The global media corporations have recognized the need to communicate through a variety of channels and, by accumulating associated companies, have used a strategy where they secure a web of interests across the world in television, radio, book publishing, newspapers, magazines and digital services.

Dooling suggests that powerful new retailer brands – such as Manchester United football club in the UK – will emerge from this steady and strategic process. Equally, he argues: 'BSkyB is a massively powerful retailer of the future. They can talk to us 24 hours a day anywhere in the world. In eight or nine years there will be retailers we have never heard of in the past.'

Furthermore, these new retailers are likely to be formed from unexpected alliances forged between companies as different as Mercedes and Swatch, and between others who understand how electronic mobility will alter the way in which consumers behave. 'It will mean that designers and retailers will have to think about how we shop, not about how they sell', Dooling adds. There will need to be a more efficient understanding and resulting exploitation of all the different channels and methods used by consumers to buy goods, as well as of the times at which they shop. The environmental experience in stores, in which they sell a 'life proposition' or lifestyle, will be another clear element essential to future success.

Digital TV

There is ongoing debate about the sort of impact that the new media – such as the Internet and digital television – will have on retail. What has emerged, however, from countless consumer surveys undertaken in both Europe and the USA, is an increasing demand from consumers for out-of-hours shopping.

The increase in remote shopping will have a number of effects, including enlarging the total advertising spend and the stimulation of brand advertising to promote new products and services into the homes of potential customers. The direct contact made with consumers through the Internet and digital TV will provide retailers with detailed knowledge about individuals and households which will ultimately allow a large degree of interactivity during the shopping process. The variety of different channels available to consumers will also allow retailers to identify niche groups and to target them individually with specific products related to their family profile. Through sponsor-

ship of programmes, the use of icons, instant purchase options and so on, retailers will be able to design a specific marketing plan for each household, based on the various responses they receive.

A new interactive age

With even the most basic children's computer games able to exploit a high degree of interactivity and action, the challenge for retailers is to recognize the demands which new generations of technologically aware consumers will make on them. The use of in-store kiosks as alternatives to catalogues (offering a range of goods not stocked in the store), website design and assimilation of all channels of shopping into one coherent identity will present a greater challenge for designers in future: it will no longer be enough

*Above **A young man collects books from the extensive Amazon.com New York warehouse for dispatch of goods. They have built huge warehouses to store and distribute the books more efficiently, thus improving their service.***

to concentrate on store environment alone. Just as designers have stretched the identity of individual retailers to incorporate graphics, packaging and advertising, that identity will need to work even harder in a number of different forms. Physical demands, such as screen size and the differing uses of various computers (such as hand-held organizers, laptops, television screens and in-car entertainment), will need to be addressed, as the format and resolution will give differing impressions which may then distort the brand message.

The Internet shows that its users' attention and interest need to be captured right from the start, because it has educated consumers to expect speed of response. Similarly, the residual effect of other media is to expect high-quality images which satisfy the imagination. With greater competition than ever for customers, stores will need to ensure that they can satisfy demand for the right product (in size, colour and style), and exploit the potential supplied by technology (either through kiosks or through other forms of stock-holding/price information points). Speed and service are essential to success. In the UK, catalogue-sales company Argos has installed simple touch screens which itemize costs and give information on merchandise units held in stock. This enables the customer

to check the availability of a product or to select another item if their first choice is not in stock, therefore saving both time and disappointment.

Website design

Having a website is fast becoming a crucial requirement for any company of significance. However the design of a website requires an awareness and vocabulary that for many is an unfamiliar one (see page 52). This is because website design for a retailer has no similarity to building a three-dimensional shop. Since there is no physical space with which to deal, this facet of design is dictated purely by information and speed of use: it needs to be expandable, intelligent and provide an easy way for customers of making a purchase. Physical metaphors within the site, such as shopping baskets, should equally be treated with caution. An electronic shopping basket into which a customer 'places' his or her desired purchases may not be the easiest solution for a virtual customer, just as browsing at a website is an entirely different experience from being in a shop. Some products, such as CDs and books, indeed lend themselves more readily to web-based shopping: music because it is possible for the consumer to hear samples

Opposite **The Diesel website is one of the most successful branded retail sites. Rather than being a two-dimensional catalogue, this is a genuine extension to the brand. The graphics and imagery have been co-ordinated to create a strong fashion look that Diesel shoppers will instantly recognize and enjoy.**

Right **American-based CDNow, the on-line music store set up by Jason and Matt Olins in 1994. CDs lend themselves perfectly to web-based shopping because the consumer can hear sample tracks before deciding to purchase the CD.**

of tracks or groups before actually buying; books because of the enormous amount of supporting information (in the form of reviews and publicity) that surrounds them.

Successful Internet retailers such as the American bookseller Amazon.com – launched in July 1995 as an on-line store that was customer-friendly, easy to navigate and offered the broadest possible selection of titles – have learned the value of large-scale marketing, as well as the benefits offered by selling on the Internet. The latter include the opportunity of populating other sites with links by offering incentives to site owners in the form of a commission (Amazon.com pays a percentage of sales if its logo and link are displayed on other websites: an inventive technique which acts both as advertising and as a mechanism for increasing sales). The company's concept of service – offering browsers the opportunity to write their own book reviews and also giving authors a voice – is unrivalled in conventional bookselling. Customers can choose from 4.7 million books, CDs, audiobooks and computer games, and around eight million people in over 160 countries have used the site. The company has other sites in the UK and Germany. Equally, US-based CDNow, the online music store set up by 29-year-old twin brothers Jason and Matt Olins in 1994, offers an outstanding depth of information about titles, as well as providing the opportunity to search by the lyric of a song.

According to designer Malcolm Garrett of London design company AMX Studios, a good website will be concerned with fulfilment: that is, with showing only items which are in stock, only giving relevant information to ensure that shoppers can use the site quickly, providing various options on delivery, and making payment straightforward. Garrett believes that a major change in future will involve retailers' ability to show a video of their products in action; there must also be a recognition that different forms of personal computers (hand-held or large-screen) will be used for different types of purchases. At home, using the television screen, the consumer is likely to browse for large items or clothes, while a hand-held computer is more likely to be used for a grocery shopping list.

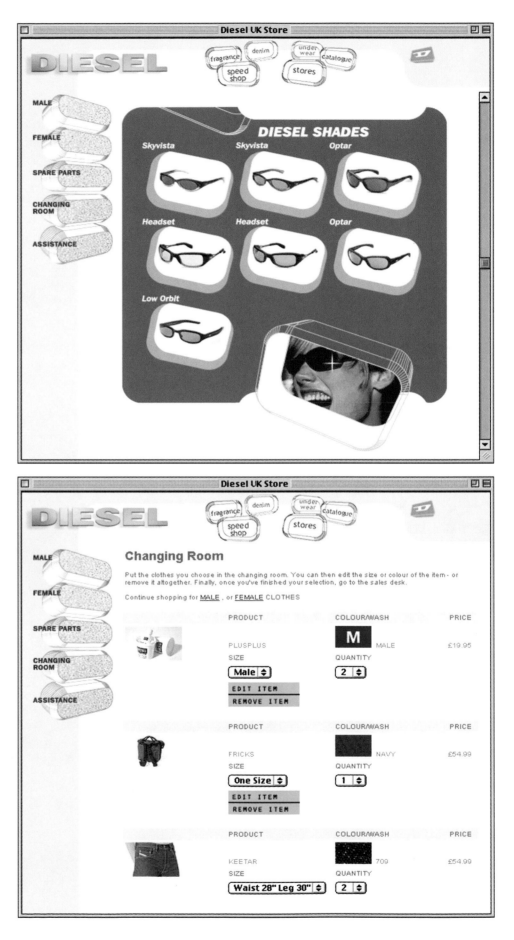

Risk-taking: the role of design

In considering the way forward for design, it is essential to refer back to the basic principles: namely, that good retail design helps to differentiate, focus and generate desire. Chapter 3 explored some of the practical methods used by designers to excite customers (see pages 78–115), and in the future this process will be even more essential to the retailer wanting to make himself heard above the raft of other interests competing for the public's time. However, the future of retail will be less risky because so much more information is available, even though innovation (as opposed to commercialization) necessarily involves an element of risk. 'Business needs designers like never before to make sense of the information they have', says British author, broadcaster and designer, Janice Kirkpatrick. She also poses the question: 'We are part of a renaissance, processing wisdom from all ages. Why are we surrounded by banality and pastiche?'.

Fitzpatrick argues that business should resist the temptation to 'watch the opposition or ask the public' because the knowledge gained will already be history. Instead, she suggests, it is time to 'innovate or deteriorate.

Risk is now less risky. There is no excuse. Innovation will become the norm – turning dreams into reality will become commonplace. Creativity has been democratized.' David Bernstein, too, has views on taking risks, and suggests that greater allowance should be made for mistakes: 'Let's increase the failure rate. There is a need for happy accidents, the freedom to experiment and connect.'

Echoing Vittorio Radice's argument that the retailer of tomorrow will be a leader, taking on all the risks associated with that position, American strategy guru Gary Hamel calls on business to give room to heretical thinkers, rather than to forecasters. Hamel, a Distinquished Research Fellow at Harvard University's Graduate School of Business Administration, and Visiting Professor of Strategic and International Management at the London Business School, comments: 'There has never been a better time to be a business revolutionary. It was never more dangerous to be complacent.' He quotes Microsoft's founder Bill Gates as saying that the company is always just two years away from failure – those two years constituting the dividing line between the leader and the laggard. Hamel divides businesses into two broad bands: the slow-moving bureaucrats, and the young, hungry start-ups. Both are of the past, he states: the former because they are struggling to catch up with someone else's future, the latter because very few companies survive beyond the vision of their founder. He argues for reinvention every one or two years but maintains that companies need to embed innovation into their organizations as deeply as they do quality and efficiency.

Even more radical is Hamel's assertion that innovation does not emanate from visionaries. The search for innovation, he says, will have to move so that it comes from every employee and, for that to happen, new passions will need to be created within organizations. The shift required here will be substantial, since he describes most companies as passion-free zones which have disconnected people emotionally from their work. Ideas will be the new trading currency. 'Draw on the hierarchy of imagination,' urges Hamel, 'because change never starts at the top.' His rallying call is for businesses to find activists within their ranks,

Below Vinopolis is a wine park themed around the consumption of wine from around the world. Built with cavernous railway arches in south London, it uses audio visual techniques to educate the public and offers specialist wine tasting, which is themed to each country and the various types of vine.

citing the example of California's Silicon Valley, which he describes as 'a refugee camp for industrial revolutionaries'. Among the top companies in Silicon Valley are Cisco Systems, Apple Computer and Intel.

Anticipating trends

Retailers know all too well that fashion is fickle and transitory and that, as Vittorio Radice points out, the speed of change is increasing. Designers, therefore, have a sensitive juggling act to manage and a brief to reconcile two forces that work at a different pace. While they need to be aware of current fashions, at a deeper level they must also be in tune with longer-term stylistic trends and be able to assimilate the vast numbers of predictions which will characterize retail in coming years. Take, for example, the forecasts of the American futurist, Faith Popcorn, author of The Popcorn Report (published in 1991) and Clicking: 16 Trends to Future Fit Your Life, Your Work and Your Business (1996). The latter reached both the *Business Week* bestseller list and the *New York Times*' list of business bestsellers. Popcorn predicted the demand for fresh foods and four-wheel-drive vehicles, and anticipated the explosive growth in home delivery, home businesses and home shopping (interactive TV), pointing out that trends are global, last ten to 12 years and can change dramatically as they evolve. She also introduced the concept of 'cocooning', which has developed from a search for warmth and homeliness to a sense of fear, represented by the public's wish to 'insulate' itself with car alarms and security systems.

The UK futurist, Lynne Franks, has underlined the need for businesses to recognize the importance of ethical trading and tangible community involvement. In February 1997, in the UK trade magazine *Retail Week*, she urged business people to 'invest back in the community. You are doing something that is of advantage to the business, but there is no reason why that cannot be used in a positive way for people you are trying to communicate with.'

Such views are also present in the thinking of the London-based Henley Centre for Forecasting. In addition, trends forecasters exist to provide a service for retailers to predict fashion colours, moods and also shorter-term social movements. These predictions may then in turn influence and determine the products that retailers choose to introduce into their stores. At a more basic level, however, second-guessing what the future may bring is much more likely to come down to an instinctive awareness, and to be critically informed by an openness to new ideas, as Gary Hamel suggests.

Trends forecasting, however essential for the future, still leaves risky decisions for a retailer on what could be merely a flash in a pan or what may become the sort of boom which will take some companies by surprise.

Above **Advances in fabric production techniques have meant that modern clothes can be works of art in themselves. These striking woven and printed clothes are by the visionary fashion designer Issey Miyake. These items were shown in Paris at the Fondation Cartier in an exhibition entitled Making Things.**

Brand effectiveness

It is clear that being ready for the future means returning to fundamentals and, in particular, understanding how brands are able to survive and reinvent themselves. The practice of brand-stretching gathered momentum during the 1990s, and has become an indispensable strategy for retailers who are looking to keep their customer base alive. Some of the best examples of brand stretch involve businesses which are entering retail afresh. Forward thinking can transform seemingly obsolete brands into cutting edge products.

Richard Zambuni of Value Engineers, a UK-based brand-strategy company, divides brands into three categories: hi-tech, service and fmcg (fast moving consumer goods). The hi-tech brand, says Zambuni, is identified with owning competence – one of the most successful examples being Cisco Systems, which has established itself as having 'brought you the Internet' through its Internet and telecom services. Microsoft has built itself on being the first company to own competences such as desktop productivity, web access, enterprise networking platforms and multi-media. Equally, Intel, while an ingredient brand in so far as it produces the components for personal computers, has achieved this 'owning competence' status for its position as the business which provides the computing power of the PC. Apple has also held on to its position as the business which provides a friendlier, more chic computer than its rivals – a reputation reinforced with the introduction in 1998 of the IMac.

A service brand recognizes that there are no limits to what it can provide. However, the success stories have been based on effective segmentation of a traditional market and on the launch of a new brand to serve those consumers identified as needing a new approach: in other words, understanding that modern imagery is necessary. A good example of this in the UK was the First Direct telephone-banking service, launched by the Midland Bank in 1989. This approach of launching the service under another name was done because it was clear that the bank's highly traditional branding would not stretch. The service offered a new image to suit a lifestyle, and First Direct became the fastest-growing bank in the UK. The Royal Bank of Scotland was equally innovative with its insurance division, Direct Line, offering a telephone insurance service; another success story is British Airway's budget-travel service, Go (launched in 1998), which recognized the demand for low-cost, no-frills flights. The Prudential's financial-services company, Egg (launched in 1998) was also, like the other financial-services companies, based on the need to separate a new brand from the image of its old, established parent; this was implemented to such an extent that many consumers may have no idea of the corporate links. In contrast to these service brands, for hi-tech brands such as Apple, Microsoft and Intel the solution was to keep their core branding stable.

For Zambuni, notable fmcg brands include Mars, for the way in which it extended the range of its familiar Mars Bar into ice cream and into different sizes, quadrupling the size of its brand in four years as a result.

Brand management

As brands move away from merely communicating information about products, their designers find themselves addressing a number of questions about how to progress in the future. At the core of all these questions lies the customer and his or her needs. In a report, 'Brand Strategies in the Information Age – the Rise of New Marketing, published in 1997 by the *Financial Times* Retail and Consumer division, the journalist Alan Mitchell identified the following four main brand strategies:

▷ Relationship branding, where the prime asset is the firm's relationship with its customers, and the core question for marketeers in their decision-making is: 'Who are my customers, and what can I sell them?'.

▷ Values branding, where the prime asset is a set of values – representing an ethos or culture – and the core question driving marketeers is: 'What values define us, and how and where can we apply these values to the benefit of our customers?'.

▷ Intellectual property branding, where the prime asset is the organization's specialist knowledge and expertise, and where the core question is: 'What do we know and how can we use this knowledge to help solve our customers' problems?'.

▷ Passion branding, where the prime asset is an internal passion that drives the firm, and where customers 'buy' the passion itself; the core question here being: 'What is my passion and how can I promote it?'.

Edward Whitefield of Management Horizons Europe argues that, as the consistency of quality in manufacturing becomes more even, the differentiating characteristics of

brands will be based on personality – the same personality attributes that will be manifested by an explosion of interests represented by value and attitude clusters (in other words by like-minded groups of people who form communities of interest based on their beliefs). These clusters, or clubs of people, are catered for by services as wide-ranging as holidays, restaurants and television. Successful brands will be differentiated by the way in which they manage the relationship with these clusters, which represent their best customers. Equally, a brand name will be successful in the future not for its association merely with a product, but rather for a complete range or package of services or customer alliances.

Non-branding: another version of the future?

It is debatable whether it is possible to subvert branding to such an extent that it becomes devoid of meaning. Branding has, in many ways, become the reference point for all other retail activity. Take, for example, the Japanese retailer Muji (see also page 40) which started out with a strong concept of non-branding but, on the strength of this, has successfully created a worldwide brand. In addition, supermarket own-labels were established to provide low-cost alternatives

Above **The iMac computer has quickly established itself as a recognisable brand. It has redefined the PC market and has been a great success for Apple. Its bright colour breaks with conventional computer design and it has brought an element of fashion into the PC world. The Imac is accessible and friendly whilst being futuristic and conveying authority.**

Above **Egg is a small specialist fashion shop in London that defines itself as a small personal concern yet has international fame. Representing a clear shift towards individualism, it edits and rejects fashion by creating its own world with a distinct set of values and relationships.**

to this desire, and the change in attitudes is also recognized by more mass-market retailers in their ambition ultimately to operate one-to-one marketing.

The rejection of branding as a global or even as a national concept forms part of a revival of localized retailing based on independent and often high-value retailing of which the London-based clothes retailer Egg is a good example. The globalization of culture inevitably has a counterpoint, evident in people's strong need to belong to a clearly identifiable community – whether that community is a geographical one or a community of shared interest. This need manifests itself in a variety of different ways: in the taking-up of hobbies, in the desire for independent travel (as opposed to mass-market tourism) and even through the polarization of communities politically or socially. The reaction of retail to this trend has centred in the emergence of independent businesses based on a clearly definable identity, and in reflecting this need for individualism perhaps through craft skills, via a naïve approach, or through amateurish statements which encapsulate non-commercial commercialism. These independent businesses will operate across the value spectrum, but at the top end – in areas such as London's Notting Hill and New York's SoHo – represent local shopping with an international appeal.

Brands for the future

Good brands tell stories which affect people. New brands such as Yahoo and Alta Vista, the Internet search engines, for instance, are exploiting their users' need to search for information and their implicit trust that these brands will supply it. So what will be the major influences in the future? Edward Whitefield, of Management Horizons Europe, believes that there will be increasing moves towards creating global critical mass in manufacturing, with certain areas of the world specializing in particular groups of products. Other key issues identified by Whitefield are instant manufacturing (manufacturing to order), customized marketing (directly related to specific consumer groups) and minute merchandising (much more closely linked to store

to manufacturers' traditional brand names such as Heinz Baked Beans and Kellogg's Cornflakes. As such they were initially regarded as 'non-branded' ranges, which were sold purely on the basis of low price, but they have subsequently evolved significantly as supermarkets (in Europe more than in the USA) have expanded their own-label products and are now actively promoting them in direct competition with manufacturers' brands. Own-label products have also evolved with the introduction of higher-value ranges such as Tesco's Finest and Sainsbury's Organics.

Nevertheless, attempts are repeatedly made by entrepreneurs to establish themselves outside the branding arena, particularly in fashion. For instance, the desire among the wealthy for bespoke tailoring – which is being revived by a new generation of fashion-conscious shoppers – feeds this trend. The shift towards individualism in Western society undoubtedly contributes in a general sense demographic profiles) – all elements which point once again to the needs of individuals, and to retailers' methods of responding to those needs.

Conclusion

I would reiterate my doubt about the value of gazing into a crystal ball. What I have tried to illustrate throughout *New Retail* is that there are a number of fundamental principles within the business which have always been followed, however and wherever people are trading goods or services. Innovation occurs when an individual recognizes a trend or a gap and then sets about exploiting it. Ron Dyson's cleaner was an example of a new approach to a well-established domestic appliance – he looked around him and saw a future which became an industry, in turn supported by an expectation now held in common by every household. The iMac, which revived Apple's fortunes, equally was an inspired reinvention of the bland personal computer.

I hope that I have succeeded in showing, through case studies, the history of retail, social trends and the impact of technology, that new approaches to retail happen when innovators are aware of what is happening in the world around them and then set about reinterpreting that reality.

It may be a long process and require considerable determination and self-belief. There may be major problems convincing others that your idea is valid, particularly if it involves questioning the status quo, received ideas and traditional ways of operating. But successful innovators instinctively understand the basic truths of their business and of human psychology.

People are basically sociable and curious. We want to laugh, play, show off, ensure those we love are happy, be respected as individuals and we want to be stimulated by new ideas, music, fashion, art, invention and food. Centuries ago, that stimulation was relatively limited because information and entertainment was not widely available. Now, the opportunities for, and our expectation of, this stimulation are seemingly limitless, and are curtailed only on a practical level by the amount of money that each of us has to spend. Retailers have to jostle within that crowded marketplace of consumers to convince each of us that they can satisfy those desires.

Below **Yahoo! has been a phenomenal sucess since its launch in the USA. It allows browsers to compare prices of products and brands from differing sources.**

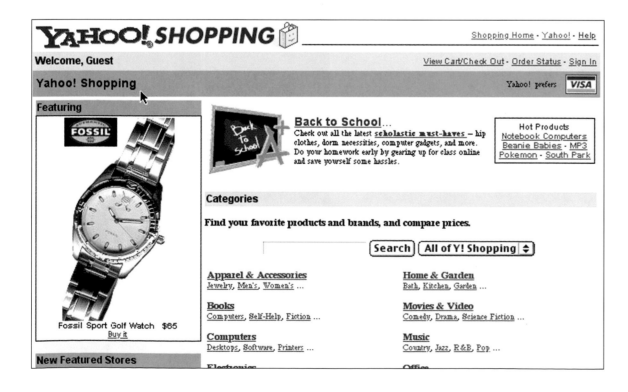

Clients' guide

Design Organizations

AUSTRALIA
Design Institute of Australia (DIA)
Employers House, 21 Burwood Road,
PO Box 21, Hawthorn,
Victoria 3122
tel: 00 61 3 819 6837
fax: 00 61 3 819 3686

Australia Graphic Design Association
PO Box 283, Cammeray, NSW 2062
tel: 00 61 02 955 3955
fax: 00 61 02 955 0566

AUSTRIA
Design Austria
Kandlgasse 16, A-1070 Vienna
tel: 00 43 1 524 4950
fax: 00 43 1 524 4949 4
email: info@designaustria.at

BELGIUM
Associatie van Interieurarchitekten van
    Belgie (AInB)
B.I. Trade Mart, Atoium Square (Dover 5),
Postbus 613 B, 1020 Brussels
tel: 00 32 2 478 47 58
fax: 00 32 2 478 37 66

BRAZIL
Associacao Brasileira de Desenhistas de
    Interiores e Decoradores (ABDID)
Av. Brigadeiro Faria Lima 1664, CJ. 113,
CEP 01452 Sao Paulo
tel: 00 55 11 814 1884

CANADA
Society of Graphic Designers of Canada
    (GDC)
c/o Gregory Gregory Ltd, 1081 River Road,
Ottowa, Ontario K1P 3VG
tel: 00 1 613 741 4027
fax: 00 1 613 744 0168

Interior Designers of Canada (IDC)
160 Pears Avenue, Toronto,
Ontario M5R 1T2
tel: 00 1 416 964 0906
fax: 00 1 416 924 4761

Interior Designers' Institute of Canada
745 Clark Drive, Vancouver,
B.C.VSL 3J3
tel: 00 1 604 251 5343
fax: 00 1 604 251 5347

CHILE
Colegio de Disenardores Professionals de
    Chile (COP/AG)
Casilla 50950 Santiago
tel: 00 56 215 2626

CHINA
China Industrial Designers Assciation
    (CIDA)
1, Alley 10, Lane 62,
Chiech-Cheng Rd. Sec.1.
Taipei 111, Taiwan
tel: 00 886 2 883 0351
fax: 00 886 2 832 3867

CZECH REPUBLIC
Design Centrum of the Czech Republic
    (DCCR)
Sekaninova 6, 128 00
Praha 2
tel: 00 42 2 692 6475

DENMARK
Danish Design Council (DDC)
HC Anderssens Blvd 18,
1553 Copenhagan V
tel: 00 45 33 146 688
fax: 00 45 33 320 048

ESTONIA
Estonian Society of Designers (ESD)
Tartu Maantee 1,
EE-001 Tallinn
tel: 00 7 0142 590 453
fax: 00 7 0142 434 172

FINLAND
Finnish Association of Designers
    (ORNAMO)
Yrjonkatu 11 E, 00120 Helskini
tel: 00 358 0 607 500
fax: 00 358 0 607 488

Design Forum Finland (DFF)
Fabianinnkatu 10, 00130 Helsinki
tel: 00 358 0 629 290
fax: 00 358 0 611 918

FRANCE
Societe des Artistes Decorateures (SAD)
Grand-Palais Porte H, 75008 Paris
tel: 00 331 43 59 66 10

GERMANY
Bund Deutscher Innenarchitekten (BDIA)
Konigswinterstrasse 675,
5300 Bonn 3
tel: 00 49 22 844 2414
fax: 00 49 22 844 4387

Design Centre Stuttgart
Landesgewerbeamt Baden-Wuttenberg,
Will-Bleicher-Str. 70174, Stuttgart 1
tel: 00 49 711 123 2685

Internationales Design Zenrum Berlin e.v
    (IDZ Berlin)
Kurfurstendamm 66, 1000 Berlin 15
tel: 00 49 30 882 3051

GREECE
Greek Designers' Association (GIDA)
Timarchou 5 Pagrati, Athens 11634
tel: 00 30 1 934 8540

HUNGARY
Design Center C. Ltd
Fazekas Utca 27, H-1027 Budapest
tel: 00 361 202 6340

ICELAND
Form Iceland
Hallveigarstigur 1, PO Box 1584,
Reykjavik 121
tel: 00 354 1 275 77

INDIA
National Institute of Design (NID)
Paldi, Amedabad 380 007
tel: 00 91 272 796 92

INDONESIA
Himpunan Disainer Interior Indonesia
    (HDII)
J.L. Melawai X/14, Kebayoran Baru,
Jakarta 12160
tel: 00 62 21 73 909 42
fax: 00 62 73 59 34

Below **Shoe market in the Central Market Hall, Alexander Platz, East Berlin in 1965.**

IRELAND
Society of Designers in Ireland (SDI)
8 Merrion Square, Dublin
tel: 00 353 1 284 1477
fax: 00 353 1 284 1477

ISRAEL
Association Of Interior Architects in Israel
  (AIAI)
17 Ben-Zion Israeli Dt.,
Giva Taim 53230
tel: 00 972 3 726 038

ITALY
Associazione Italiana Progettisti in
  Architecttura d'Interni (AIPI)
Via C Borgazzi 4, 20122 Milano
tel: 00 39 02 839 4883

Istituto Superiore di Architecttura e Design
  (ISAD)
Via Bianca de Savoia 14, 20122 Milano
tel: 00 39 02 832 1781
fax: 00 39 02 836 0098

JAPAN
Japan Design Foundation (JDF)
3-1-800 Umeda, 1-chome, Kita-ku,
Osaka 530
tel: 00 81 6 346 2611
fax: 00 81 6 346 2615

Japan Graphic Designers Association
  (JAGDA)
JAGDA Building, 2-27-14 Jingumae
Shibuya-ku, Tokyo 150
tel: 00 81 3 404 2557
fax: 00 81 3 404 2554

Japan Interior Design (JID)
Chayaz aka, T&K Bidg. 3F, 2-3-14 Ebisu
Minami, Shibuya-ku, Tokyo 150
tel: 00 81 3 5704 3421

KOREA
Korean Society of National Design
  (KSVD)
Ulchiro 3 ga. 344-4,
Jungg Seoul 100-193
tel: 00 82 2 278 0544

MEXICO
Colegio Disenadores Ind. y Graficos
  (CODIGRAM)
Apdo postal 20-308, Mexico 20 DF
tel: 00 52 5 598 8591

THE NETHERLANDS
Netherlands Design Institute
Postbus 15797, 1001 NG Amsterdam
tel: 00 31 20 638 1120
fax: 00 31 20 620 1031

International Federation of Interior
  Architects/Interior Designers
Waterlooplein 219, 1001 PG Amsterdam,
Postbus 19126, 1000 GC Amsterdam
tel: 00 31 20 627 6820

NEW ZEALAND
New Zealand Soceity of Industrial
  Designers (NZSID)
PO Box 3432, Aukland
tel: 00 64 9 776 012
fax: 00 64 9 373 765

NORWAY
Norske Interiorarkitekters Landsforening
  (NIL)
Uranienborgveien 2, N 0258 Oslo 2
tel: 00 47 22 558 586

PAKISTAN
Pakistan Design Institute (PDI)
16 Muslimabad, Karachi 5
tel: 00 92 21 411 512

PHILIPPINES
Product Development and Design Centre
Cultural Centre Complex, Roxas Boulevard,
Manilla
tel: 00 63 2 832 33646

POLAND
Stowarzyszenie Polskych Artyctow Grafikow
  Projektantow (SPAGP)
Zarzad Glowny, Nowy Swiat 7,
00398 Warsawa
tel: 00 48 22 217 819

PORTUGAL
Assocacao Portugusea de Designers (APD)
S.N.B.A. Rua Barata Salgueiro 36,
Lisboa 1200
tel: 00 351 1 521 293
fax: 00 351 1 521 046

Centro Portugues de Design (CPD)
Estrada do Paco do Lumiar,
1699 Lisboa Codex
tel: 00 351 1 716 5822

PUERTO RICO
Colegio de Decoradores y Disenadores de
  Interiores de Puerto Rico (CODDI)
GPO Box 3703,
San Juan PR 00936
tel: 00 1 809 753 0865

RUSSIA
Society of Soviet Designers
121019 USSR, Arbatskaya Square 1/2,
Moscow
tel: 00 7 095 202 5160
fax: 00 7 095 248 7894

SINGAPORE
Designers' Association Singapore (DAS)
109 North Bridge Road, Paper House,
02/04 Funan Centre,
Singapore 0617
tel: 00 65 339 6811
fax: 00 42 733 1389

SOUTH AFRICA
Society of Designers in South Africa
  (SDSA)
PO Box 39365, Bramley 2018
tel: 00 27 11 887 2444
fax: 00 27 11 887 2444

SPAIN
Association de Disefiadores Profesionales
  (ADP)
C/Valencia, 560-562, 2-3,
08026 Barcelona, Spain
tel: 00 343 265 8646
fax: 00 343 265 1946

SWEDEN
Foreningen Svensk Form (FSF)
Renstiernas gata 12,
116 31 Stockholm
tel: 00 46 8 644 3303
fax: 00 46 8 644 2285

SWITZERLAND
Vereinigung Schweizer Innarchitekten
  (VSI)
Weinbergstrasse 11, 3. Stock,
CH 8001 Zurich
tel: 00 41 1 471 686

Arbeitsgemeinschaft Schweizer Grafiker
  (ASG)
Limmatstrasse 63, 8005 Zurich
tel: 00 41 1 272 4555

UK
Architectural Association
34/36 Bedford Square,
London WC1B 3ES
tel: 0207 636 0974
fax: 0207 414 0782
e-mail: archassoc@archassoc.org.uk

Arts Council of England
14 Great Peter Street,
London SW1P 3NQ
tel: 0207 333 0100
fax: 0207 973 6590

British Design and Art Direction
9 Graphite Square, Vauxhall Walk,
London SE11 5EE
tel: 0207 582 6487
fax: 0207 582 7784
e-mail: marcelle@dandad.co.uk

British Design Initiative
2-4 Peterborough Mews, Parsons Green,
London SW6 3BL
tel: 0207 384 3435
fax: 0207 371 5343
e-mail: initiative@britishdesign.co.uk

Business Design Centre
52 Upper Street, Islington,
London N1 0QH
tel: 0207 359 3535
fax: 0207 288 6446
e-mail: bdc@dial.pipex.com

Chartered Society of Designers (CSD)
32-38 Saffron Hill, London EC1N 8FH
tel: 0207 831 9777
fax: 0207 831 6277
csd@csd.org.uk

Crafts Council
44A Pentonville Road, Islington,
London N1 9BY
tel: 0207 278 7700
fax: 0207 837 6891
http://www.craftscouncil.org.uk

Design Council
34 Bow Street, London WC2E 7DL
tel: 0207 420 5200
fax: 0207 420 5300

Design Museum
Shad Thames, London SE1 2YD
tel: 0207 403 6933
fax: 0207 378 6540

Design and Artist Copyright Society
Parchment House,
13 Northburgh Street, London EC1V 0AH
tel: 0207 336 8811
fax: 0207 336 8822
e-mail: dacs@designweb.co.uk

Design Business Association (DBA)
32-38 Saffron Hill, London EC1N 8FH
tel: 0207 813 3123
fax: 0207 813 3132
www.dba.org.uk

Interior Decorators and Designers
 Association (IDDA)
Crest House, 102-104 Church Road,
Teddington, Middlesex TW11 8PY
tel: 0208 977 1105
fax: 0208 943 3151

National Association of Shopfitters,
NAS House, 411 Limpsfield Road,
The Green, Warlingham,
Surrey CR6 9HA
tel: 01883 624961

Institute of Packaging
Sysonby Lodge, Nottingham Road, Melton
Mowbray, Leicestershire LE13 0NU
tel: 01664 500055
fax: 01664 64164

International Council of Graphic Design
 Association
PO Box 398, London W11 4UG
tel: 0207 603 8494/0207 371 6040
e-mail: 106065.2235@compuserve.com

Royal Institute of British Architects
62 Portland Place, London W1N 4AD
tel: 0207 580 5533
fax: 0207 255 1541

Shop and display equipment association
 (SDEA)
24 Croydon Road, Caterham,
Surrey CR3 6YR
tel: 01883 348911
fax: 01883 343435

USA
American Center for Design
233 East Ontario Street, Suite 500,
Chicago, IL 60611
tel: 00 1 312 787 2018
fax: 00 1 312 649 9518
e-mail: acdchicago@aol.com

American Institute of Architects (AIA)
735 New York Avenue NW, Washington,
DC 20006-5292
tel: 00 1 202 626 7300
fax: 00 1 202 626 7426
www.aiaonline.com

American Institute of Graphic Arts (AIGA)
164 Fifth Avenue, New York, NY 10010
tel: 00 1 212 807 1990
fax: 00 1 212 807 1799
e-mail: brand@aiga.org
www.aiga.org

American Society of Interior Designers
 (ASID)
608 Massachusetts Avenue,
NE Washington, DC 20002
tel: 00 1 202 546 3480
fax: 00 1 202 546 3240
e-mail: asid@asid.org
www.asid.org

Association of Store Design and Visual
 Merchandising Representatives
 (ASDVMR)
307 Cove Creek Lane,
Houston, TX 77042-1023
tel: 00 1 713 782 5533
fax: 00 1 713 785 1114

Design Management Institute
107 South Street, Suite 502,
Boston, MA 02111-2811
tel: 00 1 617 338 6380
fax: 00 1 617 338 6570
e-mail: dmistaff@dmi.org
www.dmi.org

Institute of Store Planners (ISP)
25 N. Broadway, Tarrytown,
NY 10591
tel: 00 1 914 332 1806
fax: 00 1 914 332 1541
e-mail: adminisp@ispo.org
www.ispo.org

Institute of Design
Illinois Institute of Technology,
10 W 35th Street, 13th Floor,
Chicago, IL 60616-3793
tel: 00 1 312 567 6461
fax: 00 1 312 567 3779

International Interior Design Association
 (IIDA)
341 The Merchandise Mart,
Chicago, IL 60654
tel: 00 1 312 467 1950
fax: 00 1 312 467 0779
e-mail: iidahq@iida.org
www.iida.org

Organisation of Black Designers
 (OBD)
300 M St. NW, Ste. N110,
Washington, DC 20024
tel: 00 1 202 659 3918
fax: 00 1 202 488 3838
e-mail: obdesign@aol.com
www.core77.com/obd

Planning and Visual Education Partnership
 (PAVE)
3368A Oxford Avenue, St Louis,
MO 63143
tel: 00 1 314 644 2590
fax: 00 1 314 644 2591

Society for Environmental Graphic Design
 (SEGD)
401 F Street NW, Ste. 333,
Washington, DC 20001
tel: 00 1 202 638 5555
fax: 00 1 202 638 0891
e-mail: segdoffice@aol.com

Society of Visual Merchandisers
 (SVM)
320 W. 13th Street,
New York, NY 10014
tel: 00 1 212 724 5975
fax: 00 1 212 645 0461

Other Organizations

CANADA

Retail Council of Canada (RCC)
121 Bloor Street E., Ste. 1210,
Toronto, ON M4W 3M5
tel: 00 1 416 922 6678
fax: 00 1 416 922 8011
www.retailcouncil.org

FRANCE

International Association of Department
Stores (IADS/AIGM)
4 Rue de Rome, 75008, Paris, France
tel: 00 33 1 42 94 02 02
fax: 00 33 1 42 94 02 04
e-mail: iads@iads.org

SOUTH AFRICA

Cape Chamber of Commerce and Industry
PO Box. 204, Cape Town 8000
tel: 00 27 21 418 4300
fax: 00 27 21 418 1800
e-mail: ccci@cis.co.za
www.ccci.co.za

UK

British Council
10 Spring Gardens, London SW1A 2BN
tel: 0207 930 8466
fax: 0207 582 7784

British Council of Shopping Centres
1 Queen Anne's Gate,
London SW1H 9BT
tel: 0207 222 1122

British Shops and Stores Association
Middleton House
2 Main Road
Middleton Cheney, Banbury,
Oxon. OX17 2TN
tel: 01295 712277

The Henley Centre,
9 Bridewell Place, London EC4
tel: 0207 955 1800,
fax: 0207 353 2899

Institute of Contemporary Arts
The Mall, London SWIY 5YT
tel: 0207 930 3647

Royal College of Art
Kensington Gore, London SW7 2EU
tel: 0207 590 4444

Royal Society of Arts
8 John Adam Street,
London WC2N 6EZ
tel: 0207 930 5115
www.rsa.org.uk

USA

International Association of Lighting
Designers (IALD)
200 World Trade Center, Suite 487,
Chicago, IL 60654
tel: 00 1 312 527 3677
fax: 00 1 312 527 3680
e-mail: iald@iald.org
www.iald.org

International Council of Shopping Centers
(ICSC)
665 Fifth Avenue,
New York, NY 10022
tel: 00 1 212 421 8181
fax: 00 1 212 486 0849
www.icsc.org

International Facility Management
Association (IFMA)
1 E. Greenway Plaza, Ste. 1100,
Houston, TX 77046-0194
tel: 00 1 713 623 4362
fax: 00 1 713 623 6124
www.ifma.org

International Mass Retail Association
(IMRA)
1700 N. Moore Street, Ste. 2250,
Arlington, VA 22209
tel: 00 1 703 841 2300
fax: 00 1 703 841 1184
www.imra.org

National Association of Store Fixture
Manufacturers (NASFM)
3595 Sheridan Street, Ste. 200,
Hollywood, FL 33021
tel: 00 1 954 893 7300
fax: 00 1 954 893 7500
e-mail: nasfm@nasfm.org

National Retail Federation (NRF)
325 7th Street N.W., Ste. 1000,
Washington, DC 20004-2802
tel: 00 1 202 626 8139
fax: 00 1 202 626 8145

Point-of-Purchase Advertising Institute
(POPAI)
1660 L Street NW, 10th Fl.
Washington, DC 20036
tel: 00 1 202 530 3000
fax: 00 1 202 530 3030
e-mail: rjennison@popai.org

Retail Advertising & Marketing Association
International (RAMA)
333 N. Michigan Avenue, Ste. 3000,
Chicago, IL 60601
tel: 00 1 312 251 7262
fax: 00 1 312 251 7269

Magazines

American Center for Design Journal
Design Year in Review
Design Statements
(see American Center for Design)

Arche Cree
9 Place du General Catroux, 75017 Paris,
France
tel: 00 331 42 12 8080

Architects' Journal
151 Roseberry Avenue, London
EC1R 4GB
tel: 0207 505 6700

Architectural Review
Audit House, 260 Field End Road,
Eastcote, Ruislip, Middlesex HA4 9LT, UK
tel: 0208 956 3015

Blueprint
Christchurch, Cosway Street, London NW1
5NJ, UK
tel: 0207 706 4596
fax: 0207 479 8515
e-mail: frattray@aspenmedia.co.uk

Canadian Retailer
(see Retail Council of Canada)

Creative Review
12–26 Lexington Street,
London W1 UK
tel: 0207 439 4222
fax: 0207 970 6713

Below **Man with barcode briefcase,**
computer-generated image designed by
Michelle Salmien.

Above **Changing room in Morgan at the Bluewater Shopping Mall, designed by Kinnersley Kent Design.**

Design Export News
2-4 Peterborough Mews, Parsons Green, London SW6 3BL, UK
tel: 0207 384 3435

Design Week
20 Poland Street, London W1V 4AX, UK
tel: 0207 439 4222

Display & Design Ideas Magazine
Shore-Verrone Inc., 6255 Barfield Road Suite 200, Atlanta, GA 30328, USA
tel: 00 1 800 241 9034
fax: 00 1 404 252 4436

Domus
Domus Spa, 5/7 Via Achille Grandi, 1-20089 Rozzano, Milano, Italy
tel: 00 39 02 82 4721
fax: 00 39 02 28 44282

Elle Decoration
Endeavour House, 189 Shaftesbury Avenue, London WC2H 8JG, UK
tel: 0207 437 9011
fax: 0207 208 3587

Frame
Oude Braak, 16 hs, NL–1012 ps, Amsterdam, The Netherlands
tel: 00 31 20 4233 717

FX
ETP Ltd Sadlers House, 2 Legg Street, Chelmsford CM1 1AH, UK
tel: 01245 491717

Graphics International
The Mill, Bearwalden Business Park, Royston Road, Saffron Walden CB11 4JX, UK
tel: 01799 544237

In-Store Marketing
20 Poland Street, London W1V 4AX, UK
tel: 0207 970 4262
fax: 0207 970 4295

Interiors & Sources Magazine Online
I&S, P.O. Box 13079, North Palm Beach, FL 33408-7079, USA
tel: 00 1 800 833 9056

Perspective Magazine (see International Interior Design Association USA)

Retailsource Inc.
775 Winslow Way E. #105, Bainbridge Island, WA 98110, USA
tel: 00 1 206 780 1728

Stores (see National Retail Federation, USA)

Wallpaper
7th Floor, Brettenham House Lancaster Place, London WC2E 7TL
tel: 0207 322 1177

Books/Key Texts

Architektur Fur Den Handel (Architecture for the Retail Trade), Birkhauser Verlag, 1996

Commercial Space: Boutiques, Francisco Asensio Cerver, RotoVision SA, 1996

Commercial Space: Cosmetics, Francisco Asensio Cerver, RotoVision SA, 1996

Commercial Space: Shop Windows, Francisco Asensio Cerver, RotoVision SA, 1996

Commercial Space: Shop Windows, Women's Fashions, Men's Fashions, Francisco Asensio Cerver, RotoVision SA, 1996

Designing With Light, Janet Turner, RotoVision SA, 1998

Fitch on Retail Design, Rodney Fitch and Lance Knobel, Phaidon, 1990

Nuovi Negozi in Italia 3, Edizioni l'Archivolto. 1995

Planning for Social Change 98, The Henley Centre, 1997.

Point of Purchase Design Annual, The Point of Purchase Advertising Institute, Retail Reporting Corporation, 1997

Shops & Stores, Morris Ketchum Jnr., Progressive Architecture Library, 1948

The Big Picture: Retail, Design Week, June 1998.

Visual Merchandising, The Editors of VM&SD Magazine, ST Publications Inc., 1997

Directories

Design Business Association, Directory of Members.

Professional Practice in Design Consultancy, Liz Lydiate, (ed.), Design Business Association.

RIBA Index
Shopfitting Specification International 1998/9, Nexus Media.

SDEA Directory 1998/9, (see Shop and Display Equipment Association).

UK Retail Marketing Survey 98, Portland Press.

Index

Page numbers in *italic* refer to captions to illustrations; those in **bold** to the case studies. All names are inverted e.g. Penney, J.C.; Karan, Donna; Smith, W.H

Acknowledgements

Conran Octopus would like to thank the following photographers and organizations for their permission to reproduce the photographs in this book:

1 Courtesy of Claudio Silvestrin; 2 Jeremy Horner/Hutchinson Picture Library; 5 Paul Warchol (design:Toshiko Mori)

introduction

6 Hulton Getty; 7 Melvyn Vincent Photography (Harvey Nichols window display/visual merchandising Manager: Janet Wardley); 8 left Courtesy of Rococo Chocolates; 8 right Lon Van Keulen/Interior View No.14 Blind Design (stylist: Carin Scheeve); 9 left Courtesy of Michael Nash Associates; 9 right Courtesy of the Arnell Group

principles of retail design

10–11 Kozo Takayama/Nacasa and Partners (design: Masamichi Katayama/H Design Associates Inc.); 12 Nicholas Kane (Peter Marino and Associates/Mark Alford Associates); 13 Steve Spiller (design: Thomas Heatherwick Studio); 14 left Romilly Lockyer/Image Bank; 14 right Fred Charles Photography; 15 left Alan Becker/Image Bank; 15 right Adrian Wilson/Courtesy of Carte Blanche Design; 16 Courtesy of Habitat UK; 17 below left and right Courtesy of French Connection UK; 17 above Alberto Arzoz/Axiom; 18 agency: TBWA; 19 left Courtesy of Aboud Sodano (illustration: Maxine Law/art director: Alan Aboud); 19 right Courtesy of Aboud Sodano (illustration: Maxine Law and Tim Spencer/art director: Alan Aboud); 20 Jim Holmes/Axiom; 21 Hedrich Blessing/Steve Hall (Nike inhouse design); 22 above Paul Warchol (Richard Gluckman Associates); 22 below Richard Bryant/Arcaid (Eva Jiricna Architects); 23 Lewis Moberly; 25 Michael Steele/Empics; 26 Nick Knight (agency: Bartle Bogle and Hegarty); 27 Maxwell MacKenzie (Pompei A.D. New York City); 28 left Christian Sarramon; 29 Ian McKinnell (Virgile and Stone Associates); 30 Hulton Getty; 31 Richard Glover (Corsie Naysmith); 32 left Popperfoto; 32 right Chris Gascoigne/View (Michael Aukett Architects); 33 left Peter Aaron/Esto (Peter Marino and Associates); 33 right Richard Waite/Arcaid (artist: Brian Clarke); 34 Dennis Gilbert/Arcaid (Jeremy Dixon and Edward Jones); 35 Michael Moran (design: Jack Ceglic); 36 Chris Doyle (Pompei A.D. New York City); 37 above Alex Bartel/Arcaid; 37 below Kozo Takayama/Nacasa and Partners (Masamichi Katayama/ H Design Associates Inc.);

38 left Courtesy of Virgin Press Office; 38 right Paul Warchol; 39 Chris Gascoigne/View (Morey Smith Associates); 40 Dennis Gilbert/Arcaid (Harper Mackay); 41 Courtesy of Benetton (creative director: Oliviero Toscani)

new kinds of retail

42–43 Nicholas Kane (David Chipperfield); 44 Robert Wallis/Coloritic; 45 Courtesy of Diesel Creative team; 46 Courtesy of Tesco; 47 Courtesy of Interact Design; 48 Courtesy of Rawls and Co; 49 Peter Clarke (Landini Associates, Sydney); 50 Mark McNulty/Courtesy of Wade Smith; 51 left Banana Republic; 51 right Courtesy of Alan Chan Creations, Hong Kong; 51 centre Courtesy of William Somona; 52 Courtesy of Apple Macintosh; 53 Courtesy of Granada TV; 54 Popperfoto; 55 above Courtesy of Rawls and Co; 55 below Michael Moran (design: Jack Ceglic); 56 Kozo Takayama/Nacasa and Partners (design: Masamichi Katayama/H Design Associates Inc.); 57 Evan Kafka/Gamma Liaison; 58 Courtesy of Calvin Klein, New York (John Pawson); 59 Chris Gascoigne/View (Lifschutz Davidson); 60 Graeme Williams/Katz Pictures; 61 left Fred Charles Photography; 61 right Chris Gascoigne/View; 62 left Paul Warchol (Richard Gluckman); 62 right Ian McKinnell (Virgile and Stone Associates); 63 left Paul Raftery/Arcaid (Claudio Silvestrin); 63 right Paul Warchol (Michael Gabellini); 63 above Bessard/Rea/Katz Pictures; 64 Jon O'Brien (Din Associates); 65 Chris Gascoigne/View (Wickham and Associates); 66 Paul Warchol (Torett Colaborative); 67 Richard Bryant/Arcaid (Eva Jiricna Architects); 68 Edina Van der Wyke/The Interior Archive (design: Sophie Hicks/sculpture: Tom Dixon); 69 Ed Reeves (Paul Daley); 70 Keith Hunter Photography/Courtesy of Andrea Marx PR; 71 Owen Humphreys/Associated Press; 72 Courtesy of Arthur Colllin Architects; 73 Keith Parry (XMPR); 74 Dennis Gilbert/View (Conran Design Partnership); 75 Peter Mauss/Esto (Pentagram Design); 76 Mark McNulty/Courtesy of Wade Smith (design: Davis Baron); 77 Chris Gasgoigne/View (Fitch)

practical implications

78–79 Annabel Elston/World of Interiors March 1998; 80 Courtesy of Egg, London; 81 Chris Gascoigne/View (Wickham and Associates); 82 Michael Taylor (Harvey Nichols window display/visual merchandising: Janet Wardley); 83 above Dennis Gilbert/View (RTKL UK); 83 below Paul

Warchol (Michael Gabellini); 84 Peter Mauss/Esto (Peter Marino and Associates); 85 Ian McKinnell (Virgile and Stone Associates); 86 Paul Warchol (design: Toshiko Mori); 87 Paul Warchol (Yoshi Matsuyama); 88 Chris Gascoigne/View (Gerard Taylor Associates); 89 Wayne Vincent/The Interior Archive (Future Systems); 90 Paul Warchol (Michael Gabellini); 91 Mike Tonkin (Tonkin Architects); 92 Chris Gascoigne/View; 93 Chris Gascoigne/View (Gerard Taylor Associates); 94 Jon O' Brien (Din Associates); 95 Peter Cook/View (Hugo Tugman); 96 Richard Glover (Din Associates); 97 Keith Parry (RTKL UK); 98 left Kozo Takayama/Nacasa and Partners (design: Tsutomu Kurokawa/H Design Associates Inc.); 98 right Courtesy of Watch 2 Watch (design: Cobalt); 99 left Richard Glover (John Pawson); 99 right Paul Avis; 100 Paul Warchol (Mahar Adjimi); 102 Chris Gascoigne/View (Peter Marino and Asscociates); 103 Kozo Takayama/Nacasa and Partners (design: Masamichi Katayama/H Design Associates Inc.); 104 Richard Glover (John Pawson); 105 Dennis Gilbert/View (design: Conran Design Group); 106 Paul Warchol (Michael Gabbelini); 108 left Shinichi Sato/Nacasa and Partners (design: Masamichi Katakama/H Design Associates Inc.); 108 right Peter Cook/View (Dalziel and Pow); 109 left Peter Mauss/Esto (Warren Bohn); 109 right Paul Raftery/Arcaid (Claudio Silvestrin); 110 Adrian Wilson/Courtesy of Paperchase Products (Wingate and Moon); 111 Red Dog (Tonkin Architects); 112–113 left Camper, 28 Old Bond Street, London; 114 Adrian Walker/Courtesy of Carte Blanche Design; 115 Elliott Kaufman (Haigh Architects)

new models
116–117 Nacasa and Partners (design: Kanji Ueki/Casappo and Associates); 118 Sarah Moon (design: Whitmore Thomas Angel, London); 119 Tim Street-Porter (design: Whitmore Thomas Angel, London); 120–121 Tim White (design: Whitmore Thomas Angel, London); 122–127 Jen Fong Photography (Tsao and Mckown, New York); 128–131 Courtesy of Io Corso Como; 132–135 Niall Clutton (Building Design Partnership); 136 Richard Dobson/Courtesy of Shanghai Tang; 137 Stuart Woods Photography; 138 Richard Dobson/Courtesy of Shanghai Tang; 139 above and below Marco Ricca/Courtesy of Shanghai Tang; 140 Carlos Dominguez (Kinnersley Kent Design); 141–142 Adrian Wilson (Hosker Moore and Kent); 143 above Carlos Dominguez (Kinnersley Kent Design); 143 below Adrian Wilson (Hosker Moore and Kent); 144–147 Maxwell Mackenzie (Pompei A.D. New York City); 148–149 Richard Glover (John Pawson); 150 Richard Glover (AM Design); 151 above James Morris/Axiom (John Pawson); 151 below Richard Glover (John Pawson); 152–155 Nacasa and Partners (Casappo and Associates); 156–157 Todd Eberle/Commes des Garcons (concept: Rei Kawakubo/tunnel: Future Systems UK); 158–159 Masayuki Hayashi/Commes des Garcons (concept: Rei Kawakubo/Facade: Future Systems UK); 159 below Masayuki Hayashi/Commes des Garcons (concept: Rei Kawakubo/Facade: Future Systems UK); 160 Paula Smith Designs, Inc. (Richard H.Lewis, New York); 161 An Mi Le (Richard H. Lewis, New York); 162 above Eric Rank (Richard H. Lewis, New York); 162 below Jan Staller (Richard H. Lewis, New York); 163 An Mi Lee (Richard H. Lewis, New York); 164–167 Peter Clarke (Landini Associates, Sydney); 168 illustrators: Hayes Davidson (Michael Aukett Architects); 169 Dennis Gilbert/View (Michael Aukett Architects); 170 above Benedict Luxmore (Michael Aukett Architects); 170 below Courtesy of Future Brand; 171 View/Dennis Gilbert (Michael Auckett Architects); 172 Dennis Gilbert/View (Michael Auckett Architects); 173 above (Jeremy Lindley); 173 below Benedict Luxmore (Michael Aukett Architects); 174 IDEE, Tokyo; 175 Nacasa and Partners (Courtesy of Klein Dytham); 176–179 Courtesy of IDEE, Tokyo; 180 Pieter Vlamings Architetur Fotographie (Merx and Girod Architects); 181–182 Alexander van Berge (Merx and Girod Architects); 183 above Mariette Carstens (Merx and Girod Architects); 183 below Pieter Vlamings Architectur Fotographie (Merx and Girod Architects); 184 Jon O'Brien (John Hebert and Raj Wilkinson); 185 Keith Parry (John Hebert Partnership); 186 Jon O'Brien (Din Associates); 187 Selfridges, London (Christian Liaigre); 188 Keith Parry (Din Associates); 189 Courtesy of Selfridges, London; 190 Jean-Luc Benard (Eric Khune Associates); 191–195 Michael Chittenden (Eric Khune Associates)

the future of retail
196–197 Yasaki Yoshinaga/Courtesy of Fondation Cartier (design:Issey Miyake); 198 Jeff Sherman/Telegraph Picture Library; 199 above Courtsey of ASDA; 199 below Kenneth Cole; 200 left/right Din Asscociates.; 200 (DDA); 201 Jon O'Brien (Din Associates); 202 Paul Warchol (design: Gabellini Associates); 203 left Courtesy of IDEE; 203 right Thomas Heatherwick Studio; 204 Courtesy of BSkyB/Sky Sport Active; 205 David Samuel Robbins/Sygma; 206 Courtesy of CD NOW; 207 Courtesy of DIESEL; 208 Tony Kyriacou/Rex Features (design: Studio Hagaar); 209 Yasuaki Yoshina/Courtsey of Fondation Cartier (design: Issey Miyake); 210 Courtesy of First Direct Banking (concept: Cake); 211 Klaus Lahnstein/Tony Stone; 212 Michael Nash Associates; 213 Courtesy of Yahoo! Shopping

clients' guide
214 Gardi/AKG, London; 217 Michele Salmien/The Telegraph Colour Library; 218 Carlos Dominguez (Kinnersley Kent Design)

Every effort has been made to trace the copyright holders, architects and designers and we apologise in advance for any unintentional omissions and would be pleased to insert the appropriate acknowledgement in any subsequent publication.